Acrosswater

Acrosswater

a modern adventure along the waterways and backroads of America

Paul Danforth

Acrosswater technical design produced by North River Boats. Used with permission.
Acrosswater rendering courtesy of Karl Klep. Reproduced with permission.

Maps and expedition planning documents provided by Karl Klep. Reproduced with permission.

Journal text courtesy of Karl Klep, Larry Bierman and Roxa Bierman.

Cover design by Marilee Kimball.

Schaak homestead photo generously provided by Christy Klep. OriginalPhotoBooth.com

Every effort made to contact copyright holders of *Pink Houses,* by John Mellencamp and *My City Was Gone,* by the Pretenders.

See sources for further reading.

For Karl

Contents

ONE warm, autumn day in 1951, a young boy took his father's hand and eagerly climbed the steps of a gangway to start the first leg of his adventure. He was going to New York City. The fog and light drizzle had already blown away from the Oregon coast and the weather seemed perfect for flying. Of course flying in those days was a serious undertaking, requiring nerves of steel, a strong stomach and a willingness to put one's life in the hands of pilots with rather dubious credentials. Passenger jets were nearly a decade away, so a trip of any distance required many, many stops. This one began in Astoria and then leapfrogged across the country through cities like Spokane, Milwaukee and Toledo - seven stops in all - before terminating in Port Clinton, OH.

The boy did pretty well, only suffering one bout of motion sickness along with the rest of the passengers during the descent into Minneapolis. The airline crew dispensed pills to everyone while on the ground, presumably after ingesting fistfuls themselves, and then they were back on their way with fresh airsick bags behind every seat.

At one point going across the country, the world's tallest, living man joined the ride, somehow stuffing his eight foot frame into one of the rows.

Upon landing in Port Clinton, they took a quick taxi ride to a yacht club where they were greeted outside the main entrance by the boy's aunt and uncle. "How were the flights, Karl?" Uncle Rolf asked, tousling his nephew's hair.

"I puked!" the youngster cried, beaming up at his uncle.

Sufficiently apprised about the details of the journey, the four of them headed for the dock and the motivation for the trip in the first place. Rolf and his wife Alice had recently purchased a 38-foot cabin cruiser from the Matthew's company and needed help navigating the craft from Ohio to their home near the Long Island Sound. Rolf had called his younger brother Andy and asked if he would come east; Andy agreed and brought his son, Karl, along to share in the fun.

They spent the first night dockside and dodged a tragedy right from the start. Fooling around near the edge of the boat, young Karl fell overboard and just managed to grab one of the lines tied to the pier – he had not yet learned to swim – before landing in the water. He dangled there until someone heard his frightened cries and, realizing what had happened, hauled him back on board.

They left in the morning and motored up the coast of Lake Erie to Buffalo and the gateway to the Erie Canal to start the 363 mile trek across New York. In the early fifties, the Erie Canal still handled over 5 million tons of freight annually so the Matthew's cruiser and its crew shared the water with barges and tugs, as well as other pleasure craft. Karl fished, helped tie off when they went through locks, fussed with the various cleats and winches, gorged himself on a delicious chicken dinner prepared by Aunt Alice, slept in too late and gazed in wonder at the sights all around him. Just outside Albany, he watched the private yacht of New York's Governor Dewey sail past, all trimmed in pomp and circumstance. And the locks especially thrilled him; from the first to the last he watched, mesmerized, as the water rushed in or out, controlled by the lock master.

The boat arrived at the Waterford Flight, the last set of five locks on the Erie Canal and, with a 169-foot drop, the largest lift of its kind in the world. Passing through lock #2, the cruiser began its downriver run towards New York City. Karl sat at the stern, his chin on the rail of the boat, and watched the entrance to the canal disappear into the confluence of the Mohawk and Hudson rivers. He stayed there for a long time, staring at the wake unfurling behind them until his father called him up front to have a look at West Point, silently standing guard on a cliff overlooking the river. When the outline of New York City came into view, he briefly forgot about the canal as the giant buildings and bridges passed in succession and they made their entry into the raucous harbor.

They sailed up the East River to New Rochelle, found the moorage for the cruiser and spent several days at the family farm. The ride on the water drifted even further away as they traveled to the city several times on the train to explore.

They went to the top of the Empire State Building where a man fainted, overcome by the view, the thrill and the altitude. A visit to Yankee Stadium resulted in a win over the Red Sox as well as many autographs on the ball that Karl had brought along just for the occasion. And they all sat in awe as the orchestra rose out of the stage at Radio City Music Hall to start a show.

Like all good things, their visit ended too soon and eventually Andy and Karl found themselves jammed back into a series of ever shrinking airplane seats for the return flight across the country. Their great excursion was over.

Some years later, that young man, now much, much older, had an occasion to go for a ride on a jet boat. Water travel had stitched itself into his being and over the course of his lifetime, Karl had owned a ski boat, a 27-foot Morgan Sloop and several other watercraft. An offhand remark to his wife, Rose, that he felt curious about the operation and design of jet boats touched off a remarkable series of events.

Attending college in the sixties, Rose had dated a man at Oregon State University. On a weekend trip to the campus, she brought along her cousin, Roxa, as the two were inseparable, more like sisters than cousins. One of the fraternity brothers, Larry, became quite smitten with Roxa; they eventually married and over time, Rose dumped her OSU boyfriend to marry Karl. The two couples naturally connected - prompted by the sisterly bond between Rose and Roxa - so after the aforementioned comment of a passing interest in jet boat design, Rose shared the conversation with Roxa, who in turn passed it along to Larry. Larry had stayed in touch with many of his frat brothers since graduation and one of them owned North River Boats, a builder that specialized in jet boat design. A test drive was quickly arranged.

The owner met Karl and Rose at the Umpqua River with one of the newest models. Not long into the run, he realized that his best chance for closing the deal was to win over the missus. He could have talked transoms, Hamilton propulsion or bilge capacity all day, but he had a business to run. So after a couple of passes, he suggested that they drop Karl off at the boat ramp to retrieve the trailer, giving Rose a little more time at the helm. Karl had barely regained his balance after hopping off the boat onto shore before his wife was rocketing upstream, leaving nothing behind but a vapor trail. North River had another convert.

More importantly, that little spin on the water reignited a long dormant passion, an ache that years of life and loss and success and failure had covered, but not erased. Ever since the mouth of the canal had vanished into the mist, Karl had longed to be back out there, wishing he could take just one more peek around the next bend in the river. In Rose, he happened to have the ideal companion, someone whose daring and interest in adventure rivaled his.

Newly retired, they hatched a plan to follow the rivers from Astoria to St. Louis and then jet down the Mississippi to New Orleans. Karl aspired to follow a similar strategy in the future by starting on the Ohio River and then going east to where he could float again in the rivers and waterways of his childhood, but he kept that to himself for the time being.

In the infant planning stages, they realized that more hands were needed so they reached out to Larry and Roxa to gage their interest and found them not only intrigued, but thrilled to be included. The foursome began to correspond with regularity, exchanging ideas about where to go, what to see and how to get there. None of them realized they were on the cusp of the grandest adventure of their lives, but, as they started to plan with real intent, something became crystal clear; only one name suited their boat and their expedition.

Acrosswater

Part l

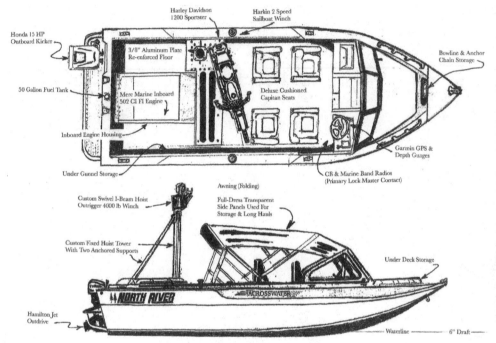

Honda 15 HP
Outboard Kicker

50 Gallon Fuel Tank

Inboard Engine Housing

Under Gunnel Storage

Harley Davidson
1200 Sportster

3/8" Aluminum Plate
Re-enforced Floor

Merc Marine Inboard
502 CI FI Engine

Harkin 2 Speed
Sailboat Winch

Deluxe Cushioned
Capitan Seats

Bowline & Anchor
Chain Storage

Garmin GPS &
Depth Guages

CB & Marine Band Radios
(Primary Lock Master Contact)

Custom Swivel I-Beam Hoist
Outrigger 4000 lb Winch

Custom Fixed Hoist Tower
With Two Anchored Supports

Awning (Folding)

Full-Dress Transparent
Side Panels Used For
Storage & Long Hauls

Under Deck Storage

Hamilton Jet
Outdrive

NORTH RIVER   ACROSSWATER

Waterline   6" Draft

ACROSSWATER

NORTH RIVER JET BOATS Roseburg, OR 97471

Renderings & Legends
by Karl Klep

Chapter 1
Renegades have timetables too

"make check or moneyorder payable to 'FAO
USAED Omaha'
Please DO NOT send cash"

Payment instructions on a Map Order Form,
 US Army Corps of Engineers, circa 1999

The *Acrosswater* team relied heavily on USACE
maps and charts to plan the expedition.

ON a day early into their journey, the *Acrosswater* convoy stopped to refuel while crossing the Bitterroot Mountains into Montana. As the other three travelers ventured inside the service station, Karl waited outside and struck up a conversation with a deputy sheriff who was also at the fuel island. He remarked to the officer that there seemed to be quite a large collection of law enforcement for such a small town; he counted at least twenty patrol cars and trucks in the parking lot.

The deputy informed him that they were preparing to escort members of a national motorcycle club from Missoula to South Dakota for Sturgis' annual Bike Week. An undisclosed number of the brothers were meeting nearby to pick up their bikes, having shipped them by train from various parts of the country. Karl imagined all the chapter presidents huddled up in the rail yard, readers perched on the ends of their noses as they meticulously checked each manifest to confirm the safe arrival of the members' Softails and Fat Boys.

The point was clear; even outlaws and anarchists, no matter the machismo and swagger displayed on the outside, rarely left home without a plan. And though you wouldn't think it by their outward appearances, the members of the *Acrosswater* party were quite like those long-haired, leather-wearing desperadoes descending on Missoula, a collection of inquisitive, counter-cultural explorers who also happened to have a grounded, pragmatic character that valued the need to prepare.

Larry, the son of an extension agent, was born near Hermiston, OR and had spent his formative years working the surrounding fields. He had grown up fishing and boating on the Columbia before moving on to become an Eagle Scout, attending Oregon State University and, ultimately, forging a career as a pharmacist. He raised champion Irish Setters and later in life, cultivated a huge garden on the property where he lived with Roxa. He was realistic and frugal, determined to make sound decisions, but was also curious about an exhaustive range of topics. Assigned to research potential points of interest during the course of the journey, Larry proved to have a knack for discovering slices of Americana that many other modern adventurers would have missed.

Roxa was nearing retirement (as was Larry) after working nearly forty years at the same organization, the Pacific Maritime Association. During her career as an administrator and manager, Roxa had helped coordinate the many, unionized tasks associated with unloading the great cargo ships that called at the docks in Astoria, Longview and Portland. She dealt with the prickly personalities embedded within each union, scheduled the appropriate manpower for each function (jobs like stevedores, linesmen, electricians and walking bosses each had separate representation) and made sure everyone was paid for completed work. She was also interested in a variety of topics, was relentlessly optimistic and shared her cousin Rose's tendency to go against the grain.

Rose was born with a pioneering, independent spirit. She loved nothing more than to visit her grandparents' ranch and spend her days riding horses or exploring the outdoors. A tireless worker, she became a registered nurse and supported her family when Karl went back to school later in life. She was also a voracious reader and more historically informed than any of the others. When she and Karl were younger and they went on family trips with their children, Rose made a habit of pointing out types of flora or places of historical significance to her daughters, so traumatizing the youngsters with quizzes about what they had seen that the girls actively avoided riding in the same car as their mother on future excursions.

Organized, intellectually curious and open minded, the three amigos formed a daring brain trust that would go anywhere and that had the administrative wherewithal to execute any plan to get there. When it came to preparation, however, the three of them put together still fell short of the maniacal attention to detail that afflicted the captain.

Before selling his company to a larger, international entity and then retiring as vice president of a division, Karl had developed the largest book of business for Boise Cascade Office Products in the country. He knew exactly how much he had to sell every hour in order to reach his own personal sales goals. Dissatisfied with simply being the top salesman in the company, he collected all of the sales data available for his accounts, manually mapped out total sales (that was back in the pre-Excel days) and then went to his manager to request that only the largest businesses stay in his portfolio. He pioneered industry mainstays such as the easy-order form (a simple, customizable purchasing document that listed only the most frequently ordered commodities), consigned inventory and on-site sales representation.

And he did not limit his meticulous habits to his professional life. Every decision required a business plan and he adored creating drawings and color-coded maps of potential landscaping decisions or home improvements. On more than one occasion, he made - by hand out of balsa wood - scale models of buildings he considered adding to his property: a work shop, a barn, a gardening shed. He had to see what it might look like before breaking ground on anything. For an experience like they were planning, the captain was ideally suited to think through as many scenarios as possible and to make sure their equipment, their route and their strategy were sound.

In retrospect, the *Acrosswater* adventure was a truly ambitious undertaking (regardless of who was doing the planning), not just for what the team hoped to accomplish, but also how it planned to reach its goal. The foursome knew that people crisscrossed the country all the time, particularly those in the retiree demographic, but during all their preparations they had not seen or heard of anyone attempting it quite like they planned.

They loosely based their traveling strategy on a journey that Rose's parents had taken about fifteen years earlier. Shortly after selling their country store and retiring, Bud and Jane Porter decided to explore parts of the Pacific Northwest, but instead of investing in a Winnebago, they loaded a scooter onto their 18-foot runabout and started upriver. During the round trip from Portland to Lewiston and back, they investigated ports of call by throwing a plank from the boat to the shore and driving the scooter onto land. From there they were free to zip into town to window shop, have lunch, visit local points of interest and generally see what else they had been missing. They rarely stayed in one place too long, slept on board the boat, kept their own schedule and reported to no one.

All the members of the *Acrosswater* party had heard Bud and Jane rave about their trip and the captain thought it formed a rudimentary framework for the day-to-day execution of how to travel. He concluded that, with the right gear, he and his mates could launch a boat into a river in the morning, travel downstream to the next campsite, return to the original launch area to retrieve their campers and then move all the equipment forward. They would effectively leapfrog their way across the country, the only snag being how they would travel from the boat's stopping point back to the original launch.

From the outset, they intended to spend as much time on the rivers as possible, but, practically speaking, they knew that traveling on water exclusively or spending nights on board a boat (a la Bud and Jane) was unrealistic. Scrubbing the jet boat in favor of a vessel large enough to house both couples (while also being versatile and durable enough to navigate the rapids and sandbars of America's rivers) was not only imprudent, but they both already owned recreational vehicles, which saved them an enormous expense.

So they stuck with the North River jet boat and, as planning progressed, the captain's decision to use such a craft revealed itself to be quite forward thinking. It could operate in shallow water, as little as six inches in the right conditions. The rivers of North America changed dramatically from year to year as sediment, flooding and wind shifted the location of sandbars, channels and snags. Having a boat that could reliably draw only a few inches of water would allow them to explore those evolving parts of the landscape without worrying about a damaged prop. And with its aluminum frame and skin, *Acrosswater* was light enough to muscle around on shore yet durable enough to handle a landing on a rocky canal bed. Karl also had North River install a 425 hp, GM engine, figuring that the extra kick might come in handy during the trip. That left how to travel from landing to launch as the final piece of the puzzle.

The captain loved the concept of a scooter as a means of transportation. It was light enough to carry on board the boat, simple to drive and theoretically conveyable from ship to shore with relative ease. But given that the Missouri River alone was almost 2400 miles long and that they estimated a fifty-mile river run per day, a scooter just did not seem robust enough to use long term. At minimum, they would have to drive the river distance with every daily transition to the next stopping point. More importantly, Karl really did not like the thought of buzzing up the dock on a Vespa, Larry balanced on the back with his arms draped around the captain's midsection..

So after considering several options, they decided on a Harley Davidson 1200, a bike with horsepower, substance and the added benefit of being an American classic. After purchase, Karl delivered the Hog to North River so accurate revisions could be made to the final boat design. To account for the added weight and corresponding displacement, the engineers extended the length of the craft by one foot and welded a thick, metal plate to the deck where the Harley would ride. Lastly, the builders had to design and install the mission-critical hoist that would be used to move the Harley to and from the boat, a complex proposition to say the least.

In addition to accounting for the 600 pounds of bike, they had to think through a long list of loading conditions: the flat, dry space of a Walmart parking lot, a severely sloped, water-slicked ramp on the Columbia, a half-rotted dock on the Mississippi or a muddy, root-tangled bank on the Missouri. The explorers might have to offload in a driving rainstorm or in brutal heat, all while trying to keep the boat steady in a swift current with a boatload of backwoods yokels bearing down on them. The mechanism had to be strong, durable, efficient, collapsible and light.

The skipper himself proposed his own design, complete with drawings. It used an I-beam supported by an A-frame that would be deployed to shore and was fitted with adjustable footings to accommodate the varying degrees of pitch that they expected to find along the rivers. Using a simple block and tackle, the lift would raise the bike off the deck and slide it across on the I-beam to shore, where it could be lowered to the ground. After inspecting the plans, the North River engineers thought it seemed viable and crafted a rough prototype. It was only during testing that they realized the grounding of the frame forced the boat downward with no freedom of movement. In the end, the winning design used a hoist attached to a simple, removable pole with a pivoting arm that cleared both sides of the boat, and paired it with a powerful, electric winch.

Karl did contribute two other designs that were used in the final product. First, he suggested installing sailing winches with dual gear ratios on both sides of the boat. That would allow he and the crew to cinch *Acrosswater* tightly to a dock, ramp or other solid surface when unloading the bike. In order to clear the gunwale of the boat, he had a friend of his build custom, aluminum blocks that raised the winches just high enough so that lines could move freely. That same friend machined cleats and brackets to secure the bike while they traveled on the water; the last thing they wanted was to wrestle with a tumbling, quarter-ton motorcycle in the middle of a squall.

Second, he insisted that the boat trailer also be fitted to accept the bike. The manufacturer engineered a channel to run down the center of the trailer that just fit the tires of the Harley and built a removable, aluminum ramp that fit into a notch on the back end. When anyone made the run from the dock back to the original launch site on the motorcycle, he could quickly run the Harley up onto the trailer and be back on the road in minutes to retrieve the campers.

While North River finished outfitting the boat, the team turned its attention to the tactics of day-to-day living on the road. One of the first things they did was to enroll in motorcycle driving lessons. Karl had the most experience riding a bike, but his endorsement had expired long ago. The group decided that they should all be certified to allow for greater flexibility during daily operations and things went really well with their initial training. Roxa led the team through extended study sessions and clearly appeared to be the most prepared of everyone to ace the written exam.

Alas, the driving component of the test did not go as well; she dumped the bike going around some cones and fractured her ankle. Adding insult to injury, the pain in her leg was so distracting that she could not concentrate during the written test and failed that too. The other three passed with flying colors, infusing everyone with optimism that they would have a large pool of shuttle drivers to select from.

Not long after the three received their motorcycle endorsements, Karl and Rose went to Larry and Roxa's house for dinner and brought along the newly completed boat and the Harley. After supper, Karl showed Larry how the lift could lower the bike to the ground and when the demonstration concluded, he encouraged Larry to take the Hog for a spin.

Three hours later, the captain was still in the driveway, this time deputizing neighbors and passersby for the search party when, thankfully, Larry limped into view, pushing the bike. The captain rushed to the end of the drive and found both Larry and the Harley with multiple fractures and patches of road rash; they had hit the deck skidding through some loose rocks while going around a curve.

After surgery to set Larry's arm, the group collectively decided to shelve their backup, motorcycle strategy for the foreseeable future. (Soon thereafter, Rose took a call from Larry and Roxa's son, Ryan. He was a doctor and he expressed some understandable concern for the well-being of his parents. Participants did not recall the conversation in its entirety, but the words "harebrained" and "dumb ass" figured prominently.)

With the trip launch still several months away (and with a key piece of equipment undergoing reconstruction), the explorers began the complicated chore of mapping out the exact route they planned to travel. Though just a scant twenty years ago, planning an expedition with that much complexity was tedious and time consuming. The technology of 2020 - things like mobile devices, GPS and Web-based, information sources - makes it easy to forget how people used to travel, but in 2000, when the *Acrosswater* team had just begun zipping across the Umpqua and careening through gravel patches, experts were still debating the merits of WiFi and predicting how the Internet might be used by businesses. Facebook would not be introduced for four more years, the iPhone for seven and the iPad for ten.

By 2020, if you wanted to research a drive from Missoula to St. Louis, you plugged the stops into your phone and in seconds knew both how many miles (choosing from a variety of routes) and how long it would take. In 1999, you ran your fingers over a road atlas and put a magnifying glass to a mileage chart.

Traveling by boat, which also required points of egress and docking facilities, added another layer of complexity to route development. In 1999, as far as Karl knew, the U.S. Army Corps of Engineers had done the only comprehensive survey of the rivers and lakes in the country, but its exhaustive publications were supremely dense and technical in nature. When the captain sent in his money order for the charts covering the whole *Acrosswater* route, he received back a mountain of topographical maps. The charts outlined the contours, water depth, acre-feet and shore miles of rivers and reservoirs like gigantic Fort Peck Lake, but listed none of the ramps. Those the team would have to discover on the fly.

Undaunted, the foursome plunged further into the detailed, granular preparations for their trip and Karl manned the point for mapping out the specific mileage between stops, portage locations, lay day locales and other mundane but crucial aspects of the journey. Applying his usual rigor to the process, he organized his library of USACE publications sequentially and numbered them to correspond to a larger map with a bird's-eye view of the route. Using their daily, fifty-mile goal as a guide, he carefully laid out the the starting and stopping points for each day, the estimated dates of travel, emergency alternate locations, highway routes, the addresses for fuel stops and the names of potential marinas.

For camping spots, he used a Trailer Life guidebook to locate the places to stay every night. Trailer Life was an imposing tome that organized parks and campsites by state. It used a three-part rating system that graded facility completeness, cleanliness of restrooms and visual appearance of the site. Karl and Rose had been members of the Trailer Life community for several years and found the guidebook not infallible, but certainly reliable. The skipper aimed for parks with 50 amp hookups and highly graded ease of parking to increase their chances of finding a pull-through camp site.

He also tried to anticipate the particularly hazardous legs they might find out on the trail, especially in the upper region of the Missouri River where navigational aids were mostly absent; he wanted to minimize the chance that the party would find itself marooned and forced to subsist on starvation rations until help arrived. As a means of creating a single guide that all of them could reference, he developed a daily worksheet that encapsulated all of the information on one page and then filled a large, three-ring binder with all the itineraries. Though unlikely that they would find serious trouble, the rural parts of the country were a bit of a mystery and thus the team had to be well prepared for anything. Karl in particular developed contingencies for as many situations as he could.

Meanwhile, Rose and Larry devoted themselves to finding both popular and obscure points of interest along the route. Rose read two books in preparation: *Undaunted Courage* by Stephen Ambrose and *River Horse* by William Least Heat-Moon. She underlined sections she found particularly moving or applicable to their excursion and shared her inspirations with the other members.

From the start, they all felt a strong connection with the journey of Lewis and Clark and all the more after Rose completed Ambrose's story of the Corps of Discovery. It resonated with them so much that they adopted the famous explorers as their historical forebears and tried to map out a route that would keep them as near the Lewis and Clark Trail as possible.

Rose and Larry suggested they visit some of the more famous spots like the Badlands, Mt. Rushmore, the St. Louis Arch and Beale Street, but they also noted as many of the rarely seen slices of the country as they could. The two of them pored over books, magazines and newspaper articles to find those infrequently seen treasures sprinkled along the way.

Although the Internet did not yet have a particularly robust infrastructure, Roxa worked with a close friend to develop a simple website that would allow her to share pictures and text with family and friends during the trip (it would be called a travel blog today). Two of the other team members planned to record the experience in journals every day so Roxa would have written resources to consult if she questioned her own recollections.

They also invested in a digital camera to record what they saw and where they went. Again highlighting how their trip took place in a different technological era, the camera's picture quality was at best 2 MP (even the venerable iPhone 4 has a 5 MP camera) and more than once Roxa lamented in her journal not having *the* camera with her; today, she would simply pull out her phone. At any rate, Roxa planned to compile the images and, when the party came to a town with Internet access, send them along with a written account to her friend, who would upload the whole packet to the Web.

They coordinated their start date to coincide closely with Larry's and Roxa's retirements in July and, as the summer neared, excitement grew in all four of them. They had planned, researched, collected, studied, packed, unpacked and packed again and finally, after a few last minute arrangements such as mail coordination and equipment maintenance, the time arrived.

200 years prior, before retiring for the night, *Acrosswater*'s spiritual companion, Captain Meriwether Lewis recorded in his journal a familiar sentiment when he wrote, "…I could but esteem this moment of my departure as among the most happy of my life." Karl expressed the exact same sense of wonder and thrill in his journal by writing simply, "AXH2O Day 1!"

They were on their way.

SHADY REST RV PARK (GLASGOW, MT pg 952)
1-800-422-8954 or (406) 228-2769

MISSOURI & MISSISSIPPI RIVERS ITINERARY
WORKSHEET

Date: _8 / 1 / 00_ Day: S M (T) W T F S Day Number: _1_ Lay Day: _No_
_{Yes/no}

Today we will begin in _GLASGOW/FT. PECK, MONTANA_
                                 City   State

Today we will end in _WOLF POINT,_   _MT._
                            City   State

Alternate or safety location: _FRAZER OR OSWEGO, MT._
                                       City   State

Lay day activity: _____

Boat Route Today: Map Name/No.: _____ Pg. ___ -

Start river mile #: _____ End river mile #: _____ Boat Hours #: _____
Boat Ramp or Marina Name: _FT. PECK BOAT RAMP_
Dam Name: _____ Lock Number: _____ Radio Channel: _____

Motor Home Route Today:

RV Park or Camp Ground: _____ AAA ____
                                                          Yes/no
Address: _____
City: _____ State: _____ Phone #: _____
Hwy. # _____ Miles: _____ (to) Hwy. # _____ Miles: _____ (to)
Hwy. # _____ Miles: _____ (to) Hwy. # _____ Miles: _____

Motorcycle Route Today:

Hwy. # _____ Miles: _____ (to) Hwy. # _____ Miles: _____ (to)
Hwy. # _____ Miles: _____ (to) Hwy. # _____ Miles: _____

Fuel Stop:

Pacific Pride or _Get topped off in Great Falls !_

Address: _3100 Tri Hill Frontage Rd._
                          Alternate name
City: _Great Falls_ State: _MT._ Phone #: _(406) 442-7202_

Directions: _Exit 277 - I 15 South side of I 15_

GLASGOW — A5 *Valley*

Daily Notes: _____

→ **SHADY REST RV PARK** (Priv) Apr 1 to Oct 31. From Jct of US-2 & SR-24N, W 1.5 mi on US-2 to Lasar Dr (E end of town), N 0.1 mi (E). Good gravel interior rds. 3 tent sites. SITES 44 gravel, mostly shaded, 7 pull-thrus (26 x 60), back-ins (26 x 50), big rig sites, 44 full hookups (30/50 amps), city water. FAC Restrooms & showers, security, public phone, ltd RV supplies. REC None. Last year's rates: $12.50 to $17.50, V, MC, D, (406)228-2769

Itinerary worksheet

Chapter 2

Beyond Astoria

"...a gravitational force pulling me toward water..."

Rolf Klep - from a 1969 retrospective published by the University of Oregon Museum of Art

He described a trait shared by much of his family.

ONCE A RIVER RAT - ALWAYS A RIVER RAT !

The River Rats

TUCKED in behind the relative safety of Point Adams, Astoria has captured the hearts and imaginations of people for generations. Even the name, Astoria, when heard for the first time, conjures visions of a warmly lit, kitchen window spied through a winter storm, a lighthouse on a rocky crag, a safe haven sought by weary souls at the end of a long, punishing trek; "God, please let me make it to Astoria!" Originally established by John Jacob Astor as a fur trading hub, it was the earliest, non-indigenous settlement on the Pacific Coast when it came into existence just six years after Lewis and Clark wintered nearby in 1805.

Astor's foray into the northwest was short lived. He had dispatched both an ocean going team and a land-based party with the intent that they meet where the Columbia River reached the Pacific Ocean. They were to arrive at roughly the same time and construct a stockade where company trappers scattered around the region could bring their furs for shipment to the Far East and Europe.

Unfortunately, the captain of the ocean-going wing could sail like hell, but when he arrived in the Northwest, he displayed such poor negotiating skills that he soon found himself clubbed and stabbed to death after he insulted a local chief while they were haggling over the price of sea otter furs. The rest of the crew that had ventured with the captain up the coast north of Astoria, suffered a similar, grisly fate, save for the one sailor who blew himself up with the ship so he wouldn't be gutted along with the others.

The members traveling over land eventually reached the tiny settlement, but much later and with a much less convivial greeting than they had hoped. Instead of roaring fires, hearty salmon stew, chairs laden with luxuriant furs and even a brandy sifter or two, they discovered a muddy complex constructed of scraggly fir trees. To make matters worse, the man who had assumed control of the community when the captain departed acted like a king, despite the abysmal living conditions. Mercifully, the War of 1812 forced Astor's men to abandon the site before things became even worse.

Control of the area and the industry that propelled Astoria's growth changed often over the next two centuries, but one thing always remained the same, the deep and abiding influence of the water. From fur to fortified defense to canning to lumber to tourism, the town's proximity to the great struggle between the mouth of the Columbia and the Pacific Ocean always attracted people drawn to a maritime life.

The ancestors of the *Acrosswater* team were certainly no different. Uncle Rolf (whose invitation to New York had planted the seeds of the *Acrosswater* expedition) descended from Norwegian lineage. His grandfather had been a ocean-going captain - ultimately going down with his ship - and his uncle on his mother's side had run away to sea. Rolf himself was an Astoria man through-and-through. When he was a boy, he befriended many tug-and-pilot skippers in the area and spent innumerable days looking for excuses to go on board every ship down at the dock. His formative teen years in the town saw him delivering papers, working summers in one of the many lumber yards and even realizing his dream of being a secondary helmsman on a boat (a Columbia River highway ferry).

He graduated from Astoria High, earned a fine arts degree from the University of Oregon, lived in Chicago and New York City and produced highly acclaimed, advertising illustrations for the likes of *Collier's*, *Newsweek*, *Life* and *Fortune*. In the later years of his career, he collaborated with Wernher Von Braun during the beginnings of American rocketry and illustrated many of the technical designs and drawings of the first, spaceship prototypes. But even with all that success and notoriety, when he and Alice retired, they returned to Astoria.

Back in town for good, Rolf teamed with other businessmen inclined towards civic preservation and founded the Columbia River Maritime Museum, still the preeminent repository of Pacific Northwest, maritime history. His work at the museum, his design of the Comcomly Memorial (King Comcomly was the chief of the Chinookan natives who lived in the area during the time of Lewis and Clark), his visionary involvement with the restoration of Fort Clatsop, his work with the Astoria Chamber of Commerce and his participation in a range of other clubs in the area firmly established his legacy in the Astoria community.

Karl's father, Andy, worked nearby painting minesweepers during World War Two and later converted an old gill-netter into a pleasure craft that he used to cruise up and down the river. Andy had creative talent himself and carved out a living painting signs. No less an artisan than his older brother, his success was more blue collar yet still depended on a keen eye, a steady hand and an exhaustive grasp of fonts, shading and scale. He was also associated with an iconic destination in town when he worked at Lawson's, a popular confectionery and soda fountain that served as a hangout for local kids. Tragically, just one year after the Erie Canal voyage, Andy lost his life when, in the mist and gloom of a darkened highway, he plowed into the open drawbridge spanning Old Youngs Bay.

Karl, as a boy, lost himself in the nautical culture. He and his friends amused themselves hanging around down by the old pilings and pier ruins - the self-described "River Rats" - and built rafts out of driftwood and discarded lumber. Ignoring the fact that none of them could swim, they poled up and down the river, fishing, exploring and dreaming.

The canning industry still had some punch back then and the River Rats loved to watch the great fishing boats offload their catches. At times there was a shortage of labor and the Rats heard rumors of desperate captains installing trapdoors in the docks in order to snare unsuspecting young men for their crews; since nobody ever disproved those stories, they kept wary eyes on every creaky deck board when they walked the docks.

Karl left Astoria at the age of eleven in the same year his father passed, returning in subsequent years only for an occasional visit. Still, his nautical foundation, just like those of his father and uncle, was irrevocably anchored on the banks of the Columbia amidst the old canneries and vast, rusting ships. Combined with the obvious link to the heritage of Lewis and Clark, there could be only one launch pad for *Acrosswater* and that was Astoria.

Karl and Rose rolled into the Kamper's West RV resort a little past noon on that first day, hurriedly hooked up the utilities to their rig and immediately took off to find a boat ramp. They were meeting Larry and Roxa at Beacon Rock further up the Columbia in three days and they had a lot to accomplish; their first order of business was finalizing the procedures required to safely convey the Harley from the floating boat to dry land. In order for the trip to succeed, the transfer of bike to dock had to go off like clockwork. The anxiety caused by approaching a dock or ramp, the range of peril they might encounter and the number of catastrophes caused by the tiniest mistake was limitless, so Karl and Rose wanted to identify clear, simple steps that they could use to instruct Larry and Roxa.

They found a boat ramp, launched *Acrosswater* and took her for a cruise into the brackish water just short of Tongue Point. They delighted in watching the commercial ships entering and leaving the river and by feeling the wind and the spray for a brief time before returning to the ramp to test one of their offloading methods. For their first rehearsal, they selected the dockside maneuver. They cinched the boat tightly to the dock and then unloaded the bike, a process that turned out to take much longer and was more unnerving than they anticipated.

With the boat on the water, the shifting weight of the Harley, particularly when hoisted on the arm of the lift, caused a tremendous amount of rock and sway. One of the benefits of the jet boat - its shallow draft and flat hull - proved to be a detriment when they had 600 pounds of Harley Davidson swinging in the breeze. Even with both winches cranking the dock lines tight, *Acrosswater* tipped dramatically. It was like being on a watery seesaw. Once they achieved a touchdown on the dock, they put the bike back on board and cautiously ran through the procedures again before reloading one last time and securing everything for the day.

Many of the people at the ramp could not help but question the sanity and purpose of what they were seeing. More curious than mean-spirited, the inaugural words of those first bystanders (changing only in accent and word choice) followed the *Acrosswater* crew throughout the course of their long journey in comments like these: "Is that a Harley on your boat?"; "I thought you had a wheelchair on there at first."; "Does the little lady polish your bike for you while you fish?" From the outset, the explorers' chosen method of travel was a conversation starter with every stranger they met.

After they secured the motorcycle to the deck of *Acrosswater* the last time, they brought the boat back to their RV headquarters, drove into Astoria for a late dinner at Cafe Uniontown and debriefed each other about the events of the day. They were pleased to discover that their waitress was a long time resident who remembered frequenting Lawson's soda fountain as a teenager and who likely had been served a frappe or two by Karl's father. When their heads finally hit their pillows that night, it was after 11:00 p.m. and they had been awake for over sixteen hours.

Another order of business in Astoria was to conduct an ancestral send-off of sorts, so the next morning, rather than smashing a bottle of champagne over the bow of *Acrosswater,* they visited places that resonated with their family. They stopped first at Ocean View cemetery and paid their respects to Andy and Rolf. The day could not have been more perfect with a cool breeze and a clear sky and they spent a long time amidst the serenity of the tombstones, enjoying the comfortable silence.

Next, they launched and made their way upriver to find a moorage near Uncle Rolf's museum. Once tied off and inside the building, they lingered amongst the displays, marveling at the detail and layout. Ranging from an up close look at the Columbia River Bar Pilots - the bar is still one of the most treacherous, river gateways on the planet - to thoughtful presentations about the Coast Guard, the building was a model for what a museum should be: tasteful, informative, interactive and well maintained. They felt immensely proud that their family had played such an enormous role in CRMM's inception and development.

Returning to *Acrosswater*, they realized they had docked near the USCGC *Steadfast*, the 210-foot Coast Guard cutter based in Astoria. The uniqueness of their planned journey and method of travel had attracted another set of admirers; some sailors from the *Steadfast* had come down to investigate why the motorcycle was on the boat.

It was one thing to have day trippers give you a hard time down at the public ramp, but it was another thing entirely to speak with people who worked on and around the water as a profession and have them tell you that you were onto something special. None of the sailors had seen or heard of anyone attempting an odyssey of the kind Karl and Rose described and the conversation filled the two adventurers with excitement, optimism and pride. They bid farewell to their new fans, pushed off and boated the fifty miles to their next stopping point in Cathlamet, WA.

In Cathlamet, they tried a different variation for unloading the bike by pulling into a boat launch and lowering the motorcycle directly onto the concrete ramp that sloped gradually into the water. In what became their preferred technique, they slid the boat sideways into the ramp, tied off the stern and bow lines and then set the motorcycle into roughly four inches of water. Quick, simple and with an immeasurably more stable platform, the ramp procedure was clearly the one to use.

They secured the boat in a rented slip at the marina and then rode back to Astoria to retrieve the rest of the gear. They ran into a slight delay when they realized they were missing the ramp used to load the motorcycle onto the boat trailer; they had mistakenly left it on board *Acrosswater*. They managed to back the trailer flush with an embankment and then loaded the bike into its channel, but it was difficult and dangerous. The bank had a lot of loose sand so it made wrestling the motorcycle into place a struggle.

When they finally had the bike trailered, they drove by a few, last, memorable landmarks on the way out of town - there was the grammar school Karl attended, that was the soap box derby hill he roared down as a kid, there was where all the old hospital and liberty ships were left to rust - before leaving Astoria for good. Arriving back in Cathlamet, they checked in at the RV park, dusted as much of the sand off the trailer as they could, had dinner and finally turned out the lights after another fifteen-hour day.

On the last day of their practice run, Karl and Rose planned to bring the land equipment forward to Kalama and then bike back to pick up the boat so they could try loading the motorcycle and departing directly from the ramp. They knew they could not test every scenario, but they at least wanted to have the basics under their belts.

Before heading out, Karl went to the office of the harbor manager to confirm he could purchase some fuel, make sure he did not owe any additional fees after spending the night and confirm he could leave the boat in its slip a little longer. Although common courtesy prevailed at most marinas, this one seemed semi-private and as such it might have had restrictions regarding the use of the fuel pumps. The attendants at the office were not enthusiastic about allowing a non-member continued use of the facilities (even after the captain sweetened the deal by offering to let them sit on the Harley), but they finally acquiesced.

They forwarded the rigs to their next campsite then rode the Harley back and picked up the boat. The loading of the bike went fine, but once on the water, rough conditions in the main channel made the going slow and choppy which forced them to stay closer to shore. It took them nearly twice as long as the previous day to travel a similar distance. To top it off, the travel sequence they had planned necessitated an extra hoist of the Harley.

When boating first and driving second, they unloaded and loaded only two times: once to ride back to pick up the land gear and once to put the bike back on the boat. If they moved the rigs to that day's final destination first, they found they had to conduct the operation three times: once to take the bike off the boat to go on the trailer, once to put it back on the boat to travel on the river and a final removal off the boat at the ramp so they could ride to the RV park. (This tactic had the potential for a fourth hoisting if they elected to go back to the ramp and haul *Acrosswater* back to camp the same day.)

Usually, the extra step was a minor inconvenience, but after enduring the drawn out trip up the Columbia, with every wave and swell hammering them through the flat bottom of the boat, they were somewhat relieved to find that the ramp in Kalama was too steep to unload the Harley; they would have to leave the bike on board.

They rented a slip in the Kalama marina and left the boat and bike on the water for the night. After they cinched all the lines, secured the Harley to the deck and zipped shut all the openings of the cockpit enclosure, they trudged back up the hill to their camper.

Day three of their adventure felt like a struggle from start to finish and by the end of it, they just wanted a quick bite to eat and a good night's sleep. Tomorrow, they would reunite with the rest of the corps and begin the next step of their journey, passage through the Columbia River Gorge.

Chapter 3
Through the Gorge

"Comment.
-Strangest thing I ever saw/Pats Karl on
Back Thought that it was a special
wheelchair"

Larry's journal - July 23, 2000

Larry recorded comments someone
made about the Harley on the boat at
Hat Rock. The motorcycle's presence
on the boat fascinated everyone they
met during the journey.

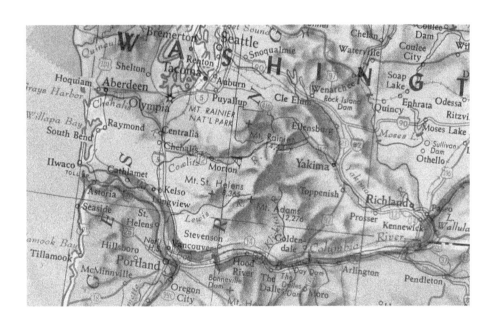

The Columbia River

THE wail of old number 755's air horn jolted Karl and Rose awake early the next morning, the tenth interruption during a restless night. Without realizing it during check-in, they had parked their camper within twenty-five yards of the busy, Burlington-Northern railway.

The sleep deprived travelers had rustled through every cabinet and closet on their RV to find something - anything! - to muffle the constant rumblings of passing freight trains, but even with earplugs, earmuffs, a University of Oregon apron, two scarves and sixteen pillows of all shapes and sizes stacked over their heads, they found that nothing could dull the thrum, honk and clatter of the railroad. Seeing no hope for rest after that last wake up call, they brewed an extra strong pot of coffee, left a note on the door of the office that they would return later that day to break camp, shuffled down the hill to the marina and puttered out into the river with the rest of the insomniacs.

A little rough initially, the ride from Kalama to Beacon Rock smoothed out nicely once they passed the confluence of the Columbia and Willamette rivers. They performed the Harley offload like a couple of seasoned longshoremen, checked in at the marina office to rent a slip for several hours, made the white-knuckle ride back to Kalama (unbeknownst to them, motorcycles must drive approximately 132 miles per hour to avoid being run over on I-5), retrieved the rest of their gear and then returned to that night's bivouac.

It sounded easy on paper, but their little commute was comprised of eighty river-miles, sixty miles on the bike and then another sixty miles in the RV. They managed to arrive back at the park at the same time that Larry and Roxa did (burning through nearly all their cell phone rations trying to find each other). The foursome had dinner together in the shadow of their campers and then brought the boat up to camp for safe keeping; someone had already stolen the family crest from its stanchion at the stern of *Acrosswater* while the boat was unsupervised during the equipment retrieval. Karl and Rose filled in Larry and Roxa about all the events of the past three days and the marathon conversation ran late into the night. So distracted were they that nobody save for the captain seemed to notice the trees overhead being whipped around by the growing breeze. The Columbia, it seemed, was starting to show its teeth.

Packed with howling winds, whitecaps, misty waterfalls, sweeping vistas and towering trees, the Columbia River Gorge is a different land all together, with every curve in the road and every scenic overlook giving observers a peek into an earlier, more rugged age, like a John Muir painting come to life. Travelers who approached the Gorge by driving along the highways that run parallel to the river may not realize what a geologic masterpiece is before them - think of seeing the Grand Canyon for the first time from the vantage point of a raft on the Colorado River instead of from the top of the South Rim - and the landscape can appear somewhat unassuming because the river itself is so vast and the sheer cliffs so distant.

To better appreciate the wonder the Gorge deserves, fly out of one of the tiny communities on the surrounding highlands. As the plane clears the acres of orchards that line the top of the canyon, the ground suddenly plummets away and the abrupt, angry chasm of the Gorge stretches into the distance as far as the eye can see.

Consensus about the Gorge's creation centers on the Columbia River. Geologists have made a strong case that the canyon was formed gradually - almost gently - over years of steady erosion. Some experts believe, however, that the primary instrument responsible for the abrupt and jagged nature of the area was a series of floods in the distant past. In his field guides that covered the geological underpinnings of the region, Bruce Bjornstad described cyclical ruptures in ice dams holding back giant Lake Missoula (a freshwater sea that existed years ago and was formed by glacier melt). Each time the dams broke, a violent series of floods let loose and, over time, carved the Columbia River Gorge into its present state.

Having taken place some 10,000 to 15,000 years ago, the floods were far beyond human comprehension. Using surveys and satellite imagery, other researchers estimated that Lake Missoula was roughly the size of present day Lake Michigan (holding an estimated 500 cubic-miles of water) and when those glacial dams broke, the mile-high runoff churned through the landscape at speeds up to seventy mph, obliterating every rock, tree and mountain in its way. Geologist and former Professor Emeritus David Alt once suggested that the floods roared through an area known as the Eddy Narrows at 9.46 cubic miles per hour. Keeping in mind that the maximum discharge ever measured on the Mississippi was .05 cubic miles per hour, the deluge running through the Narrows would have been ten times the combined discharge of every river in the world.

Today, 265,000 gallons of water per second pulse along the Columbia making it the fourth largest river on the continent in terms of volume of output. The enduring influence of its ancient, watery heartbeat on the Pacific Northwest is everywhere and primal reminders seem to lurk around every bend in the river and road; a simple yet often overlooked example resides just forty miles east of Portland on I-84 at the Bonneville Fish Hatchery.

Since 1909 the hatchery has helped mitigate the decline of different fish populations caused by commercial fishing and dam construction. The facility has picnic benches, plenty of shade and a peaceful atmosphere so rest-stoppers often linger at the site longer than normal. Holding ponds absolutely teeming with Coho, Steelhead and Chinook in various stages of development guard the walking paths throughout the complex and visitors can even throw a few bits of fish food bought from a well-positioned dispenser into a feeding lagoon to watch the masses swirl this way and that.

The true eye-opener on the property, however, is found in a little white building to the left of the feeding pools underneath some large evergreens. A set of concrete steps descends into a gloomy viewing area, with one whole side dominated by an underwater perspective of the pond adjacent the building, and it is there that someone traversing the Gorge for the first time starts to understand how old - how prehistoric - the region is. For eventually, after only a few moments, and after a number of fish of considerable size swim by the glass, out of the murk will emerge a sturgeon, a freshwater monster over ten feet long and weighing more than 500 pounds, a creature little changed since it first appeared on the scene some tens of thousands of years ago and a beast many visitors to the Gorge had no idea existed.

Just as the hatchery itself acts as a counterweight to the effects of the nearby dam, many of the landmarks along the river serve a similar purpose as planners and engineers tried to balance modernization with preservation; few other places in the country blend nods to the past and innovations for the future as neatly as the Columbia River and its Gorge. Near the Bonneville Hatchery, the glorious spray of Multnomah Falls draws the awestruck eye of everyone passing on the highway below. Just two exits later travelers find The Bridge of the Gods neatly conveying traffic from Oregon to Washington, all while tipping its hat to the older, fabled, natural arch for which it was named.

Further on, Hood River takes advantage of the reliable, howling winds that barrel from one end of the Gorge to the other and the town has positioned itself as one of the premier, wind surfing destinations on the planet. And The Dalles, the setting of a series of abrupt falls that vexed the Corps of Discovery two centuries earlier, became a site of controversy when the installation of a hydroelectric dam sacrificed one of the oldest, continuously inhabited communities in the world for the convenience of clean, reliable power.

Indigenous fishermen netting salmon from a teetering platform, pioneers, lumber barons, railroad titans, active volcanoes, Google server farms, petroglyphs, tugs pushing acres of floating timber, a Cold War nuclear waste dump and dams producing over half of the country's hydroelectric power, the Columbia River Gorge abounds in vitality, intrigue and mystery. Like the Corps of Discovery before them and though they had spent years of their lives on and around the river's banks, the *Acrosswater* foursome approached a trip through the Gorge with equal measures of wonder and respect.

The next morning, while the rest of the team slept, the captain stepped outside his camper and immediately knew that they would have to travel on land that day. The wind had risen to a gale, making it impossible to risk a trip on the river. He broke the news to the crew over breakfast and the team moved to their secondary plan without complaint. Rose, Larry and Roxa hiked Beacon Rock after eating, but the skipper took the opportunity to visit the Bonneville Lock & Dam Visitor Center to confirm standard procedures for locking through on the river.

Although well-seasoned on water operations, Karl did not want to take anything for granted, particularly around locks and dams. He needed a clear understanding of which VHF channel to use to reach the lock masters, in which common areas they should tie off to wait for lock entry and how the lock masters ranked lock priority. Many recreational boats treated commercial traffic with indifference and even worse, flirted dangerously with dams until it was too late. The *Acrosswater*'s commander had all the respect in the world for both and firmly believed he could always learn more.

Given the frequent installation of dams along the planned route of the entire trip, he could not think of a better way to invest in the safety of the crew.

More often associated with canals, locks have been used for years on rivers. In places where engineers dammed water flow to cover rapids or falls, designers had to find workable solutions to keep traffic flowing in both directions, even where the upstream and downstream water levels differed drastically. Early models allowed downstream boats to career into the lock at the velocity of the river itself, while travelers using the lock to move upstream had to fight against a deluge when the lock flooded. Often going around the dam on land - or portaging - was the preferred or only choice. Today, even the most state-of-the-art facilities still follow the same basic principle: a boat moves into a controlled space with gates that allow water to flow in (raising the water level in the lock and the craft with it) or to flow out (lowering the craft).

On the Columbia, the U.S. Army Corps of Engineers constructed a series of dams along the course of the river to make the waterway navigable to commercial traffic. The USACE's efforts created a shipping channel from Lewiston, ID (and its proximity to major grain producers in the West), all the way to the Pacific Ocean where the products could be exported around the globe; some publications ranked the Columbia-Snake River route as the top, wheat gateway in the country. Additionally, the hydro-power grid of the Pacific Northwest dams accounted for sixty-three percent of all such energy produced in the U.S. The upshot of all that infrastructure for the captain of *Acrosswater* was the need to fully comprehend the procedures and protocols in and around the locks and dams. He did not want to find himself and the crew making a poor decision around a 14,000 ton, 4-barge tow.

Following his exploratory visit to the Bonneville Visitor Center, the skipper made a quick pit stop at a golf course he had passed along the way. While fiddling with the newest model of Pings in the pro shop, he happened to notice the leftovers of a breakfast buffet on a string of tables towards the back of the room. Realizing a tournament must have just kicked off, he glanced out the window to make sure the convoy of golf carts filled with players was indeed heading out to the course and then edged over to check out the selection. He was just tucking into a plate of warm apple danish when he heard, "Karl?" behind him. He whirled around to find himself face to face with Larry and Roxa's son-in-law.

"Trevor?" he asked, choking down a chunk of crust and wiping the crumbs from his mustache. "What are you doing here?"

"Work event," Trevor replied, pointing to the corporate logo on his hat. "I'm running the putting competition when the players start coming off the course. Are you playing today?"

"Me? Ah...no. We're just passing through on our trip. Larry and Roxa are hiking Beacon today with Rose so I decided to check out the renovations." He gestured to the front of the pro shop with one hand and discreetly tried to slip the plate behind his back onto the table with the other.

"Oh, I see." Trevor paused and glanced up and down the buffet line. "Nice spread, huh?"

"What? Oh. Yes. Very nice." Karl dusted away any remaining evidence.

They stood there quietly for a few moments, studying the picked over remains. Trevor broke the silence. "Well, I better get back to work. Too bad you're not playing today. Give my love to everyone!" The skipper smiled, said goodbye to Trevor and then moseyed back out to the parking lot.

After lunch, the party members stowed their gear, cleaned up camp and headed east. The captain led the convoy in his and Rose's camper (towing *Acrosswater*), while Larry and Roxa followed in their RV hauling the SUV. Because they had all spent many days in and around the Columbia, they had excluded this leg of the journey during their pre-trip research. Even so, the thrill of their new adventure inspired them to take in the familiar landscape with a fresh outlook as they drove deeper into the Columbia River Gorge. Members of the *Acrosswater* motorcade were firm believers of the glacial runoff theory and the unplanned portage along the river was the perfect chance to discuss the merits and counter arguments.

They stopped for lunch and fuel in The Dalles and then kept moving until they reached the Umatilla RV Park and Marina, their encampment for the night. The wind was still wailing steadily with gusts up to forty-five mph by dinnertime so the outlook for time on the river the next day was poor. Before locking the door to the RV for the night, the captain took one last look at the flag flying at the front of the park. It was horizontal, cracking in the wind.

When dawn broke, and much to everyone's surprise, the banner at the park entrance lay limp; the wind had ebbed considerably overnight. The troops closed up camp immediately and headed for the river to take advantage of the lull. They were close to McNary Lock & Dam so that was where Larry and Roxa locked through for the first time. Considerably less well known than the other structures along the river, McNary still represented a formidable engineering achievement within the USACE's catalog of projects. The lock itself was more than two football fields long and contained seventy-five vertical feet in its single lift. Though the dam had not been significantly updated since its construction in the early 1950's, it produced enough electricity to power over 650,000 homes and allowed more than 5 million tons of cargo to safely pass through its lock annually.

The dance of locking through would eventually become second nature to the entire crew, but the first day was a big learning curve for the newest sailors. The skipper patiently guided them for the duration of the process on where to stand, what line to hold, where to tie off, what to watch for, what signal to listen for and what not to do. They exited the lock on the east side of the dam without incident and then cruised over to Hat Rock to offload the Harley. Since Larry had grown up in nearby Hermiston, he shared stories with everyone as they went. He gestured in the direction of some lands where he used to hunt and informed his listeners that, though the land was private, his father had relationships with most of the farmers so Larry was allowed to shoot on some of the choicest grounds in the area. He also pointed to a spot where he had taken a spill trying to water-ski barefoot, something he had no inclination to try again.

At Hat Rock, Larry and Roxa experienced both the delicate act of winching the bike onto shore, as well as the good-natured comments from other visitors at the ramp about the team's choice of locomotion. Perhaps had they not been distracted by the technical aspects of the lock, the stories of the past and the wisecracks, they all might have realized that it was the last time *Acrosswater* would feel the cool touch of the Columbia on her hull; they were moving forward to Pasco for the night and planned to put the boat into the Snake River in the morning so they could continue east. They had covered over 300 miles, worked out an indeterminate number of kinks in their procedures, reconnected with ancestors, rendezvoused with friends and launched their adventure as successfully as they could have hoped. They pulled out of Hat Rock and drove towards Pasco, drops of the Columbia trailing behind.

The Harley and the hoist

Chapter 4

Footsteps of the past

*"Mom was born there on Sept. 5, 1919.
These folks led a tough life, no question."*

Karl's journal - July 30, 2000

McCone County, MT, a landmass twice the size of Rhode Island, had no recorded inhabitants during the Census of 1910. By the Census of 1920, that number had increased to 4800, nearly all as a result of homesteading.

IDAHO is enormous. Perhaps underestimated because of its slender top, the state has 20,000 more square miles than all of New England. If it was a country, it would be the eighty-second largest in the world, bigger than Syria, Greece, Austria, Jordan and Hungary and all that acreage ranges from valleys filled by glacial drift to snow-capped peaks of 12,000 feet. Hells Canyon National Recreation Area, sitting on Idaho's western edge and the centerpiece of *Acrosswater*'s next stop, is the deepest gorge in North America and the very definition of backwoods. Even a sprained ankle would be a serious cause for concern because, not only is Idaho big, it is so sparsely populated that help could take hours if not days to arrive.

So uninhabited is the Hells Canyon region that mail arrives once per week via Beamer's jet boat. Ranchers, rangers and other rural inhabitants travel (often on horseback) to a series of stops along the Snake River to collect their mail and to interact with other human beings. Since the *Acrosswater* team had done its homework, the lay day planned in Lewiston, where the Snake meets the Clearwater, included an excursion with the aforementioned Beamer's. If they ran into trouble heading up the whitewater, they would have professionals close at hand.

Their trip to Lewiston was half water, half portage and their first day on the Snake, traveling from Pasco to Lyons Ferry, checked all the boxes of their vision for travel: everyone drove the boat, the lock master at the Lower Monumental Dam went by the book and the accommodations at Lyons Ferry were top notch. On the run shuttling equipment to the forward camp, they had a scenic ride past tapestries of wheat, corn, potatoes and Walla Walla sweet onions. In his journal, Larry remarked that he could tell the harvest stage of the wheat by the color of the field, from the blond of a fresh cut crop to the dark chocolate of a just-cultivated furrow.

After connecting all their utilities, they made time for a quick tour of Starbuck, WA, a town whose primary attraction was a home with a mule on the front porch. Starbuck had a 10:00 p.m. curfew, but still maintained a stable populace of 130 souls, despite its draconian, lights-out policy. The team had planned to travel on the river from Lyons Ferry to Lewiston the next day, but the wind blew so ferociously that they instead chose to drive. The gale had ebbed by the time they arrived in town, so they dropped *Acrosswater* into the drink for a quick run upriver, just to feel a few, small rapids. Following their dip in the water, they docked the boat, dragged the gut of Lewiston for dinner and then turned in just before midnight.

The adventurers stepped on board Captain Dan Fleshman's commercial jet boat just after eight the next morning. They felt instantly at home as the craft resembled their prized *Acrosswater*, from its sleek, aluminum hull to its sensible layout to the throaty rumble of its engine. The commercial vessels used on the Snake - in order to safely make the runs into the belly of Hells Canyon - came equipped with either twin V6's or supercharged V8's. This one had two, 400 hp Cummins and when the skipper turned the engines loose after motoring out of the marina, the passengers were pressed helplessly into the cushions of their seats, their cheeks rippling like they were being launched on an Atlas rocket.

Shortly into the voyage (after asking a few introductory questions), Karl realized he had a gold mine of information on his hands in the form of Captain Dan. For the remainder of the trip, which was seventy miles in both directions, he handcuffed himself near the helm and soaked up all he could about river navigation.

The Beamer skipper shared how to watch for rocks protruding from shore and how a wrinkled crest exposed a slightly immersed boulder. He gave color commentary on sand bar pitch and pointed out clues given away by certain land formations. He demonstrated how to traverse Class III rapids by either riding a fall of water or powering up a trough. And he explained how to identify pools and sections of river that might conceal a sleeper (a fully submerged rock normally unseen from the surface). The rest of the crew basked in the impressive surroundings, marveling at the courage of deer and wild sheep, which, unintimidated by the approach of the boat, tramped near the water's edge.

Back in Lewiston, Captain Dan extended an invitation for a return visit and a private lesson up and down the Snake, Salmon and Clearwater rivers, a session guaranteed to give Karl the navigational tools needed to negotiate all but the most severe rapids. The

Acrosswater skipper declined for the time being (citing his team's demanding itinerary), but sincerely thanked the Beamer captain for the excellent and noteworthy tour, shook his hand and then turned and walked up the wharf to where his crew waited on shore. They were leaving for Montana the next day. It would be nearly 700 miles before *Acrosswater* would be in the water again.

At mile post 174.4 on U.S. Route 12, the sign for the Lolo Summit sits 5,223 feet above sea level. Provided that the pass is clear enough to allow traffic, countless travelers cruise by every day, oblivious that they are driving past a marker of breathtaking importance in U.S. history. In 1805, the Corps of Discovery went over that very spot during a forced march across the Bitterroot Mountains. They were starving.

They were relying on a Shoshone guide because the Lolo Trail was so faint that not even the seasoned woodsmen within the Corps could follow its trace. They had already butchered their spare horses for food and their hunting attempts had only brought in a few grouse, a coyote, a beaver and two deer. The horses themselves were suffering because snowfall had covered most of the high elevation grass and they had to be rounded up daily from increasingly distant plots of forage. The Corps' guide lost the trail at some point, adding days to the journey before he realized the mistake.

When they crested the peak, Captain Clark, in desperation, took a smaller group of six soldiers and went ahead of the main party to find food at lower altitudes. He hoped to make contact with a tribe rumored to be living in the foothills to the west. After two days of slow marching, the remaining contingent led by Lewis came upon a half-eaten horse - a stray, not one from the expedition - and a note left behind by Clark. Their spirits lifted slightly after eating, and by the encouragement of their guide that the plains were close, they forged ahead. On day twenty-one of their punishing hike over the Bitterroots, they were met by one of the men from Clark's band. He had food and the news that a native community was just seven miles ahead. Shortly thereafter, the entire Corps reunited amidst the lodges of the Nez Perce. Their westward journey was back on track.

The *Acrosswater* party was fully aware of the significance of the Lolo Pass since Rose had read the rest of the crew some underlined tidbits from *Undaunted Courage* just two days prior. Appropriately - almost reverently - the insides of the RV's were absent the normal chatter and CB traffic as they left Idaho and drove into Montana. They paused briefly to fuel up in Lolo itself and then continued on to Missoula where they spent the night.

The next day, Rose and Roxa piloted the rigs to the town of Anaconda so the guys could polish up the golf clubs. They all had a tee time in the early afternoon at Old Works, the first, highly anticipated golf course of their journey. They rolled into town before noon, checked into their campsite, hooked up the utilities, choked down a quick lunch and then made tracks for the course. Larry had not swung a club since he had injured himself trying to stop the Harley from hitting the blacktop back home, and Karl had not been near a green in two weeks (unless he counted the one near Beacon Rock) so they were both eager to be on the course along with their two favorite playing partners.

When it opened to the public in 1997, the Old Works golf course was the first cooperative effort of its kind found anywhere in the United States. The course served a dual purpose; it was a renowned golfing destination and, more importantly, a protective barrier over a registered Superfund site. First listed on the National Priorities List by the EPA in 1983, the Washoe smelter stopped processing raw mining materials long ago, but the area still contained toxic levels of arsenic, millions of cubic yards of flue dust and piles of other smelting wastes.

After an extensive study and the evaluation of proposed remedies, the EPA and the Atlantic Richfield Company (then owner of the old, smelting site) agreed on an action plan to clean up the area. Part of the EPA's documented strategy required the construction of "...engineered covers over waste materials..." and the use of "...innovative revegetation techniques." The community of Anaconda petitioned the EPA and ARCO to consider building a golf course as a way to rehabilitate the site. Town leaders believed a course would promote economic growth, all while meeting the government's stringent, environmental goals.

Following long negotiations, all parties agreed and in 1994, Jack Nicklaus broke ground after being selected as the designer of choice. He made good use of the smelter footprint, winding the layout between the upper and lower works and preserving the historic remains of many of the old buildings. In place of normal sand in the bunkers, Nicklaus reused benign slag which gave the course its unique, black traps. For irrigation, engineers embedded a series of pipes that collected runoff, filtered it through several layers of cleansing strata and then emptied the water into holding ponds. The course opened to immediate praise and maintained its renowned status over the years. (It was listed among Golf Digest's top 100 courses in 2016.) More significantly, the EPA audited the site in 2015 and found that, aside from minor, expected maintenance, the property was serving its purpose by protecting the land from further degradation and toxic runoff.

Well, the Golden Bear and the founding fathers of the Old Works may have provided a world class barrier against the toxins trapped under the turf, but they had no answer for players thrashing about topside. Though Rose and Roxa were happy with their rounds, the men knocked the rust off their games by methodically carving a series of potholes and divots the entire length of the Old Works' 6,000 yards. Larry's wrist held up to the pummeling for ten holes before he had to call it quits. He barely mentioned the outing later in his diary, remarking simply and bitterly, "...hand hurts."

The captain noted in his journal that he shot ninety, however, the Old Works scorecard was curiously absent from expeditionary archives. Research turned up scores from all other courses played during the *Acrosswater* campaign - most cards were simply stapled to the historical record - but nothing from Anaconda. The skipper even listed on a separate document every round played by town, state and score - with accompanying starred ratings - but, again, no mention of Old Works. The card was likely too toxic, having been saturated with arsenic dust kicked up by the frantic swinging, and thus had to be destroyed.

After a quick shower back at camp, the foursome made their way to Barclay Steakhouse for dinner where they were greeted like celebrities. Karl and Rose had stopped in Anaconda two years prior and had dined at Barclay. The owners had been so smitten with them that they had insisted that the couple use the restaurant parking lot as a base of operations; when the travelers showed up in 2000, everyone at the restaurant welcomed them like soldiers returning home from war. Barclay was an institution in town and the *Acrosswater* party soaked up the familiar atmosphere for several hours, swapping stories and dining on a parade of classic, steakhouse dishes like shrimp cocktail, relish trays, prime rib, baked potatoes and fresh bread.

After supper and suppressing satisfied burps with handfuls of mints on the way out the door, the party bid farewell to the Barclay family and motored into the heart of Anaconda to investigate the town before calling it a night. Just a few blocks from the restaurant, the group turned onto Main Street and had not driven very far when they screeched to a halt in front of a building that was decidedly out of place for an old mining town. They had stumbled upon the Washoe Theater.

Designed in the early thirties by B. Marcus Priteca, the Washoe shared its architectural bloodlines with other, distinguished buildings across North America: Radio City Music Hall, The Orpheum Theatre in San Francisco, The Admiral in Seattle and Pantages in L.A. The Washoe did not show its first film until 1936, but it had remained a treasure in the community, eventually being listed on the National Register of Historic Places in 1982. When the *Acrosswater* party peeked inside an unlocked door nearly twenty years after that milestone, the theater still had the original paint, the original seating, some of its original carpeting and all of its original splendor. David, the theater janitor, was delighted to give them a personalized tour and proudly showed them a trove of behind-the-scenes rarities typically missed by the movie going public.

They were led into the ushers' room and its wall of lacquered wooden lockers. They saw the huge silk curtain that rarely made an appearance for fear that its ancient, frail construction would not endure being raised and lowered. They listened to the back stairs creak as they went up to the projection booth where David showed them the old projector. He let them poke their heads into the attic to see the original trusses and smell the sixty-four-year-old dust. He pointed out the craftsmanship of every guild, mural, chandelier and sconce.

When they were done touring, they all agreed that they had been transported to a different era and felt like they had just spent an hour strolling with the ghosts of Bette Davis, Gary Cooper, Jean Harlow and Jimmy Stewart. After insisting that David enjoy dinner at Barclay Steakhouse on them, they stepped back into downtown Anaconda, blinking in the glare of the modern streetlights. It had been another long day and they turned in close to midnight with plans to rise early to make the long drive across the Montana plains to Glasgow.

Their route the following morning took them to Butte, then to Helena and then to Great Falls for a pit stop and their first glimpse of the Missouri. Far from becoming the silt and snag filled waterway found miles downstream, the river at this juncture was clear and shallow, attracting scores of fly fishermen either wading or in drift boats. It certainly gave no hint of the menacing obstacles that were miles ahead.

Even cruising ten mph over the speed limit, the commute from Missoula to Glasgow took all day. It was like being on the open ocean except the waves and watery swells were replaced by endless, rolling plains. When they eventually tired of the monotonous hum of the road, they turned off at Chinook for a break, but instead of a quick stretch of their legs, pulled into the Blaine County Museum. Though the museum closed in fifteen minutes, the kindly curator ushered them into the video interpretive center where they had an experience as unexpected as it was moving.

Chinook sits less than thirty miles south of the Canadian border and just sixteen miles north of the Bear Paw battlefield where, in 1877, the Nez Perce tribe finally surrendered to the U.S. Army. Up to that point, the tribe had enjoyed a collaborative relationship with representatives of the U.S. government and had figured prominently on more than one occasion. For instance, without the support of the Nez Perce, it is doubtful that the Corps of Discovery would have survived its trek over the mountains in 1805. Not only did the tribe provide food from its own scarce reserves, members of the Corps convalesced in safety amidst the Nez Perce dwellings for over a week before continuing to the sea.

Then, when John Jacob Astor tried to establish the western branch of his burgeoning fur empire on the Pacific coast, his envoys experienced the tribe's hospitality as *they* limped towards the ocean; once settled in Astoria, trappers counted on the Nez Perce as peaceful trading partners. And fifty years later, as western expansion continued unabated and the Federal Government held treaty discussions with several of the tribes in the Oregon Territory, the leader of the Nez Perce, Old Chief Joseph, supported the negotiations. Even when the United States allowed Anglo settlers to pour into the area much earlier than planned, the Nez Perce still honored their agreement and assisted in subduing the Yakima peoples.

Still, the tribe's reserve of patience was not bottomless and in the 1860's, the government tried to renegotiate for ninety percent of the natives' remaining land. Old Chief Joseph - by all accounts a pragmatic, humble man who wanted peace at all costs - refused to sign the treaty and tore up his Bible in disgust. Hope flared briefly in 1873 when a federal inquiry determined that the Nez Perce held the rights to the land and President Grant declared the Wallowa Valley a reservation. Sadly, it dimmed almost immediately as settlers continued to flood the territory, abusing and terrorizing the natives.

Four short years later, the government reversed course and gave the Nez Perce just thirty days to evacuate the region. A burst of skirmishes commenced, forcing Young Chief Joseph - he had assumed the leadership mantle from his father - to gather what remained of his people and attempt a flight for the safety of Canada.

Over the course of 1700 miles, the tribe forded the Snake River at flood stage (the *Acrosswater* party had seen the location of the crossing during its ride with Beamers), crossed the Bitterroot Mountains via the Lolo Pass, traversed a corner of the newly designated Yellowstone Park and navigated much of Montana from south to north. Accounts vary as to the exact number of people in retreat, but it is indisputable that the vast majority were elders, women and children. With twice as many ponies also in tow, the natives eluded the U.S. Cavalry for as long as possible, but ultimately, starving, exhausted and with many having already died en route, Chief Joseph surrendered near Bear Paw. Most of his people were allowed to resettle on a reservation near their ancestral home, but Joseph was barred from returning for fear he would instigate an uprising. He died in 1904 in exile on the Colville Reservation in Washington, having never returned to his place of birth.

Despite its brevity, the movie in the Blaine County Museum captured the plight of the Nez Perce tastefully, emotionally and with surprising depth. Using a combination of music, videos, pictures and classic paintings, the film thoughtfully chronicled those last few weeks and how the conflict between the tribe and the U.S. Army was a microcosm of the unstoppable march of settlers across the West.

The *Acrosswater* crew exited the theater feeling profound admiration for the people of Chief Joseph and their indelible stamp on the nation, mixed with a gnawing sadness at the inability of the two cultures to coexist without one suffering at the hands of the other. They mingled a few more minutes among the other displays, then trooped back onto their campers and finished the rest of the drive to Glasgow. They had another date with history in the morning.

The picture was as iconic as any seen on a Hollywood billboard. If its subject was Barbara Stanwyck or Katharine Hepburn or Vivien Leigh, the photo would have been celebrated for its rugged authenticity. Instead, it was Jane Schaak (Porter), a young woman on break from school, sitting on a giant steer, a flop-eared dog in her lap, her hand shielding her eyes as if searching for something off in the distance. In the background, a stand of tall trees cast shadows on a simple, wooden home and beyond the home, the horizon stretched on forever. There was snow on the ground, no leaves on the trees and viewers could almost feel the bite of the cold and the wind.

But the picture was not of a movie set or remote film location. It was a homestead out on the vast plains of Montana and it was Jane's birthplace. Since the *Acrosswater* expedition was putting into the Missouri just downstream from Fort Peck, and the old homestead was settled in that very region, captain and crew decided they could not pass up the chance to try to find it. If they successfully tracked it down - which was in no way guaranteed given the size of the area and the scarcity of property records - it would be a touching finish to an already unforgettable start to their odyssey.

The Homestead Act of 1862 paved the way for thousands of settlers to acquire real estate. For the price of a licensing fee, five years of labor, the construction of a modest dwelling and the

Jane Schaak at the homestead

commitment to reside on and work the soil, homesteaders received in return the deed to 160 acres of formerly public land. Migrants were eligible as well and could satisfy some requirements of citizenship simply by completing the steps to property ownership.

Among the European settlers who swept into the West to take advantage of the Homestead Act were members of the Schaak family. Originally from southern Russia, they were hard-working, entrepreneurial and German speaking, and John and Rose Schaak (Jane's parents) would eventually parlay their first homestead into a huge ranch near the Wolf Mountains in central Montana; however, in the early 1900's, that little foothold out on the plains was barely beginning.

The *Acrosswater* convoy made the drive from Glasgow to Circle in just over an hour and met up with the Porters. (They were out on an expedition of their own and had broken course to join the hunt for the homestead.) They all piled into one SUV so that Bud could guide the search party with some old maps and notes he had. They drove south for several miles and followed approximate markers Bud had written down: take a left at Wadkins; bear right on Old Skull; go straight ahead on Chalk.

Soon they were driving in ruts and faint impressions carved across the savanna and looking at scores of fence posts disappearing in all directions; the fences were straight as arrows, following the county surveyor lines. Every so often the SUV would reach a gate and Larry would hop out, open the gate and then shut it behind them. At some point, Bud said that he thought they were close. Then, at the brow of a hill, after the latch of the gate fell into place and Larry jumped back inside the SUV, the vehicle inched over the crest and a cry of joy went up from the crew. There below them, in a little valley next to a stand of scrubby trees, was the old homestead.

The people who took advantage of the Homestead Act and dared to carve out a life on those windy prairies did so under back-breaking conditions. In the same collection of photographs that held the one of Jane on the steer, a formal, family snapshot displayed the whole clan in its grim, weather-beaten glory; the only person who did not seem to mind posing for the photo was the baby asleep on the lap of the matriarch. Everyone else appeared to have been marched in front of the camera at gunpoint and they were clearly not a family that had time to waste sitting for a photographer. They had a life to scratch out on the plains and from the youngest to the oldest, they had work to do.

They had to clear the land of brush and try to prepare it for farming. They had animals to raise, sell and butcher. They had crops to gather and food to preserve for each long winter ahead. There were latrines to dredge, clothes to mend, fence posts to set, wood to stack and hides to scrape. Any dwellings they built were constructed of whatever materials were readily available: tar paper, sod, discarded lumber and sheet metal. They only went to larger communities a few times yearly to sell livestock and buy or trade for supplies. The rest of the year, the family lived alone in vast, wind-blown, utter isolation.

Hardship was commonplace. In a compilation of oral histories gathered by historian Donna Gray, Montana ranch women recalled what it was like to grow up during that time. They told of traveling by stage coach as late as 1920. They described living in the barest of homes with earthen floors and drafty walls and the satisfaction of figuring out how to cook on a wood stove without scorching everything. One reported about the time a blizzard blew in just after her father went to town, stranding her and her younger siblings. They managed to survive by wading through the snow to a neighbor's house, miles away.

They talked about collecting water by punching through the ice of a frozen stream, about the excitement of having a plain cabinet to store kitchen utensils in, about living without electricity or heat for over twenty-five years in the same two-room house and about the messy business of butchering animals they had grown attached to. One thing they did not seem to do was complain. Not ever.

That was the backdrop that the *Acrosswater* SUV rolled into as it maneuvered slowly down into the gully and stopped in the clearing in front of the main residence. Jane, thrilled to be home, escorted everyone into the ancient house, a three-room building still standing and the affirmation of a rugged, pioneering existence. It was hard to believe that she had been born there.

They strolled over the entire acre, examining smaller outbuildings, sheds, dilapidated farm machinery and broken-down, rusty cars. What struck all of the first-time visitors was the absolute desolation and seclusion. The Schaaks had deliberately built the home down in a vale as they sought whatever protection they could from the howling winds that swept across the prairie and that setting, combined with the sheer distance to the nearest neighbor, clarified the fierce, independent nature of Jane's side of the family. They had needed that determination and resourcefulness just to survive.

Jane's memories came in waves as they toured the property. She pointed out the shed where her best friend (a small, black sheep) was born. She showed them the shelter for the Shetland pony her father had bought for her. She rode it like hell to school and back, clutching its mane with one hand and her lunch box in the other. It always infuriated her on the return home when the pony went too close to the barn and Jane's shins banged against the wall as they cantered inside. She described the connection she shared with the ranch hands who worked for her father over the years as the small property expanded into a legitimate enterprise. And she talked about the pain of leaving the little ranch when her parents sent her away to boarding school.

After seeing her birthplace, they traveled the short distance to the homestead of her grandparents (Erdman and Christina). Jane told how her grandmother had died one winter of pneumonia and the family kept the body in a shed until April, when the ground was soft enough to dig a grave. The gravesite was still there.

They continued their visit, first in Wadkins where they saw the old post office that Jane's uncle had built, and then back in Circle where they were surprised to meet an old cowboy during lunch who had known the Schaak family. He and Jane exchanged stories of the old days. Particularly chilling was the memory of Ed Schaak's death; he perished when static electricity ignited some fuel while he was filling the tank of his tractor.

After eating, the *Acrosswater* four said goodbye to Jane and Bud, thanking them for a day none of them would ever forget. They had connected with the past in a way that few people are privileged to do over the course of an entire lifetime. Not only had they walked on a classic stage of the American West, but they had mingled with relics of their own rich history, their biography brought to life.

To a person, they noted their extraordinary, good fortune. The next day would be July 31 and they had planned a lay day. They needed the time to reflect on their journey so far and to perform some maintenance before hitting the river. Karl would write in his journal that morning, "...tomorrow we officially begin our adventure to New Orleans." They had already traveled over 1000 miles of road, navigated three rivers and several locks, visited multiple touchstones of their heritage, reunited with old acquaintances, made new ones and flabbergasted countless fishermen with their Harley, offloading process. And yet, they had not formally started their adventure. The captain summed it up in his diary, recalling the word he whispered as he stood looking at Christina's simple headstone out on the sweeping, windy tundra of Montana.

"Wow."

The Schaak homestead

Chapter 5

The woes of Wolf Point

"300 acres of alfalfa & weeds - get 4 ton/AC & 65$ a ton"

Larry's journal - August 2, 2000

While exploring Montana, the crew observed firsthand the struggle of the independent farmer to eke out a living. Larry recorded these rough estimates after visiting with a family living near Wolf Point.

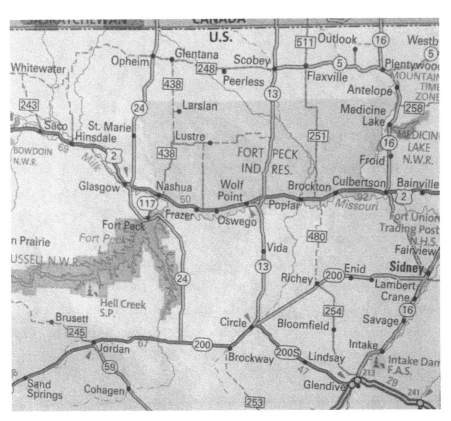

Fort Peck region of the Missouri River

SOMETIME in the early evening of Wednesday, November 26, 1930, the owner of an outdoor recreation company set out in a boat to retrieve a group of duck hunters from a sandbar on a stretch of the Missouri River. He had built up his business over a number of years by catering to the varied interests and whims of the men who hired him so to find himself motoring across the waves at anytime of day or night was commonplace. The wind was whipping strongly over the water - gusts of seventy mph had been reported downstream - but his knowledge of the area, experience on the river and confidence in the craft he was piloting gave him reassurance that he would be back at home in just a few hours.

He might have given his rescue trip a second thought had he known that a little earlier in the day, a hunter a few miles away had to navigate five-foot swells in order to make it to shore after being stranded alone on a sandbar for fourteen hours. Although witnesses in the area would later claim they had seen a fire burning on a tiny island near the owner's last known location, he was never seen again.

Nearly seventy years later, the river still presented a perilous challenge for visitors of all ages, regardless of the modern conveniences available. In late July of 2000, a grandfather-granddaughter team found itself stranded for several days during a fishing trip before being rescued. They were seasoned boaters, locals, well prepared and had fished on the river near Fort Peck many times. Despite all those advantages, they ran aground on a sandbar in a remote section of the river and with no cellphone at their disposal, could only wait for help to arrive once they did not return home at their appointed time.

Members of the *Acrosswater* party had poured over stories like those during the preparation phase of the trip so they knew that traveling on the water carried big risks, especially on the stretch of river between Fort Peck, MT and Sioux City, IA, where navigational markers were nonexistent and settlements were sparse. Still, they had done their research and prepared as best they could and therefore, they launched on August 1 just east of Fort Peck with extraordinary optimism. The captain's log started with the words "The Missouri River First Day!", perfectly reflecting the upbeat mood of the entire team as they headed into virgin (for them) territory. They had enjoyed several good days of practice on other rivers, the skipper had received some impromptu training on the Snake from a professional, jet boat captain, their equipment was in tip top shape, they had a full tank of gas, they had the most up-to-date maps and charts available, the weather was fine and their spirits were high.

The first sign of trouble appeared on the Harley ride back from forward base camp. The planned sequence for the day called for them to drop the boat into the Missouri, Karl and Larry to move the RV's ahead to Wolf Point, the girls to stay behind at the dock to polish the chrome on *Acrosswater* and then for the guys to ride back to the boat ramp so they could all travel on the river together. On the return trip, the men found themselves in the middle of a rainstorm that soaked them for almost thirty miles. When they finally sloshed their way to the ramp, they discovered that the same front had forced Rose and Roxa to seek refuge under a picnic shelter.

That brief setback aside, the weather seemed to brighten for good after lunchtime so they wiped down the seat cushions, pushed off from shore and began their downstream run. They needed to travel seventy-three river miles that day and things went well for more than sixty. The captain had been successfully following the deep channel of the river despite the absence of marker buoys, but as he turned into a corner near the south bank of mile sixty-two, the water beneath *Acrosswater* disappeared before he could react. They ran aground.

Attempts to secure a line to the river bottom using their anchor only succeeded in stirring up the mud and it was no wonder. The banks and shores in that area were more like dust than dirt because the sediment was so fine, and it quickly became clear that they would need to use different tactics to pull themselves free. They cobbled together nearly all the rope on board and then searched the edge of the river for something sturdy they could lash onto. One of them spotted a group of trees at the top of an embankment about 200 feet away. All they needed was some way to bring the rope from the boat to the trees.

One of the least celebrated heroes of the Corps of Discovery was the woodsman Charles Drouillard. An accomplished trapper and hunter, he was a crack shot, spoke English, French and several native dialects, knew sign language and regularly proved to have an endless supply of diplomacy and resourcefulness. Time and again over the course of the expedition, Captain Lewis called on Drouillard to help rescue them from thorny circumstances. Had a member of the party become lost hunting? Drouillard tracked him down. Had the horses run off? Charles had them back in an hour. Is that a hostile war party approaching? "Charlie, go see what they want." It is not too much of a stretch to suggest that had he not been along, the great trek would have ended in tragedy on more than one occasion.

On the *Acrosswater* team, Larry served as the group's "Drouillard," so when they found themselves stuck on the sandbar during their first try tearing down the Missouri and the captain, after putting the last sheet bend in the line, turned around with eyebrows raised, Larry wordlessly allowed the working end of the rope to be tied to his waist, put on his old sneakers and plunged into the frigid current. (Important note - a dip in the freezing, muddy river was never mentioned when Rose informed Dr. Ryan that his father's safety and well being were the highest priority on the trip.)

Once on shore, Larry clambered up the bank and secured the rope to one of the trees. They tried to winch the boat free, but it simply would not budge. Seeing no other choice, Larry used some sign language of his own to alert his mates that he was going for help and set off over the surrounding hills.

Two hours later, Larry came upon a farmhouse at the top of a long, gently sloping field. He first circled the home four times looking for a water spigot (he later recorded his sentiments in his journal with the grim, desperate words, "...thirsty! Hot!") before giving up and banging at the screen door. When nobody answered, he turned his back and resigned himself to another baking walk to the next ranch. He had made it only fifty feet when he heard a creak behind him and a quiet, nervous voice asked, "Can I help you?"

Whirling around, he saw a teenage girl peeking through the cracked door. From his vantage point he could clearly see that she was spooked (and with good reason since she had been watching his erratic behavior the whole time through the home's thin curtains), so he made what he thought were reassuring motions with his hands and calmly explained the dire circumstances unfolding at the river. She stared at him in unblinking silence for a moment and then abruptly slammed the door. It may have been the heat and dehydration playing tricks on him, but he swore he heard something heavy like a gun safe or upright piano being slid against the other side of the entrance. He took off his hat and sat on the stoop to contemplate his next move.

"Charlotte tells me you're having some trouble down at the river."

He looked up to find a small, leathery man in socks and dungarees standing on the porch putting suspenders over his shoulders. Larry hopped to his feet. "Why, yes...yes!" We're stuck on a sandbar!"

"Yeah, they'll gitchah. Name's Sam. I'll fetch my boots." Sam shuffled down the porch, opened a previously unseen door and disappeared inside. "Charlotte! Bring our friend some water!", Larry heard him holler. A few minutes later they filled up the back of an old Chevy with a pile of lariats that were stacked around an outdoor pen, pulled out of the drive, immediately veered sharply off the road and roared across the range towards the river.

Back at the shipwreck, the other members of the crew had more than one cause for concern. They were primarily worried about Larry, given the rural nature of the landscape around the river and the stifling August heat. At least on the boat they had some shade and water. They also noticed that storm clouds were building again in the distance and the thought of wind, rain, lightning and thunder in their exposed situation was unnerving. Even more worrisome, a group of locals was gathering on the north side of the river, clearly more interested in consuming the cases of beer they had with them than offering any assistance.

In fact, the clearing in which the crowd was setting up seemed well-worn, as if people frequently observed marooned sailors from that very spot. As the number of vehicles arriving at the clearing grew, so did the sophistication of the camping apparatus: portable braziers, kegs with custom taps, elevated lifeguard chairs, a smoker, five hammocks and propane lamps should the event run into the night.

On board *Acrosswater*, and after several tries without success, the captain finally reached the sheriff's office using the cell phone. The deputy who answered said they would send out a boat to help. Karl thanked him and rang off, watching with growing alarm as the mob on the north shore became louder and larger.

"Larry!" Roxa shouted. Karl turned and saw Larry waving languorously from the top of the bank as he emerged from the passenger side of a truck. A sense of relief flooded across the group. Their party was back intact and they had made contact with some authorities. Things were looking up.

Larry and Sam unloaded a mound of rope from the truck bed and then, through a series of hand signals, the two groups hatched a plan to shuttle lines between the boat and the truck in order to establish a more secure tow. After tying off and receiving the all clear, Sam tried to pull the boat free with his Chevy, without effect. Whether it was the lack of traction or the sheer weight of the boat, they were still stuck, even with Sam pulling in four-wheel drive. When one of the lines snapped under the strain, the crowd on the north bank cheered while the captain and crew groaned. Again using sign language, the *Acrosswater* team concocted a new strategy involving the retrieval of the SUV from the forward camp as well as some additional rope from Sam's ranch. This time Rose swam ashore with the keys to the SUV, along with some drinking water, and then Larry and Sam were off to the RV park in Wolf Point.

A short while later, Larry arrived back at the river with the SUV and some more rope just as two officers puttered up in a small boat; even they had struggled under the existing conditions to make it through with any vessel larger than a dinghy. This time, with the extra pull of the SUV plus a push from the officers and the *Acrosswater* crew all standing on the sandbar, they succeeded in freeing the jet boat.

The storm clouds seen earlier were almost on top of them so the captain consulted with the deputies about next steps. Because of the way the jet boat operated, they would have to go through a purge ritual to safely evacuate all of the sediment that had been sucked up the intake and with both the lightning and darkness swiftly approaching, there simply was not enough time to run through the checklist. They all concluded that the safest course of action was to tie off on the southern shore, batten the hatches and trust that the boat would be secure overnight, despite the storm and the throng on the other side of the river.

Using the little Honda outboard on the stern of *Acrosswater*, they motored over to the bank and selected a spot as sheltered as possible. After unloading any necessities and locking up the boat as well as they could, they trudged up to the SUV, none more slowly than the skipper. They all cast one, last, forlorn glance at *Acrosswater*, exposed to the elements as she was, and then drove away towards Wolf Point. On the north bank, the revelers were firing up the propane lamps and tapping a new keg, clearly unconcerned about the approaching weather. It seemed it would be a sleepless night for both groups.

Early the next morning, the members of the *Acrosswater* party raced through breakfast and then set out for the river. After a quick pit stop at a tack and feed store in Wolf Point to buy a new lariat for Sam, they made a painfully slow drive back to the boat. The road was being resurfaced and there was a pilot truck leading the construction processional; it maxed out at twenty miles per hour with intermittent, anxiety-inducing waits sprinkled in. With tensions running high, captain and crew finally crested the bank at the scene of the wreck and saw their precious craft, still tied off just as they had left her, bobbing safely in the current. The party on the opposite shore had cleared off at some point over night, leaving nothing behind but an expanded venue for future galas.

The team immediately set about restoring *Acrosswater* to full working order. Rose and Roxa cleaned up all the ropes while Karl and Larry started to flush the intake and cooling lines. For all of its benefits, the jet boat had one huge drawback: the intake purge. In order to generate propulsion, the engine drew water through the bottom of the boat and forced it out the jets at the rear, enabling both locomotion and steering. By running aground, the engine had sucked up sand and other detritus into the jet, both fouling the lines and threatening to permanently damage the primary means of thrust.

The process to fully clean the intake called for the removal of two screws securing a plate on top of the jet assembly, which allowed for the plate to be detached. That maneuver granted access to flush the sediment, but it also created a giant hole in the bottom of the boat through which water would geyser. Although they had a high-capacity, bilge pump on board and a hand brace that expedited the bolt extraction process, they still had to work quickly - and God help them if they dropped one of the screws.

They successfully ran through the purge checklist and then Karl, Rose and Roxa used the outboard to motor into deeper water while Larry waited by the SUV. The water-based team started up the jet engine to confirm it was running properly and then idled over to the north side of the river, which the deputies had recommended because it seemed to have a better channel. The plan called for the boat crew to navigate to a bridge a few miles down river, where they would meet Larry with the trailer and pull *Acrosswater* out of the Missouri.

Had they known that the deputies themselves had become stranded after helping rescue the expedition from its first shipwreck (the constables had also been forced to abandon their boat overnight), the river crew might have opted for more conservative tactics or, at the very least, eased back on the throttle a bit. In any event, the water was much deeper on the north side of the river - just as the deputies had predicted - which allowed the craft to reach the optimal speed required to skim through the shallows and guarantee its arrival at the bridge ahead of the ground crew.

Or, as in this case, the optimal speed to firmly lodge the boat in the center of the next, much larger sandbar.

Larry had just arrived at a field gate on his way to drop off the lariat to Sam when he heard a faint cry over the CB. "Larry! We're stuck again!!" He could just make out Rose's voice crackling over the airwaves and they carried on a garbled conversation, much like the variety enjoyed by ham radio enthusiasts the world over.

After a time, he was able to confirm that they could see three silos from their position and that they were near the Long family ranch on the north side of the river. (A government worker surveying in the area happened upon *Acrosswater* and provided the details to Rose who relayed them via radio to Larry.) He acknowledged the information, signed off the CB, delivered the lariat to Charlotte (apparently, Sam was off rescuing another ship of fools) along with lavish words of appreciation and gratitude, and then drove several miles to the three silos as described by Rose.

Turning into the drive, he met a van coming off the property, slowed to a stop and explained who he was to the woman driving the vehicle. Her name was Juleen and she was the matron of a family ranch, but not the Long family ranch. As luck would have it, she knew both where the correct silos were and the Long's phone number. Larry once again threw himself on the good graces of a complete stranger and was soon rattling over the fields again, enveloped in the dust kicked up by the van leading the way.

The two vehicles slid to a stop in sight of *Acrosswater*. (It was not nearly soon enough for the folks on the boat. They were mystified and, frankly, a little irritated that it had taken Larry so long to find them, especially after they had provided the brilliant and obvious landmark of the three silos. They had no idea that all 417 farms in the area had three silos.) Using the CB, the teams coordinated their next steps. Larry would take the trailer back to the RV park (a clear sign of everyone's brimming optimism that a trip down this part of the river was still in the cards), fuel up the

SUV, drive to the Long home in case the water crew could not reach the ranch by phone and then lead an ensemble of heavy machinery back to the river to free the boat.

Given the spotty track record of all the other plans to that point, it came as no surprise that the new strategy ran into some snags immediately. Right after Larry left the party at the water, he was again held up by the pilot truck and endured a painstaking crawl back into town. He dumped the trailer at the RV park and then, like the retired pharmacist that he was, followed with exacting precision the directions Juleen provided. He roared back out of town and took a right on Indian Road. She had warned him that the driveway to the Long ranch was long, dusty and washboard-like and she was right on every count - except for the name of the road. After offering sincere apologies for waking yet another napping cowboy, Larry inquired if the man could point him in the direction of the Long property, which he could. Following two, filling-rattling rides up and down the wrong and right drives respectively, he found himself rapping on the screen door of a farmhouse. Janice Long answered his knock. "You just missed the boys," she said. "They already left for the river after your captain called a few minutes ago. Just follow their tracks across the field."

He arrived at the site of the wreck to find *Acrosswater* and all hands on shore along with Bernard Long, Bernard's son David, David's son Keith and Keith's dog Tank. The Longs had brought a tractor and an ATV, and they had used the tractor to successfully pull the boat off the sandbar into about three feet of water.

After surveying the water depth up and down river from their present location and finding it just as shallow, they concluded that the best course of action was to trailer the boat and haul it back to camp. Because it did not appear as if they could back the SUV close enough to the water to load the boat conventionally, Bernard suggested using an old, D7 Caterpillar he had back at the ranch to provide additional lift. The skipper liked the idea and the two parties agreed to meet up back at the Long property after the *Acrosswater* team retrieved the trailer. Being that another storm was almost upon them, they shook hands and parted ways, promising to meet up shortly.

Scant visual evidence of the remainder of the day's events exists save for some renderings scratched out in the captain's log because, after lunch and just before departing for the Long property, the men had decided that Roxa (the official trip historian and photographer) and Rose should stay behind at HQ. They forbade the women from accompanying them on the grounds that they did not want the girls offering them any words of unfounded optimism during the reclamation procedure and, more importantly, because they expected the afternoon to be punctuated by excessive cursing. After all, their dear, priceless *Acrosswater* was hopelessly marooned on the banks of the fucking Missouri.

So leaving their better halves behind, they pulled onto the Long's property with trailer in tow and went into the barn where they found Bernard and David crawling over the D7 trying to start its engine. Keith stood nearby with an assortment of tools at the ready. "Either of you boys a mechanic?" Bernard asked.

Following his visitors' admission that they were not, Bernard instructed David to run over to the neighbor and try to borrow the "...big..." tractor. Ten minutes later, they heard a deep, mechanized thumping, the ground began to shake ominously and trails of dust fell from the rafters in the barn. "Oh, good," Bernard said, "he's back." Just as he finished the sentence, impossibly large tires rolled past the barn door.

Karl and Larry hustled over to the entrance, mouths agape, and watched as a mountainous John Deere, all decked out in University of Oregon green and yellow, chugged away towards the river. They estimated that the tires themselves were taller than both of their RV's and they could barely make out David, perched high up in the cockpit, motioning for them to follow. They piled into the SUV and fell in behind.

Finding the boat just as they had left her, the men first selected the best landing site available and, with David driving, used the big tractor to tow her upstream to a relatively flat area. Immediately satisfied with the progress they were making, and with the benefit of having the much larger John Deere, they decided to attempt a full extraction. Karl happened to have on board 100 feet of 1-inch, double-braided nylon rope with a 25,000-pound tensile rating, so they tied one end to the bow and the other to the tractor. With the crew applying some weight to the nose of the boat to keep the front end down, David threw the the tractor into gear and gently touched the gas.

In an instant, the line broke and whistled under the belly of the tractor, the report echoing like a rifle shot. Counting themselves lucky that the rope had miraculously missed everyone, they realized that they would need something a little stronger. Bernard raced back to his barn on the ATV and returned with a steel cable, which, when put to use, immediately began to unravel. While Bernard wove a new eyelet, David used the bucket on the smaller tractor to carve out a makeshift ramp on the shore to level the gap between the height of the trailer and the bottom of the boat.

The cable repaired, they hooked it to the stern and dragged the rear of *Acrosswater* around until it was at a right angle to the shoreline. Then, using a sling fashioned out of chain, Bernard hoisted the boat out of the water with the big tractor, while Karl and David unhitched the trailer and manually wheeled it down the improvised ramp until it was under the hull. As Bernard lowered the boat onto its cradle, the front of the trailer rose into the air until it was almost level with their heads. Bernard hopped out of the cockpit of the tractor to help Larry pull down the tongue. That allowed Karl and David to connect the trailer hitch to the ball on the rear of the SUV (they had backed the SUV closer to the scene of the wreck) and to secure the winch line from the trailer to the bow of the boat.

They cranked the winch to add some tension and, with the boat balanced like a seesaw but secure for the moment, positioned the two tractors on either side of the SUV. After they rigged lines from both sides of the stern to the tractors and with Karl cranking the trailer winch, they eased the boat fully onto the trailer. Finally, they used the giant John Deere to pull the SUV, trailer and boat far enough away from shore for the SUV to tow on its own. At long last, *Acrosswater* was safely out of the river.

Impossible for me to draw. If there were a diagram B it would show two tractors pulling the boat up into the trailer. Oh hell I'll show it from a birds eye view.

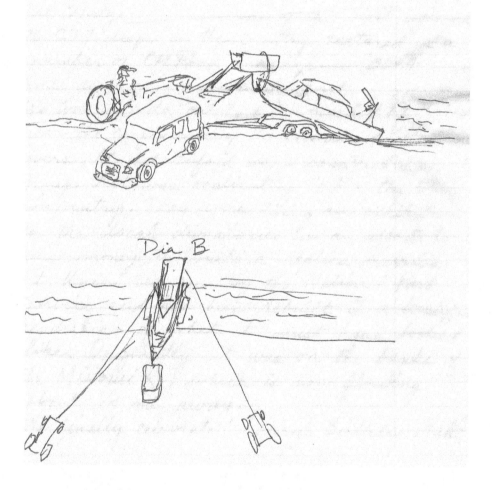

Acrosswater sandbar rescue

Back at the Long farmhouse, with the heavy machinery put away, Karl and Larry sat at the kitchen table and talked with Bernard and Janice about their lives on the ranch while Janice shelled peas she had just picked that morning. The Longs had raised seven children on the property and eked out a living growing alfalfa on their 300 acres. Due to the depressed value of silage at that moment, they were forced to depend more than they liked on Bernard's social security; his children joked that when he died they would tie him to a tree down at the river with a fishing pole in his hand to keep the income alive.

When it came time to head back to camp and Karl and Larry bade them goodbye, the Longs steadfastly refused any kind of compensation as a way of thanks and said they would tell all their friends and family about their cousins from Oregon. They were still on the front porch waving when the farmhouse disappeared into the dust behind *Acrosswater*.

Seeing the boat caked in Missouri River mud irked the captain to no end, so shortly after he and Larry pulled into camp, and despite the fatigue brought on by the day's events, he insisted that Rose accompany him to a do-it-yourself car wash he had noticed in town so they could restore their prized vessel to some semblance of normalcy. Arriving at the facility, the skipper went inside the convenience store attached to the wash to exchange some dollars for quarters while Rose drove the SUV around back and pulled the boat into the bay.

Change in hand, Karl met her near the control panel, inserted five dollars worth of quarters into the machine and the two of them spent the next several minutes hosing, scrubbing and talking about the day. Finally satisfied with what he saw, the captain asked his wife to pull the boat forward while he holstered the brush and spray nozzle.

What neither of them realized was that the exit to the bay was slightly shorter than the entrance. As the boat pulled forward, the crane stanchion that was used to hoist the Harley was protruding just high enough to catch the header beam running across the exit. Karl noticed what was happening first because he could see the tires of the SUV starting to slip.

"No! Rose, No!" he yelled, waving his arms to grab her attention but it was no use. Smoke and steam poured from the tires of the SUV, obscuring the vehicle and the boat. The pole of the hoist finally bent under the strain, allowing the truck and trailer to tear out of the bay in a shower of splinters and shingles. The captain ran to the cab to make sure that his first mate was alright and as he reached the door to check on Rose, he glanced through the windshield of the SUV; a sheriff's cruiser was gliding toward them through the smoke.

"I says to myself, 'I know that boat.'" It was Bruce, one of the deputies from the sandbar rescue. "How're you doin' Karl?" He had his elbow resting on the window of his car as he came to a stop next to the SUV.

"Well, Bruce? What are you doing here?" The skipper took off his cap and smiled at the deputy.

"Stanley's car wash is the only place in town that sells Tab. Trying to lose some of this gut." He patted his belly and winked at the captain. "My little lady likes a big man, just not this big."

"Been there, done that!" the skipper agreed, motioning with his head back at Rose.

"Man," Bruce said looking out the window, "did a tornado roll through here or something? Look at all this kindling."

"No, we just misjudged the clearance a little." Karl looked up at the stanchion, which was clearly not in any shape to hoist a motorcycle. "We'll be high and dry until I can have it repaired."

"It's probably for the best. You need to stay off the river."

The skipper couldn't believe his ears. "Excuse me?"

"The water's too low. Neil and I got stuck ourselves after we helped you last night. You never should have gone on the north side."

Now you tell me, Karl thought to himself. "You don't say?"

"Yeah. I heard at the office that another guy got stuck on at least thirty-five sandbars between the dam and the bridge, just last week. I would stay off until you reach the next, big lake. I'd hate for anything to happen to that gorgeous boat of yours."

"You and me both. Say, hang on while we park this thing. We'll go with you and see if we owe Stanley anything for the damage."

"Alright, but I doubt he'll be worried about that old wash. He has to slap up new shingles every time the wind blows." They both parked their vehicles and all three of them went inside, just as a tornado siren started to whine in the distance.

Forced off the water by the conditions on the river and the bent stanchion, the travelers portaged to Williston, a part of their original itinerary. The captain located a place in town to look at the hoist and when he paid the shop a visit, found that it specialized in aluminum repair and custom welding. Parts were ordered and the owner, Pat Helgeson, promised to fix the stanchion the following day. They used the extra lay day to belatedly celebrate Larry's birthday, do laundry, send an update for the Web page, play golf, pay some bills and catch a 6th Infantry reenactment near Fort Buford. Mostly, though, they took the time to marvel at the good fortune they had experienced in Wolf Point.

Just as the members of the Corps of Discovery had depended on the Nez Perce for food and sanctuary following their harrowing march across the Bitterroots, so too had the *Acrosswater* team found itself amidst a community of selfless, good-hearted people. Under what circumstances today would someone answer a phone call in the middle of the day and, upon receiving the crackling summons of a complete stranger on the other end, immediately dispatch her entire family with a convoy of heavy equipment to help.

The Long family, Sam, Juleen and the deputies all buoyed the *Acrosswater* expedition at a time when it needed it most. Sure, the boat became stranded and they had to evacuate the river, but their luck was uncanny. *Acrosswater* was abandoned overnight and then torqued during the pull from the river in ways never imagined by its engineers, yet it emerged unscathed. The Long's neighbors happened to be home when David called on them for the big John Deere. The snapped rope missed every head and limb on its whistling journey under the tractor. And Pat Helgeson just happened to specialize in welding aluminum alloys. Perhaps the trip from Fort Peck to Williston did not proceed exactly as originally drawn, but in the end, they had launched semi-successfully into the upper Missouri, made some unforgettable memories and bonded with kind, compassionate people.

Chapter 6
South to the Badlands

"Ain't that America, we're something to see."

Pink Houses

By John Mellencamp

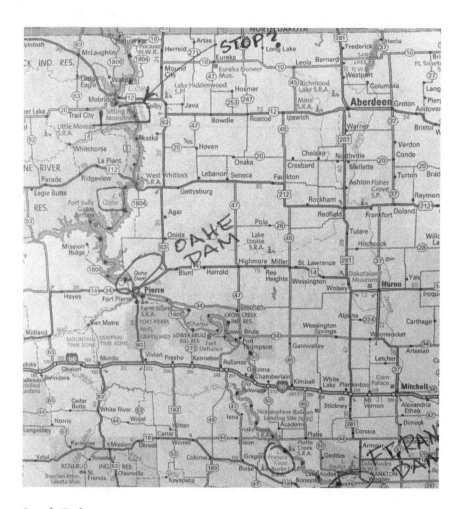

South Dakota

ON a Sunday morning in 2011, campers in Waterford, ME awoke to shouts and flashing lights. Police officers from nearby Bethel had tracked a fugitive to Keoka Lake after the suspect led them on a high speed chase over dark, twisting roads, sometimes at speeds nearing ninety miles per hour. The officers managed to flatten the getaway car's tires with a spike mat, but the driver fled on foot and eventually tried to escape by swimming across the lake.

When the residents of the camp found out what was happening, a few of them joined the posse in their paddle boats. The owners of the park loaned the police their party barge (Tiki torches and all) and soon, the unorthodox band of law enforcement plus civil servants was gently churning its way across the pond, closing in on the tiring escapee. He finally gave up, cornered and exhausted. The police offered high praise for the campers' support, noting that without the use of their boats and their hands-on assistance during the pursuit, the final outcome most certainly would have been different.

Truthfully, had the suspect dove into the water near any number of camps or RV parks throughout the country, the same sense of spirited generosity and civic responsibility would have spontaneously appeared. People in the RV community, whether permanent or part-time, can be ridiculously tight-knit and they often coordinate their travel with friends they have made over the years, becoming, in effect, modern nomads. They celebrate holidays together, decorate their tiny homes with flair, organize both recreational and humanitarian clubs and support their favorite organizations, bringing considerable, combined clout to those in need. The winter residents of a park in Yuma, AZ once donated more than $12,000 to a local hospice center, even though they were in the midst of a recession and many of them were struggling to pay their own bills. Many RV enthusiasts are retired or semi-retired and with all those miles under their collective tires, it takes something eye-opening to stir them from a late lunch or game of dominoes.

So imagine the startled murmurs that swept across the parks in the summer and fall of 2000 when the *Acrosswater* caravan rumbled into the campsites. Larry and Roxa owned a 1989 Sportscoach IV and it had served them well. They had purchased it years before the foursome ever conceived of their adventure so they had already taken it on many outings.

It was thirty-five feet long, painted neutral colors and had most of the standard fittings that made RV travel convenient and comfortable, but it resembled the majority of the other rigs on the road and in the parks. None of the other campers would even look up from their potato salad when Larry and Roxa rolled past because, frankly, they were sitting in lawn chairs right next to a coach of almost identical make, model and appearance. However, not once, even if you added up all the experiences of all the occupants at every KOA or state campground the *Acrosswater* party passed through, had anyone ever seen another set-up like Karl and Rose's.

They owned a Marathon, the 280th that had come off the assembly line, forty feet of shimmering chrome. Though used, the six-year-old Prevost still looked brand new due to the skipper's meticulous attention to maintenance and his investment in regular, forensic scrubbings. He had forged a relationship with an auto detailer who shared the same maniacal obsession with cleanliness, a detailer who would show up with an armload of Q-tips to make sure he removed every particle of dust and every molecule of filth from the rig's many crevices. Additionally, the team's towing configuration had Larry and Roxa dragging the SUV, leaving the trailer and boat to Karl and Rose. With their matching paint and gleaming aluminum, the Marathon, boat and Harley made for an eye-popping combination.

The Marathon (or the Bus, as it was affectionately called) contained stylish, but practical, living quarters. It had a nice sized master bedroom in the rear, a bath with a shower, a complete kitchen and dining bench and a small sitting area directly behind the front seats that collapsed into optional beds. The bedroom and the living room both had televisions and the entire residence had full and mood lighting. Someone blindfolded and dropped off on the inside would find the arrangements pleasant and well appointed, but not pretentious.

It was a home in which someone could entertain friends for a game of cards, watch college football on a crisp, fall afternoon, prepare a contribution for an evening potluck or dry camp for weeks if needed. And as finely crafted as its interior was, the Bus hid even more value in the engine compartment, behind its lower bay doors and in the intuitive, complementary systems sprinkled throughout.

The driver side held most of the technical infrastructure. A compressor with 140 PSI output and fifty feet of hose resided inside the front wheel-well, a thoughtful inclusion for owners needing to top off any of the tires. Bay one contained the main generator, a 20 kw, 4-cycle diesel. In bay two, the inverter sat adjacent the generator on a slide out with 50 amp power cords and connectors. The final door on the driver side concealed the plumbing array which included inputs for city water, outputs for sewage, valves that managed gray water and black water and a faucet for washing up after completing a dump. Marathon 280 could carry 120 gallons of fresh water and its black and gray water tanks could hold 120 and 140 gallons, respectively.

On the passenger side, the Bus's primary storage sat in the middle bay and came complete with slide outs and plenty of cargo room. The water heater and pumps were stowed in the rear bay and the front bay held drawers, a tool chest and equipment locker, but still made room for the 12 volt, marine-grade, house batteries. At the very rear of the coach sat the engine, a Detroit Diesel Series 92 V8 which generated 500 horsepower. It, along with the patented, stainless steel, unibody, Prevost chassis, was rated for over 1 million miles. The Bus ran like a top.

She was filled with imaginative engineering that made driving, camping and maintenance better and more convenient than every other coach on the road: pneumatic leveling bladders, a powered stairwell cover, a gel battery for the generator that was connected to a rooftop solar cell and flexible nozzles inside the sewage tanks that washed off the inner walls during a deep clean.

Strategically placed control panels inside the living quarters kept dimmer switches within arm's reach while hasps and locks secured all the inner doors for travel so that a jar of mayonnaise did not inadvertently roar up the aisle while the Bus was in motion. A variety of shades prevented prying eyes from watching the skipper when he tip-toed to the front to hang an if-the-Bus-is-a-rockin'-don't-come-knockin' sign on the door.

The team preferred pull through spaces with 50 amp power. On a day that included river travel, they tried to arrive at a site in mid to late afternoon, just when the other campers were waking up from a nap or perhaps throwing hot dogs on the grill. Without exception, all the tenants stopped and stared as the Bus, towing the Harley on the trailer, cruised past, followed closely by the Sportscoach and SUV. Occasionally a small crowd might gather - but not too close - and watch as the two rigs hissed to a stop in their spaces. Karl and Larry hustled around with the initial set up of camp and then hitched the boat trailer to the SUV and zoomed back out to the road. The other residents stood there in the dust and flying leaves, looking at each other and wondering, "What the hell just happened?"

When they first bought the Bus and started to travel, Karl would disclose to onlookers as he set up camp - oftentimes in hushed tones so that it seemed he was letting them in on a secret - that Rose was in fact a celebrity. He could not say exactly who she was of course (discretion was required in his job), but if they looked closely, they might figure it out. It was not long before Rose emerged to find curious campers ogling her suspiciously over their cans of RC.

When the team threw in a few arrivals into camp on a Harley in full leathers or if Roxa tapped away on a laptop with a headlamp deep into the night or if they made a dramatic entrance into the park of the entire, 100-foot convoy, it was no surprise that the other residents wondered about their mysterious neighbors.

While Helgeson's shop worked on the hoist, the team used its layover in Williston to its advantage to investigate historic Fort Buford and Fort Union Trading Post. Buford had seen the surrender of Chief Sitting Bull and Union had at one time belonged to the Astor fur empire so both places had significance for *Acrosswater*. The two sites had not been restored completely, but the team liked seeing the authentic, military provisions and armaments. The wandering nature of rivers came into focus for everyone when they discovered that Fort Union had originally been built on the banks of the Missouri; by the time of the crew's visit, the river was but a watery smear on the horizon.

A local club was raising money to rebuild a section of barracks at Buford and the members of the club happened to be performing a procession and presentation of colors the day of the *Acrosswater* visit. The reenactment ceremony made it special, even absent a proper museum. Roxa and Karl also searched around town for more than three hours looking for a place to e-mail photos to Roxa's Webmaster for uploading, but they were unsuccessful. Williston was still very much on the electronic frontier.

Captain and crew closed camp on August 5 and, having collected the boat from the repair shop and finding it like new, drove about twenty miles out of town to Lewis and Clark State Park. They had received a tip about a gorgeous golf course near the Missouri River called Red Mike's and soon found out why it had earned such high praise. Carved into the rolling hills and with a view of the water on most holes, the layout enchanted the foursome from the start, even though the knee-deep prairie grass just off the fairways swallowed sleeves of Titleists over the course of their round. A passing shower drenched them on the sixth hole and they had to take shelter on the back nine because of a powerful thunderstorm passing through the area (the air temperature felt like it dropped twenty degrees), but neither cloudburst squelched their enthusiasm for the outing. The sight of the water, the majestic, never ending skies and the rippling grass that flowed as far as they could see easily overcame any misgivings they may have had about their scores.

They launched the next day out of Lewis and Clark into Lake Sakakawea, the third largest reservoir in the United States and the second of a series of massive impoundments constructed on the upper Missouri by the USACE. That whole stretch of river had served as a proving ground for the U.S. Army Corps of Engineers over the years.

Dating all the way back to the Revolutionary War, the USACE evolved from only having the responsibility for military construction - projects like roads, bridges or coastal fortifications - to being indelibly linked to the creation and upkeep of national infrastructure. Competing opinions and political disagreements slowed the integration of a military organization into public works, but the country's leaders eventually could not ignore the importance of well-designed waterways and byways to the growth of the nation. In particular, the Flood Control Acts of 1928 and 1944 influenced the development of dams along the upper Missouri by ceding control of the waterways to the USACE and granting the U.S. Department of the Interior the authority to sell power generated at federal facilities.

The various projects received predictable criticism at times, particularly when communities or sacred grounds were inundated by man-made reservoirs, but the leadership of the USACE took pains to carefully compare the losses to the benefits before green lighting a proposed project. According to its mission, the Corps strived to "Deliver vital public and military engineering services...energize the economy and reduce risks from disaster." The stretch of the Missouri from Fort Peck to Fort Randall exemplified that mission.

Divided among regions of the country and beginning in the early thirties, the construction projects of the USACE employed thousands of people during a time when work was scarce. In the Omaha District, Fort Peck Dam alone needed over 10,000 men during the height of its fill operation. The wild Missouri, with its unpredictable floods and shifting course, became measurably more predictable as each dam came on line and the power plants at each site increased the USACE's twenty-four percent share of total, U.S. hydro-power output.

Once the giant reservoirs of Fort Peck, Sakakawea and Oahe filled to capacity, they accumulated more shoreline than California and covered almost as many acres as Rhode Island. The reservoirs and dams provided noticeably greater control of the ebbs and flows of the river, allowed for better access to irrigation, generated more power production and added thousands of acres of recreation. In fact, the only criticism leveled by exploring parties like *Acrosswater* was the absence of locks - the engineers deliberately left them out of dam design - so travelers needed to portage from lake to lake. With its expertise hauling in and out of water and its intended strategy to travel on land as well as the rivers, the *Acrosswater* crew was barely inconvenienced.

They ran down the lake for almost two hours. From their time spent in the southwest on Lakes Powell and Mead, the captain and first mate found the meandering arms of Sakakawea relatively familiar. The wind and chop generated by such a large body of water prevented them from maintaining their top speed of thirty knots, but they still rated the leg an eight out of ten. Karl and Larry made the fifty-seven mile motorcycle ride back to pick up their rigs and then parked the RV's at their camp for the night, Four Bears Indian Reservation RV Park. They reunited with their wives at the boat ramp and dropped the boat at HQ. Even after seven hours of travel, they still had enough time and ambition to explore the area.

An initial reconnaissance led them to an historic emblem hidden down an access outlet to the lake. Referred to as Reunion Bay, it was the spot where Lewis and Clark reunited after separating at the Lolo Pass during their return from the West Coast in 1806. It was a remarkable moment in the country's history, a place where the nation's greatest explorers had found each other again in a vast, unmapped wilderness and yet it was mostly overlooked, a mere footnote marked with the most understated of monuments. The *Acrosswater* adventurers never would have seen it except they noticed a parade of SUV's hauling boats out of an old, dirt track and decided to investigate.

They also journeyed up to a bluff overlooking the lake. Upon completion of Garrison Dam in 1953, the three communities in the area merged onto the remaining high ground and were rezoned as New Town. As the four mates took in the view, an elderly man on a Honda Goldwing (along with three kids riding shotgun in the sidecar) pulled into the parking lot beside them. They found out that he had lived in Sanish, one of the towns flooded after the dam was built. He shared some stories of the area and pointed to locations in the distance where ghostly foundations appeared when the water receded far enough.

The high winds stuck around overnight and when the commodore walked out to the end of the dock to assess the day, he saw whitecaps already forming and thunderheads building in the distance. The group wisely elected to stay off the water. Instead, they traveled over land to their next stopping point and satisfied their watery urges by camping near the lake at Fort Stevenson State Park. The place was deserted except for their exploration party and they found it so fetching that they stayed two days. They took their usual tour of the nearby town - Garrison - and discovered it was the walleye capital of the world, complete with a gigantic, fiberglass fish named Wally. They snapped some pictures posing with Wally and felt sufficiently inspired to try their hand fishing.

As luck would have it, the wind died down enough for them to go out on the lake and soon they were reeling them in by the net full. Curiously, they could not identify the type, not even using the guide book they had picked up when buying their licenses, but they kept filling the hull like they were on a commercial trawler. They flagged down a passing fisherman to show off their catch and to see if he recognized the kind of fish. He took a glance at the one Roxa held up for display. "Yeah," he said, "that's one of those Skipjacks. They're shitty garbage fish. You'll want to toss those." He twisted the throttle on his little, Evinrude motor and puttered away.

They set out the next day and crossed the Garrison Dam with the intent of cruising part of the Missouri all the way to Washburn. The water at the boat ramp seemed quite shallow and an old timer launching at the same time remarked that he had not seen the river that low in fifteen years. The crew spotted a few sandbars lurking ominously nearby, so they idled around – barely drifting really – and used the depth finder to sound the area. Just 100 yards from the launch apron, the water level fell to three feet, causing the captain to call for an immediate retreat lest they find themselves beached again. Still a little jittery from the mayhem near Wolf Point, the team was perfectly happy to travel on land to Washburn.

The adventurers found another picturesque camp site called Cross Branch which overlooked the river and which they again had to themselves. The road leading to the park passed under a railroad trestle, which proved quite harrowing to drive through. They stationed spotters as the rigs rolled by to confirm that the opening had enough clearance for both the vehicles themselves and for the roof-mounted equipment. They could not launch *Acrosswater*, so they settled for an investigation of various attractions in the area that were tied to the trailblazing of Lewis and Clark.

They first explored the Knife River Indian Villages, a historic site associated with the Corps of Discovery. The Mandan community consisted of large, earthen lodges, built by the women of the tribe and durable enough to last ten years without extensive renovations. Lewis and Clark recognized the Mandans as the last, cooperative connection to the "known" frontier when they started their westward journey and the Mandan people actively traded with many Europeans. The *Acrosswater* party walked around the site in reflective admiration before taking a short drive to the Lewis and Clark Heritage Center. There they were caught off guard by replicas of the craft used by the Corps to navigate the rivers. Stout and rustic, the primitive canoes looked marginally capable of traveling the waterways of a frog pond, let alone the upper Missouri. Having sailed those currents themselves, the admiral and company found it impossible to believe that people traveled the length of the river in vessels like that.

Low water levels kept *Acrosswater* in her trailer for the next two days so the crew rented canoes themselves and navigated the river for a few miles. Though a fraction of the distance covered by their predecessors in the early 1800's, paddling the Missouri elevated their appreciation for the physical achievements of the Corps.

The members of the team also amused themselves by golfing and investigating another spot of historical significance, Fort Lincoln. There they found that the buildings themselves were replicas of the originals (frontiersmen had looted the abandoned fort for materials years ago), but the guides working that day acted with sincerity and enthusiasm, loaning credibility to the production. The fort was the last residence of General Custer and displayed his home, barracks and other outbuildings. Since they were in the area, they also took a quick run about 100 miles to the east to visit the Jamestown National Buffalo Museum. Karl and Rose had an authentic, buffalo robe on loan to the museum and they wanted to make sure it was well tended.

The team concluded its pause from river travel with a maintenance day for their equipment and half the crew. Larry took his rig to have it washed and while Rose and Roxa had their hair done, Karl hustled over to River City Sports to collect some intelligence on the river conditions (the hairdresser had casually mentioned that her husband worked for the boat dealer). The skipper was advised that he and the crew had two choices to avoid another shipwreck. Either putz along behind a local fisherman - stopping where he stopped and idling when he idled - or portage to the next, safe body of water, Lake Oahe. They chose option number two.

They put into the lake close to Mobridge, SD. The day was clear and windless so it was safe enough for them to travel more than fifty miles on the water. So mesmerized were they by the hum of the engine that they actually passed their intended camp site and had to choose between going back for fifteen miles or pressing ahead fifteen miles to West Whitlock State Park. They pushed onward and as they approached what they hoped was the entrance to the camp, they coasted near a fisherman who confirmed that they had indeed found Whitlock.

Later that night, after they had retrieved the rigs and set up camp, captain and crew received a visit from the fisherman and his wife. Lloyd and Carol had lived in the area for many years and were so enthralled by the snippet of the *Acrosswater* story that they had heard earlier in the day, they had to hear some more details. The six new friends chatted into the night about the *Acrosswater* adventure, retirement in general and life in South Dakota. Lloyd told them how a large release of water into the lake five years earlier had ruined the fishing by washing out all the smelt and walleye. The density of smelt had dropped from forty-two pounds per acre to just two pounds per acre.

The weather failed to cooperate again the following day as high winds kept them landlocked. They explored nearby Pierre, which turned out to be quite a nice surprise. The state capitol was built in 1908 and the visitors found it stunning. It incorporated Greek stone and tile and was capped with a gorgeous, stained glass dome. (It helped that no legislators were sullying the floors.) The group also made a stop at the Natural History Museum, a building equally noteworthy in its own right. Partially built into the side of a hill, the museum had been recognized by President Bush as one of the most environmentally-efficient facilities in the nation.

Since low water continued to frustrate much of their progress, the team decided to detour away from the river for a few days, portaging toward Rapid City to explore the wealth of American history tucked into the southwest corner of South Dakota. First up was The Badlands National Park, a mysterious wilderness that Frank Lloyd Wright once described as "...an endless supernatural world more spiritual than earth." Larry and Roxa felt similarly enamored by the terrain and happily led the way along the park loop. The region was relatively small, covering barely more acres than Fort Peck Lake, but it was packed with stuff. Created over tens of millions of years through sedimentary layering and subsequent erosion, the park held otherworldly rock formations, sweeping vistas and expanses of prairie that made visits three parts religious experience and one part tour.

The crew spotted bison and sheep along the way, but mostly felt entranced by the surreal, exquisite views. They made time to stop at an old homestead carved out of some embankments to see how it compared to Ma Porter's home in Montana. Homesteading came late to South Dakota, starting in the early 1900's and only lasting until 1930. The lure of 160 acres was not enough to keep immigrants on the land because the sterile soil and harsh climate made only the poorest existence possible; even the hardy indigenous tribes in the region found it mostly uninhabitable, using the area for hunting in the summer, but evacuating to their villages along the Missouri in the winter.

The Badlands homestead was sod built and dung heated and the site had undergone renovations to allow for tours. Though they reinforced the structure, the engineers who rebuilt the display tried to follow the original blueprints; furnishings, implements and the general layout had all been retained to help clarify what life was like. Since the *Acrosswater* team had already visited the Porter home out on the prairie (an actual homestead and not a rebuilt facsimile), the visitors felt only middling admiration for the Dakota abode - and the overwhelming satisfaction of being just one generation removed from true homesteaders. They finished inspecting the piles of manure and hay at the site and then moved along to Heritage Village Campground in Custer with three primary goals: play a little golf, visit Mount Rushmore and audit the ongoing construction at the Crazy Horse monument.

Without minimizing the efforts of the untold number of people who worked on Rushmore, the monument exists primarily because of three men: Doane Robinson, Senator Peter Norbeck and sculptor Gutzon Borglum. Robinson, a South Dakota historian, started the giant project in motion when he proposed having colossal sculptures carved into the Black Hills as a way to attract tourists to the state and as a tribute to the American West. He envisioned a rocky tapestry of western figures and floated ideas that today would be considered both progressive (as when he suggested a carving of Sakakawea) and offensive (like the proposal to include a stone mural of Custer and his cavalry in the heart of Sioux country).

Still, he was no doubt persistent and patriotic and his plans soon caught the attention of Norbeck, a respected, senior, U.S.

senator who had strong political connections and a deep understanding of how best to move bills through Congress. Though it helped that the project launched at a time when the public strongly believed in American superiority (and what better way to reflect that might than in a giant, immortal carving of national heroes), without Norbeck's talent for securing federal funding at various times during the fourteen years of construction, Rushmore never would have been completed. It also helped that he seemed wonderfully adept at tactfully managing the ups and downs of Borglum's eccentric personality.

Gutzon Borglum was born to carve a mountain. Wildly gifted, he burned with passion, creativity, dramatic flair and an unwavering confidence in his personal talents. He was stubborn, prone to outbursts and could be unapproachable if crossed, but he was also fiercely loyal to his family and his friends.

He first attempted to carve an oversized sculpture when the Daughters of the American Confederacy commissioned him to turn the face of Stone Mountain in Georgia into a monument dedicated to the Confederate Army. Contract squabbles doomed that job not long into the project, but it gave Borglum the chance to develop his sculpting technique on a canvas of scale. When he received Doane Robinson's letter, which inquired about Gutzon's interest and availability to build a monument of similar size in the Black Hills, the sculptor jumped at the chance.

Kicked off with a dedication in 1927, the memorial developed in fits and starts over the next fourteen years. Though Borglum himself predicted otherwise at the outset, financing proved to be the biggest hurdle throughout construction. Modest, private donations trickled into the treasury of the Mount Rushmore National Memorial

Commission and haphazard, fund-raising schemes over the years ranged from the minting and sale of commemorative coins, to a statewide call to all South Dakota children to donate ten cents during the start of a school year.

Named Mt. Rushmore Week, the plan called for the kids to learn about early U. S. History and civic participation and then put that knowledge into action through their donations to the commission. Forecast to raise $10,000, the unpatriotic, little shits only came up with $1,700.

Without money to pay workers (for Rushmore was far and away a civil engineering enterprise), there were some years when little progress was made at all. Borglum and others mortgaged their own assets to keep the project perilously afloat until, finally, Norbeck was able to push through a series of bills that made the whole affair solvent.

Once commissioned, Borglum retained final say regarding the layout of the monument. He developed a series of models during the run-up to the dedication, trying different looks and arrangements before settling on what became the working blueprint. He was at the mercy of the mountain to a degree - Jefferson's bust started to the left of Washington (from the perspective looking up at the monument) before fissures necessitated moving it to Washington's right - but the craftsmen under his charge painstakingly blasted and chiseled away the stone largely in concert with the mercurial sculptor's vision. They took exacting measurements on the much, much smaller creation in Borglum's studio, transferred the scaled up dimensions to each craggy face and then removed the layers of rock.

The project had its own power plant, pneumatic drills, winches, scaffolding, dynamite, lifts and blacksmiths. Gutzon's stubborn will threatened the completion of the monument on more than one occasion, but it also fueled its relentless progress. He died in March of 1941, seven months before the project was completed. His son, Lincoln, oversaw the final stages.

Just twenty-three miles southwest of Mount Rushmore, construction on another massive monument began in 1947. The Crazy Horse Memorial was the Native American answer to Rushmore and the tribe that initiated the commission found the ideal sculptor in the person of Korczak Ziolkowski. Born in New England, Ziolkowski displayed artistic gifts from an early age and found success as a woodworker before transitioning to sculpting. He set up an independent studio and supported himself producing commissioned pieces, eventually earning first prize at the 1939 World's Fair. He worked that same summer in South Dakota with Borglum, gleaning insights into sculpting as a whole and large scale works in particular.

Following a deployment overseas during World War II, Ziolkowski allowed himself to be lured back to South Dakota for good by Chief Henry Standing Bear and he dedicated the rest of his life - thirty-five years - to the design and construction of the Crazy Horse Memorial. Likely because of the fiscal constraints he observed while working on Mount Rushmore, he refused to accept any government support to help build the memorial. He had noticed that the ones who controlled the money also controlled the project, so he and the Lakota people who commissioned him decide early on to choose independence over any government's largess.

Unlike Mount Rushmore, which was designed as a relief with the figures protruding out from a flat surface, Crazy Horse was to be a true statue, albeit a mountain-sized one. Ziolkowski intended to carve the entire peak into the figure of the great Sioux warrior riding on a horse. Clearly unable to complete the work during his lifetime (optimists suggested completion by 2050), the sculptor nonetheless pushed on tirelessly and created a clear mission for his descendants to follow.

The *Acrosswater* crew felt naturally drawn to both monuments, but for different reasons. In Mount Rushmore, they found a tangible expression of their love of country and could not help but swell with pride when they first glimpsed the four figures presiding over the surrounding hills. In Crazy Horse, they felt immense respect for the entrepreneurial spirit of people who dreamed big, but never once considered asking for a handout from the Feds.

Given the size of the monuments, the crew thought they might appreciate viewing the sites from the air and with that in mind, they made their first stop at a heliport to secure a thirty-five minute aerial tour of both Mount Rushmore and Crazy Horse. Unfortunately, the captain boarded first and felt too trapped between the bulkhead and the other tourists to continue. He opted out of the confines of the helicopter and decided to settle for as many pictures as the other three could snap. First mate and crew loved the overhead view of the mountains and provided a complete report to the captain once back at HQ.

They visited Mount Rushmore up close early the next morning before the crowds arrived. They were able to hike the Presidential Trail and took many photos without the usual interruptions of other people stepping into the frame. The views were indescribable and the scenery painfully picturesque.

Afterward, they squeezed in a round of golf, driving through Custer State Park to reach the course and scattering herds of buffalo along the way. They walked all eighteen holes, but still made time to dash back to Mount Rushmore for the 9:00 p.m. light show. It alone was worth their swing away from the river.

The evening was cool and comfortable even in the crowded amphitheater. The presentation began with recollections from some of the rangers on duty and then transitioned to videos describing the life of each of the men carved into the mountain. When the narrator finished the last description, he invited everyone to stand and join in the singing of the National Anthem. The song moved to the final crescendo, spotlights hitting the incredible backdrop of the four presidents and the crowd roaring the last strains with all the give-em-hell-boys gusto it could muster. The members of the *Acrosswater* crew sang at the tops of their lungs, eyes gleaming, hearts full of gratitude at their good fortune to be out on the trail, exploring their beloved country from such an up close and personal point of view.

Something to see, indeed.

Chapter 7

A 5 star day

"At 1457 head to 45 degrees (favor S shore) Pass around Independence Point Green [sheet 16]"

Karl's journal - August 7, 2000

The reservoirs along the Missouri River were so massive that the boaters had to use navigational practices better suited for the open sea. The skipper wrote out these guidelines so the others did not become disoriented.

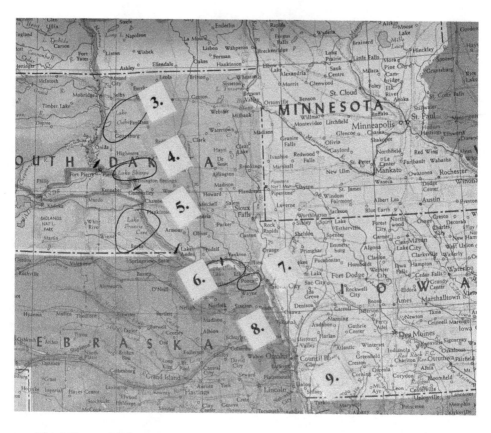

The Missouri River

The numbers corresponded to individual, USACE charts.

ANYONE who has spent any time at all in a motorhome has a black water story. "So embarrassed to post this but I need HELP!!!" wrote one desperate soul on a message board. "Tank backed up and ran down the vents. Today is hot and humid. Smell horrid!! Any ideas?" Respondents offered a number of helpful suggestions ranging from dealer intervention (have *them* clean it out) to a sprinkling of coffee grounds (worked great for fish water!).

Perhaps the worst, motorhome, sewage story in history involved the bus of a touring rock band, a grated bridge and a poorly timed, sightseeing excursion. In August of 2005, tourists on Chicago's *Little Lady* were taking a ride on the river. Sitting in the open seats of the upper deck, the breeze from the boat's forward motion and the wind off the river helped cool the travelers on a muggy, summer day. They had just passed into the shade of the Kinzie Street Bridge when, according to a report in the Chicago Tribune, passengers were showered in "...a downpour of foul-smelling brownish yellow slurry." In the subsequent legal proceedings related to the calamity, the driver of the band's tour bus admitted he had discharged 800 pounds of excrement from the septic tank as he crossed the bridge, thinking that the sewage would fall harmlessly into the Chicago River below. Mercifully, nobody suffered permanent injury or long term illness passing through the effluent waterfall, though most immediately destroyed the clothes they were wearing that day and few returned to the river again with any enthusiasm.

The *Acrosswater* captain's favorite, waste-management mishap took place when he and Rose had just returned from one of their jaunts into the countryside. They lived in Sunriver, OR at the time and their house did not have a garage large enough for them to park the Bus. Instead, they rented a storage facility and used it to hold the coach, *Acrosswater* and other assorted belongings that they did not use daily. The space sat on private property, along with a fueling station and a convenience store, and was part of a stand-alone warehouse that was sectioned into smaller units. The owner, Jerry, had offered many times to let Karl use the dump site on the property. So, when the captain and Rose pulled in after their trip, they decided to take advantage of the offer rather than make an additional stop somewhere else to evacuate the tanks.

While Rose went to unlock the roll-up door to their unit, Karl opened up the bay that housed the plumbing controls. He had his discharge process down to a science and, after donning his gloves, connected the sewer line to the pipe sticking out from the side of the warehouse. He always dumped the black water tank first (so he could rinse the sewer line afterwards), but he would generally let loose some gray water during set up to make sure all the fittings were snug. He had learned over the years that park managers frowned on sprinklings of poo around their dump sites. He opened the gray water valve and then shut it off, checking the connections on both ends of the hose. He gave it another shot of gray water and, satisfied that everything was in order, closed the valve and switched to the black water tank. He had his hand on the faucet when Rose came around the corner from opening the garage.

"What are you DOING?!?" she asked, clearly horrified.

"What? I'm dumping the tanks."

"That's not the waste dump. That's the waste dump!" she said, pointing to a slightly obscured inlet recessed into the concrete apron.

"Then where did….?" His voice trailed off as he realized he had come within seconds of pumping Jerry's warehouse full of manure through an exhaust vent. Jerry had outfitted the garage so that he could run a hose from the tail pipe of a vehicle to the vent and work with the bay door closed.

Karl immediately called to ask for a key and found that Jerry was out of town. Jerry's wife, Janice, came over and opened the garage, but Karl and Rosemary insisted that she not go in. Jerry was an inveterate clean freak whose shop gleamed like a freshly sanitized operating room; Karl and Rose did not want Janice to be traumatized by what she saw. They spent the next several hours, armed with squeegees, rags, bleach, buckets, mops, spray bottles and paper towels cleaning up the mess, gagging quietly to themselves and offering thanks that Karl had not opened that black water valve.

Full of convenience, RV's seem to have solved many of the effluvial puzzles that confounded designers in other industries for years. The earliest campers were nothing more than fancy covered wagons constructed by individual travelers, but by the early 1900's, builders like Pierce Arrow produced a limited collection of exclusive motorhomes. According to RV historian Al Hesselbart, developers of the first, truly prestigious vehicles built them to include running water, onboard generators, undercarriage storage, forward seating for a chauffeur, collapsible beds, showering attachments, cooking equipment and, of course, a private toilet (essentially a secluded chamber pot).

The Great Depression significantly delayed further advancements as well as mass production, mainly because travel trailers were rightly viewed as an extravagance. It was not until after World War Two that engineers began figuring out how to include many indispensable, modern comforts in their mobile campers at a cost that the middle class could afford. Eventually plumbing, refrigeration, propane heating and, most important to this discussion, sewage management all became standard accessories on even the most basic, RV designs.

In fact, with a vast network of campgrounds, parks and private facilities at their disposal (as it were), motorhomes are arguably more sanitary than any other form of mass, recreational travel. Take cruises for example. Today's sailing behemoths carry an average of 3,000 passengers on every excursion and those revelers produce tons of crap. Vessels accumulate up to 30,000 gallons of sewage and 250,000 gallons of gray water every day. That would not necessarily be a problem if the carriers held the waste until they reached port and drained their tanks into a suitable processing facility, but instead, ships legally jettison their slops without treatment so long as they are sailing more than three miles from shore. Within the three mile buffer, ships abide by guidelines last updated in 1979 which allow them to use aging technology to treat black water prior to discharge. Regardless of treatment, current laws allow the ships to eject unfiltered gray water at any time. Friends of the Earth filed a lawsuit against the EPA in 2014, calling for updated rules governing the treatment of all sewage released from passenger vessels in U.S. waters, but until changes are made, bathers might want to keep their mouths closed before they take that refreshing plunge into the surf.

On land, train travelers making a pit stop in the loo often find a sign urging them to delay flushing until they leave the station. The reason for the notice becomes quite clear when the relieved passenger ultimately pushes the lever and sees the tracks passing beneath the car. With as many stops as trains make in city centers, taking the time to safely and cleanly evacuate a septic tank seems not only reasonable, but expected in a modern society. Instead of that strategy, the locomotives roam the countryside without a care in the world, liberally spreading filth wherever they go. Remember those silent movies with the mustachioed, cape-wearing madman tying the damsel to the tracks? She wasn't screaming because of the oncoming train. She was hollering because she was lying in a pile of shit.

Fortunately, the communities and citizens along the path of the *Acrosswater* expedition could sleep soundly. Aside from the occasional mishap involving the storage shed of a dear friend, all members of the party paid close attention to dumping rules and regulations throughout their journey.

And their sense of courtesy extended far beyond the requisite sluicing of wastes. They recognized that their itinerary left them vulnerable to arriving late in the day to each campsite so they took great care to maintain a schedule that had them setting up long before quiet time. The basic rules for camp courtesy seemed fairly intuitive: respect others' spaces, be quiet, check-in and check-out on time, keep your area clean and obey local regulations. All the members of the *Acrosswater* team did their best to follow those rules at each stop so that, should they ever return to a site again, they would enjoy a homecoming from the permanent residents akin to their Barclay reunion, rather than being ostracized. On August 21, having tidied their encampment near the Crazy Horse Memorial and leaving it more polished and scrubbed than they found it, the convoy pulled out of the park and made tracks for Chamberlain, SD and a rendezvous with Pa and Ma Porter.

After the homestead tour outside Circle, Bud and Jane had taken a trip to Chicago before meeting up with the *Acrosswater* crew to take a ride downriver. They had even scouted out the best ramp to launch from within Chamberlain so when the two groups convened that evening, they had dinner together and reviewed their boating plans for the next day. Just before 5:00 a.m. the next morning, however, a lightning storm hit and the sky opened, dumping one and a half inches of rain in less than two hours.

The expedition members had grown used to their plans being interrupted by weather; a tornado klaxon was their afternoon soundtrack across much of the plains. Sometimes during torrential interludes, Rose recited lines from a poem entitled *Mountain Storm* that she had found in volume three of *Thunder over the Ochoco*, Gale Onkto's series about the Shoshone people. Originally penned by Ethel Jacobean, the ominous phrases became a familiar refrain for the travelers:

One lamb white cloud appeared to browse
In the azure above the aspen boughs,
When suddenly on the western rim
Thunderheads loomed, majestic, grim,
As lightening forked through the stormy wrack
And black was piled on deeper black.

The only time a forecast threatened to dampen their spirits was when they had specific plans for the day and in this case, they had all been excited to share their adventure with Bud and Jane. The team collected on the docks throughout the morning to search for any break in the clouds, but about 11:00 a.m., they ventured out once more, took a look at the whitecaps on the river (and the exodus of locals yanking their boats out of the water) and quickly voted to scrap the launch in favor of portage. The Porters drove with them as far as Platte before bidding the team farewell; their ride on the river would have to wait for another day.

Had Bud and Jane held on for just twenty-four hours, they could have experienced a model day, with the launch playing out seamlessly and the cruise uninterrupted by snags or wind or rain. With a month of practice under their belts, the crew and captain performed each task quickly and flawlessly, allowing them more time to spend touring and less time dancing through the technical ballet of a boat launch. They ran downriver to Fort Randall Dam on pristine waters, a distance of about fifty miles, after which Karl and Rose drove the Harley back to Snake Creek to retrieve the rigs. They had the Randall Dam State Park mostly to themselves and spent the rest of the day visiting Pickstown (population 190) and touring the ruins of the former military post from which Fort Randall Dam derived its name. The post was in service for thirty-six years before being abandoned in 1892 with only a small cemetery, parade grounds and chapel left behind.

In the morning, Karl and Larry did some recon at the boat ramp. They brought with them aerial views of the region from their planning documents and polled several of the local fishermen to get a feel for water levels. They had learned that some of the best and most accurate briefings were provided by the guys finishing for the day. All the anglers they spoke to advised them to stay away from that part of the river due to the preponderance of snags and sandbars. In fact, the residents told them they should not even consider water travel until they reached Sioux City, roughly 125 river miles away.

With the updated intelligence in hand, they retrieved the rest of the crew, packed up camp and moved their headquarters to North Sioux City. They planned to launch the next morning into the first section of the river not dammed by the USACE since leaving Fort Peck and a stretch of the Missouri that was far more navigable due to the presence of channel markers. In the meantime, they visited two landmarks noted during their trip research.

In 1985, following an inspirational visit to the Blessed Virgin Mary statue in California, Father Harold Cooper began the process of developing the refuge of serenity and reflection known as Trinity Heights. Finding that the cost of acquiring a suitable parcel of land prohibitive at the outset, Father Cooper's prayers were eventually answered in 1987 when the savings and loan collapse cut land value by more than half, enabling the foundation that he had established to purchase the acreage previously occupied by Trinity College and High School.

Six short years later, the organization formally dedicated the thirty-foot-tall statue, the Immaculate Heart of Mary Queen of Peace. In 1999, the slightly taller Sacred Heart of Jesus was installed as a reverent bookend to its Mother across the green. Over the years, Trinity Heights continued to add gardens, memorials and walkways and it remained an oasis for visitors of all faiths. What attracted the *Acrosswater* party to the grounds in 2000 was not either of the colossal statues of divinity, however, but a unique display whose kind was reportedly found in only two other places worldwide.

Housed in the St. Joseph Center at Trinity Heights, the Last Supper sculpture represented the culmination of a twenty-year devotion to amateur wood carving. Jerry Traufler began working with wood in 1975 and proved to be so gifted and accomplished that he won numerous, nationwide competitions, despite only pursuing the craft as a part-time hobby.

In 1986, he turned his attention to Da Vinci's Last Supper and, using only a chisel and mallet, spent the next seven years shaping over a ton of wood into a life-sized depiction of the famous painting. Rather than simply copying the portrait, Traufler used his wife and friends as models so he could capture the expressions of the disciples as they sat at the table listening to Jesus. The result was an experience that placed viewers in the hallowed room itself and enabled them to envision the possible reactions of the Apostles as they sat listening to their Lord for the last time.

During his travel research, Larry had dog-eared the page in one of the guides that described Trinity Heights. He had taken up carving in recent years, working first with hand tools to form smaller figurines before moving up to sculpting with a chain saw. Not only did he retain all his digits while pursuing his new hobby, he also diagnosed a previously unknown cedar allergy; he noticed an onset of pulmonary distress when he worked with that specific type of lumber. Though Larry was the only one of the four travelers with more than just a passing interest in carving, once the rest of them heard his description of the Last Supper sculpture, the SUV was soon screeching off the main drag and pulling into the Trinity Heights parking lot. Deeply impressed with both the detail and scale of the sculpture, Larry was able to convey to the rest of the team the labor and persistence needed to create what they were seeing.

The other point of interest in the area was the Charles Floyd memorial. For all of the peril the Corps of Discovery faced during its harrowing trek to the Pacific and back, only Sergeant Floyd perished over the course of the three year odyssey, an astounding achievement considering the obstacles the expedition encountered. They traveled much of the way with an infant in tow and they were pushing into territories without the benefit of accurate charts or maps. They subsisted primarily on what they could find through hunting or foraging, they endured exposure to punishing elements and they had to diplomatically interact with groups of people who could not understand what they were saying and likely saw them as a threat. They faced starvation, bitter cold, venereal disease, dysentery, exhaustion and frost bite. Their boats swamped, they were thrown from horses, they nearly plunged to their deaths over cliffs, they waded through ice filled streams wearing nothing but leather moccasins and they navigated rapids in supply-laden canoes.

On one unforgettable day during the return trip, Captain Lewis took Private Peter Cruzatte with him to find some game. Hunting while wearing deerskins was a dubious proposition anyway, but doing so with the notoriously nearsighted Cruzatte was doubly risky. Shortly into the hunt, Lewis was struck just below the hip by a shot and, despite calling for help from his partner, was forced to dress the wound alone. Eventually the private sheepishly emerged from the undergrowth and admitted that it was he who had shot the beleaguered captain in the ass.

Remarkably, it was not one of those other hazards that proved fatal, rather it is thought that a burst appendix killed the sergeant. Originally recruited by Captain Clark, Floyd had been a vital member of the team during the run-up to the launch; he led the Corps through drills, dispensed punishment when called for and acted as a liaison between the officers and the privates. After Floyd died, Captain Lewis presided over a ceremony at which he recognized the sergeant with Honors of War. The other members of the expedition buried Floyd on a bluff overlooking the Missouri River, marking the spot with a simple, cedar post.

By the time the *Acrosswater* party arrived in the area, Floyd's final resting place had been moved back over 500 feet from its original location and had been listed as a National Historic Landmark. The large obelisk commemorating the site struck the group as both moving and tasteful and they took their time reading all the plaques on the grounds. While on the property, they encountered a reporter from the local ABC affiliate who was preparing a story about Lewis and Clark.

When she heard about *Acrosswater* and the efforts of the adventurers to trace the path of the Corps from the Pacific to the Mississippi, she asked if she could interview one of the members for her report. The captain gave a rousing account of their journey to that point and, as the photographic record unquestionably attests, felt as comfortable with a microphone in his hand as he did at the helm of the ship.

The skipper scored his journal the following day with five stars, the first and only such designation he gave amongst all his writings. With all of the miles under their tires and hull, and with all of the exploits already enjoyed since the departure from Astoria, August 26 most stood out to him as their vision come to life.

It began with the launch into the Missouri River proper, not a tame waterway in between artificial lakes. The current was swift and turbulent, even down near the boat ramp, and the members of the crew had to work in harmony in order to safely put their craft into the water. As usual, they did so with an audience, the onlookers standing with mouths agape at the sight of the boat and the Harley.

Once out into the channel, the captain opened the throttle up to 3200 RPM without fear of slamming into a sandbar or submerged stump, making for a ride free from angst. The navigational aids provided clear boundaries to follow, a relieving contrast to the fitful boating they had struggled through upstream. Karl piloted *Acrosswater* more than fifty miles, slowing to a crawl when they passed fishermen at drift and bringing the same courteous outlook from the land of RV encampments to the river. One of the perspectives they had planned for their journey was a view of as many cities from the river as possible and, though it was not a large city in the traditional sense, the silhouette of Sioux City gave the crew a preview of what they could expect further downstream.

Shortly after noon, they cruised into Decatur and found their disembarking point for the day, the Pop-n-Doc marina. By that time in the journey, the motorcycle offload had become so commonplace to their daily routine that they could have done it wearing high heels and tuxedos, but onlookers still gathered to watch and wonder when the Harley swung out over the water.

Within minutes, the men were rumbling up the ramp on the bike, goggles in place, silken scarves snapping in the wind, Larry saluting the passersby. Rose and Roxa set to work scrubbing and polishing *Acrosswater*, erasing every water spot and blemish until their beloved craft sparkled in the sun. After they were satisfied with the condition of the boat, they set up their lawn chairs on the dock to catch some sun, read or apply a liberal spritz of pepper spray into the face of a saucy fisherman. Karl and Larry returned with the rigs and, in front of a crowd that had doubled in size, the crew reloaded the motorcycle, pulled the boat out of the river and drove off.

After they established base camp and took a brief detour to the Decatur cemetery (not out of reverence, mind you, but because it afforded an outstanding view of the river and had the best cell reception in town), the couples went their separate ways to explore the area.

Instead of joining Larry and Roxa on a survey of Decatur proper, Karl and Rose drove north on the Harley to find the Blackbird burial mound, another site of importance and antiquity. (It held the remains of the legendary, Omaha Chief Blackbird and had been visited in 1804 by Captain Clark when the Corps of Discovery passed through the area.) A short hour later, the bikers roared back down main street bearing news to Larry and Roxa that, not only had the captain and first mate located the fabled Blackbird resting place, but they had also stumbled upon an extraordinary event in nearby Macy. The 196th annual Powwow of the Omaha Nation was underway.

Realistically, the tribal celebration visited that day by the *Acrosswater* four had been taking place for many more than 196 years. The communities in the region had gathered annually for generations to trade, dance, exchange stories, sing, pray and eat with each other. When Lewis and Clark visited in 1804, they observed a dance festival and recorded it in their journals, forever establishing the formal starting date of the event.

What was unique about the gathering in Macy, however, was the fact that, unlike many of the other tribes in the country (who were scattered to reservations far from their native lands) this powwow had been held in Macy for as long as anyone knew. Because the Omaha people still resided on their original, tribal lands, they had the rare pleasure of dancing, literally, in the footsteps of their ancestors.

When the two couples drove onto the grounds, they quickly found a spot in the stands around the arena where the dance competitions were already in progress. Incredibly colorful and graced with beads, feathers, bells and braids, the costumes captivated the *Acrosswater* crew almost as much as the dances themselves. They sat amazed as they looked around at a cultural event that had endured across centuries. They stayed until the dances ended and finally crawled into their campers after midnight, happily exhausted as usual.

So, what was it exactly about August 26 that moved the skipper to rate it so highly? Was it the marriage of planning and drama-free execution that stood out to him? Instead of begging for a tow off a sandbar or dispatching Larry on horseback to some distant ranch or wearily scanning the shallows for a threatening snag, Karl was able to pilot the boat at a reasonable clip. Perhaps it was because he and the crew had so keenly honed the choreography of launching *Acrosswater* and loading the Harley that his heart no longer skipped a beat every time the bike swayed on the hoist.

Or maybe it was because, after a month into their grand adventure, he grasped how rare, how extraordinary their trip had become. Every day, they alternated between glimpsing artifacts of the country's very beginnings and walking beside the souls who formed the fabric of present-day, American culture. Without exception, strangers learning of their trek expressed undisguised envy and a remarkable willingness to sell the family farm so they could join the *Acrosswater* journey. Whatever the source of his enthusiasm, it was pretty heady stuff for a guy from rural Oregon and he certainly did not take his good fortune lightly.

Captain and crew modified their agenda slightly over the next few days; they had plans to meet up with Karl and Rose's daughter in Chicago and wanted to be closer to Kansas City by the end of the month. The morning after the powwow, they stopped in at the Lewis and Clark Park in Onawa and toured through the replicas of the different watercraft used by the Corps. Particularly stunning to the members of the *Acrosswater* team (since they had just tried to navigate the upper Missouri themselves) was the keelboat. Reading about the vessel and even seeing pictures did not compare to standing next to the boat and then imagining its occupants using it to conquer an untamed waterway like the Missouri.

Always suckers for local claims to fame, they next drove through downtown Onawa to see if its Main Street really was the widest in America, as alleged. They acknowledged the thoroughfare with an appropriate measure of wonder and then headed east to the Loess Hills National Scenic Byway and took a drive amongst rare, but under-appreciated geologic formations. Formed over eons, the piles of glacial dust called loess can be found all over the world but only in Iowa (along the National Scenic Byway) and in China do they top 200 feet. With appreciation akin to their earlier recognition of the cataclysm responsible for the Columbia River Gorge, they savored their surroundings and noticed the subtle indicators in the landscape of the glacial influence of long ago.

Their final pit stop found them in the DeSoto National Wildlife Refuge. They took a stroll along the boardwalk that wound through the refuge and visited displays devoted to the wreck of the steamboat *Bertrand*, a vessel that sank in the Missouri in 1865. Preserved by the mud of the river, the artifacts at the site were recovered just over 100 years after the stern wheeler went down.

The *Bertrand* was located and excavated from its resting place by the salvage duo of Corbino and Pursell. Their reclamation contract allowed them to keep sixty percent of the mercury, whiskey and gold recovered at the wreck, but the rest was the property of the federal government. Finding that the precious metals had long since been removed (presumably at the time of the original disaster), the salvage effort focused primarily on the supplies and personal effects carried on the ship. With over 250,000 total artifacts recovered and thousands displayed, the *Bertrand* exhibit proved fascinating to every member of the *Acrosswater* team. They could not believe how well the mud had protected the different keepsakes and implements that had gone down with the boat.

Destined for the Montana gold fields at the time, the steamship carried families traveling north to reunite with other relatives as well as necessities for the mining communities upstream. The preserved stockpile included textiles, tools, lanterns, mining equipment, jarred vegetables, journals, dolls, pictures and Civil-war era clothing, all in pristine condition. The couples also noted with wonder the changes in the landscape since the *Bertrand* sank, each of them independently describing in their journals a lush, wildlife sanctuary in a space where a river had once flowed. (11 years after the *Acrosswater* party passed through the site, the Missouri threatened the *Bertrand* again when a flood forced the evacuation of all the artifacts housed in the museum, a rescue effort carried out mainly by tireless volunteers with caretaker oversight. The museum sat flooded and empty for weeks until the waters finally withdrew.)

Had they known that morning what August 29 had in store, the couples certainly would have driven straight to Missouri, especially after Larry delivered the ominous news that the SUV had a flat. They wasted the better part of the morning searching for an auto shop with the correct tire, but after a successful repair, they still threw caution to the wind and hit the river just after lunch. The engine would not start (even after adding some spare fuel from a can on board) so they muscled the boat out of the water and drove to a gas station, only to discover the tank nearly full.

When they returned to the ramp a second time, the motor roared to life but the delay had already taken some of the wind out of their sails. They gamely took a rushed cruise over near Nebraska

City to see the town from the water and then, with evening upon them, hauled *Acrosswater* back out of the river. They followed their maps religiously along U.S. Route 75 and exited at the proper junction with high hopes of plugging in their utilities before it was completely dark.

With Karl in the lead, the convoy rolled down a main boulevard and then took a left onto a road that, according to the map, would terminate at the RV park. It seemed a little too residential to be a thruway, but the captain pushed on after double checking the route in his Trailer Life book and seeing that the street was reasonably wide. About a mile down the road, he regretted that decision. Not only had the street narrowed considerably, but trees that had been growing full and majestic since the Grant administration lined each side, creating a tunnel of foliage with a maximum clearance of roughly four feet. Eventually, rather than watching the road ahead, the skipper was spending all of his time looking up so he could curse the branches that were scraping off his antenna arrays.

To make matters worse, they had attracted an audience. Never before had such a parade of campers, SUV's and Harley-bedecked watercraft ever driven down that street and the residents flocked to their porch swings in varied states of bemused curiosity. Up and down the lane, sounds of phones ringing, neighbors hollering and screen doors banging echoed among the sycamores as people spread the news of the unfolding fiasco. Porch lights flicked on for as far as the eye could see and the aroma of fresh brewed coffee filled the neighborhood as generations of families settled in to watch.

Since Larry and Roxa were in the rear, they were able to unhitch the SUV from their motorhome which allowed Larry to reverse his smaller RV out of the neighborhood. (Later estimates pegged the distance at sixteen miles, give or take.) The rest of the crew had successfully unhooked the boat and hauled it to the side of the road with the SUV by the time Larry returned. With painstaking care and absent any streetlights or real illumination to speak of, the skipper inched the Bus backward for what seemed like an hour before he was safe. He expected to feel the crunch of a tree branch at any moment or find himself backing into the parlor of one of the houses along the way, but with the help of his dedicated ground crew providing rudimentary hand signals, he finally made it to a clearing.

The team reconnected the SUV and the boat to their prescribed campers, blew a few kisses to their adoring fans still gathered on the porches and then drove back up the highway to an RV park they had passed along the way. Well after curfew by that time, they nonetheless managed to rouse the superintendent from a deep sleep, stuffed a few extra bills into the pockets of his robe for his trouble, parked their rigs without disturbing too many of the other residents and fell into their bunks for some well-deserved rest.

They closed out the month of August with a short drive into Missouri. At their camp that last night before going to Chicago, Roxa compiled their notes and tried several times to perform an upload to her web guru. After sunset, Karl ran fifty feet of telephone wire and an extension cord to a little camp table, constructing a makeshift office. Donning a headlamp for light, Roxa tapped away until early morning, but was stymied by her inability to connect to her ISP. The upload was finally successful when the park ranger learned of the need for connectivity at that spot in the camp and switched on the circuit. Satisfied that the wider world would soon be able to catch up on their travels, the adventurers left for Chicago, eager to return the trail, especially with a plunge into the Mississippi only a week away.

Roxa updating the travel blog

Chapter 8

Buried treasures

"CIVIL WAR TODAY: (in Corvallis)
U of O = 13 (9-2)
OSU = 23 (10-1)

Karl's journal - November 18, 2000

Oregon State football had a banner year in 2000, finishing the season ranked 4th. The poor skipper endured a serious ribbing after the Beavers beat his beloved Ducks, but he was able to look back with joy at Oregon handing the hated Washington Huskies their only defeat earlier in the season. The loss ruined Washington's chance at a national championship.

COLLECTING has been popular for a really long time. Scientists suspected that a 130,000-year-old rock found in a Croatian cave served no functional purpose, but was just the precious heirloom of the cave's occupant. According to professor emeritus David Fayer, the Neanderthal possessed the limestone simply because it "...was an interesting rock." More recently, an article in the Economist described how, in 1740, the son of the British prime minister swept up all the Roman paraphernalia he found during a trip to Italy, declaring, "I would buy the Coliseum (sic) if I could." And though the collectibles industry had ebbed and flowed over the years, by 2014 (according to the National Association of Resale Professionals) resale businesses were still pulling in a healthy $15 billion in revenue, with antiques commanding thirteen percent of the total.

In 2000, during the *Acrosswater*'s march to the Gulf, people certainly searched for keepsakes with commendable fervor. There did not seem to be a particular pattern then, as now, regarding the types of items that attracted collectors. In a study funded by the Small Business Administration in the mid-2000's, aside from the usual categories like books, furniture and clothing, objects making the top ten most coveted list ranged from vintage plastic sunglasses to depression-era paper crafts. (Fanatics surrendered as much as $350 for belts made of old chewing gum wrappers.)

Many treasure hunters sought after items that fit into broad, mainstream classifications like 1920's shop signs or Elvis memorabilia, but others rummaged with a curiously specific trinket in mind. Newspaper ads recorded a desire for everything from safety ashtrays removed from the scuttled cruise ships of Ronson Ellerman to Uncle Sam-shaped banks produced in the 1800's. A few of the interests had a creepier feel, like the old bits and braces used in neurosurgery or amputation kits from the Civil War. Where exactly would the more macabre artifacts be displayed in the house? Next to family photos or in the den near a bowling trophy? Would they be shown proudly to guests before serving dinner? ("You have a good eye, Steve. That *is* a walrus-tusk handle on that cranial auger!")

In any event, the vintage industry was healthy in 2000 and members of the *Acrosswater* party, though not all of them, had interests of their own that they actively pursued. Roxa had an assortment of antique drying racks and was quite eager to add to her stockpile. Rose had an affinity for sleigh bells and Larry willingly joined the other two as they strolled through antique cooperatives so he could search for objects like axes, adzes, hand-rung school bells, farm equipment and cooking utensils. One of the three had even purchased an antique trail guide in advance of their journey.

The captain, on the other hand, would rather have bamboo splinters jammed under his nails than stop and look at old junk so when the team drove back towards Missouri to rejoin the trail after their Chicago detour, he roared past several antique shops before finally giving in to the clamoring. The group split up at a mall in Illinois with the skipper driving off to find a golf course to play that afternoon, and the others ecstatically sifting through the wares piled at each stall.

Three hours later, Karl returned to retrieve the rest of the crew. He walked into the bazaar and stopped at the front counter. "May I help you?" the woman tending the register asked as she took off her glasses and let them dangle from the slender chain around her neck. The admiral looked over the assorted knickknacks loosely organized at the front of the store and rubbed his chin thoughtfully.

"I'll give you thirty dollars," he said finally.

"Thirty dollars for what?" she asked.

"Thirty dollars for the whole store," he said, making a sweeping gesture with his right arm. She stared at him for several seconds, her eyes narrowing slightly. "I'm just kidding," he said, chuckling. "I'm here to pick up two lovely ladies and my friend Larry."

"Ah," she replied, "they warned me about you. You'll find them over in housewares, just past the Victorian incontinence pads."

He tipped his hat and strode to the back of the store where he found his companions pondering over a choice of drying racks. "Oh there you are Karl. Which one do you like better?" Roxa asked as she pointed to her two favorites.

They looked the same to him. "Can't you get one of those at Walmart?"

"No, you can't get one at Walmart. These were made over ninety years ago and they're twice as expensive. Now which one do you like?"

"Will they even hold anything? They look like they're ready to fall apart and they are filthy."

"That's the patina. Honestly." She turned to the first mate. "Rose, I think I'll get this one." The two of them trotted towards the register to pay for the rack.

Karl and Larry looked at each other. "It won't take up too much space, Larry," Karl said, putting his arm around Larry's shoulder. "At least it's not a lobster pot or a church pew or something." And with that, they followed their wives to the exit.

They arrived back at their Higginsville camp on September 7 and devoted a day to checking all the systems on their rigs, doing laundry, flushing the dump tanks, catching up on correspondence and grocery shopping. The next day, while Rose and Roxa poked through every vintage boutique in Higginsville, Karl and Larry explored the surrounding villages to find a boat ramp large enough and safe enough to handle *Acrosswater*. They discovered that the river was paradoxically swift and shallow, a combination the crew had always found especially hazardous.

The men spoke to a sheriff in town who suggested looking at the launch in nearby Wellington, but he suspected none of the ramps in the area would be suitable. Karl and Larry concurred after they visited the Wellington site and saw that it was too secluded. Neither of them felt comfortable leaving their spouses or the equipment alone at the ramp for any period of time while they leapfrogged the RV's to the next stop.

They went to the end of the dock to check out the current and, seeing that it was dangerously brisk and muddy with a poor egress, concluded that dropping *Acrosswater* into the Missouri in this area would be unwise. (They later learned that just a week earlier, a boy and his father had been swept away while the pair tried to haul their fishing boat out of the river. The boy was carried off first and then the father when he jumped in to help. Both perished.)

Rather than risk harm to themselves or their craft, they visited the site of the Battle of Lexington, the first of many Civil War battlefields they would investigate throughout the South. Several of the Civil War spots the *Acrosswater* group toured were not as well known as places like Gettysburg or Antietam, so even for informed travelers like Karl, Rose, Larry and Roxa, a site like Lexington was an eye opener.

The conflict occurred when Confederate forces advanced on a fortified field hospital used by the Union Army. Approximately 3,500 soldiers from the North had dug a series of trenches as deep as twelve feet on eighteen acres with the hospital at the center. After three days, the Rebels, under the command of Major General Price and advancing methodically over the terrain by pushing water-soaked bales of hemp in front of themselves, forced the Union forces to surrender by cutting off all sources of water to the hospital and leaving no room for escape. Known historically as the Hemp Bale Battle, none of the *Acrosswater* visitors had heard of it prior to their impromptu call and it stoked their curiosity for what might lie ahead.

Following the visit to Lexington, they pulled up stakes in Higginsville and moved closer to Kansas City, optimistic that they would be back on the river soon. But, because of the uncertainty of water access, they shelved their river dreams for one more day while they took in a few attractions in the area and carried on the search for a launch site. First up was the museum dedicated to the steamboat *Arabia*. Reminiscent of their earlier visit to the *Bertrand*, they spent several fascinating hours browsing the displays and hands-on presentations.

The *Arabia* sank in 1856 a few miles west of Kansas City. Like many of the vessels that went down in the Missouri (there were over 400), she had hit a submerged stump and foundered instantly. The boat carried over 200 tons of supplies headed for the frontier towns along the river and her lost cargo tempted treasure seekers for years.

In 1988, an amateur archaeologist named David Hawley tracked down a potential resting place for the steamship and, after subsequent core samples confirmed the find, he teamed with friends and family to complete the excavation. Using only private funds, the Hawley conglomerate opened the museum just three years after the initial discovery and it instantly became a must-see destination in the Kansas City area.

The *Acrosswater* four were thrilled by the whole visit. They loved seeing the exquisitely preserved artifacts and they were smitten with the entire layout of the exhibits. The categories were intuitively organized and the tour flowed through the museum with precision and logic. Reported to be the largest, pre-Civil War collection on display, the museum managed to show off its treasures without seeming too crowded. The crew saw the old walnut tree stump that had doomed the vessel, they examined part of the tiller that steered the ship, they smelled replicas of the 150-year-old French perfume recovered from the hold and they watched scientists in the lab as the restoration process of the discovery continued.

Of particular interest to the skipper was his conversation with Flo Hawley, the matriarch of the family behind the *Arabia* museum; she happened to be on site the day of the *Acrosswater* visit. Given his own entrepreneurial background, Karl felt a strong kinship with those who were able to eschew government assistance in favor of private enterprise. To that end, the *Arabia* partnership proved especially resourceful, establishing and operating a private, profitable museum that was just as compelling as the *Bertrand* (a federally subsidized dig) yet cost $20 million less to fund.

After their exhausting stroll at the *Arabia*, the entire crew felt famished and to their good fortune, they had reached the part of their journey where they started to indulge in some of the finest comfort foods in America. The chroniclers of the trip had already recorded some memorable meals in their journals and Larry in particular rarely let a day pass without jotting one down. Even in the middle of the chaos surrounding the shipwreck on the upper Missouri, when *Acrosswater* was chained to a tractor and a lightning storm crackled across the skies, he dutifully registered a lunch of chili dogs and salad. The captain also documented a few experiences and helpfully added some ratings - "Pork chop dinner was A plus!" - so the adventure to that point had not been without culinary highlights.

But they were entering a whole different territory. Far in the rearview mirror were the Omega-3 offerings of Pacific salmon or the lean buffalo steaks of the Plains. They were heading into Southern-fried country, a land filled with burnt ends, dry rubs, chitlins, hogs smoked for eighteen hours, ribs, fried catfish, fresh corn bread, tea so sweet it made their fillings ache and fierce disagreements over the merits of tomato-based, barbecue sauces.

First up was Strouds, an establishment that had been filling the bellies of KC residents since 1933 and that claimed to have the "Best Fried Chicken" (of exactly where was unclear). In 1998, Strouds became the first restaurant in the category of American Classics to earn a James Beard Award so its confident proclamation was not without merit. It had served a list of luminaries from across the social spectrum, sating the appetites of athletes (Bret Saberhagen, Brooks Robinson, Jan Stenerud), musicians (Eric Clapton, Ken Osmond), television stars (Kirstey Alley, Phyllis Diller) and political heavyweights (John Boehner, Rush Limbaugh). The *Acrosswater* troupe added their names to the list of satisfied diners, unanimously signing off on the "Best of" claim.

The last stop for the day found them at the ballpark where they attended a game between the Kansas City Royals and the Texas Rangers. The captain recorded a victory for the away team with the Rangers winning six runs to four, but truthfully, he conceded that he and the rest of the *Acrosswater* crew were the real winners. They had another day soaking in the culture of America on their journey and additionally, they had finally discovered a viable boat launch east of the city just off U.S. 291. By that point on the map, the Missouri ran west to east on its way to meet up with the Mississippi and the team was hopeful the ramp they had found would provide the safety and access they needed to go back on the water.

Their launch lead turned out as promised and on Sunday, September 10, they were back in the boating business. The captain clearly felt thrilled to find himself at the helm again; his notes for the day included a "Yes!" within the opening lines and he ultimately graded that river excursion a nine out of ten. They cruised upstream through Kansas City to take in the skyline from a Missouri River perspective and then turned slightly southwest onto the Kansas River. They found that tributary snag-filled and exceedingly muddy, but they could not have been happier.

Acrosswater's purring engine was music to their ears and they basked in the wind and sun as they hummed along. They encountered only one other boat that day, a kayaker, and they concluded that the rest of the Missourians in the vicinity did not know what they were missing. The haul out of the water proved somewhat challenging because the ramp terminated immediately in the current without a jetty for protection, but the crew performed admirably as usual.

After a quick refresh back at camp, they returned to Kansas City proper to try another dining landmark, Arthur Bryant's. The local gold standard for barbecue, the restaurant's cooks had been perfecting their technique for sixty-seven years and they regularly assumed a spot near the top of any reputable list of pit masters. Captain and crew found the recommendation in the same guidebook, *Road Trip USA*, that had led them to Strouds and they began to think its writers might never lead them astray.

The travelers consumed racks of ribs, homemade pickles and fresh slaw and sopped up every juicy dripping with bushels of bread. They seriously considered moving their rigs to the restaurant's parking lot in the event they had a craving later that night, but ultimately thought the better of it. Still, they drove back to camp full and content and turned in earlier that night than any since leaving Astoria.

Events over the next few days juxtaposed the rural towns and waterways of central Missouri with the surprisingly modern opulence found on the Lake of the Ozarks. First, the team broke camp near Kansas City and journeyed east to Boonville. They tried to follow their map to a boat ramp near the intersection of State Route 5 and U.S. Route 40 but finally had to stop and ask a highway worker for directions. He pointed them back towards the correct turnoff and they were soon rattling down a road so dusty that Karl could not see the boat in tow behind the SUV. They fretted over their bearings until they reached the terminus, a long, steep, concrete slab with a crumbling launch pad, but as usual, found serenity once on the water.

They toured the region for almost three hours, including a short diversion down a smaller river that flowed into the Missouri from the south. Larry took the opportunity to embrace his inner bumpkin, steering the boat with the small, Honda outboard by using the extended tiller and removing his shirt to expose his shipmates and the world at large to an outstanding farmer's tan.

Back at the launch, the boat extraction proved difficult due to the current, but given the crew's well-developed, sailing chops, they managed the removal in only two tries. The first time Rose backed down the ramp, she had to gun the SUV out of the water almost immediately because the river threatened to float the trailer away. On the second run, and after a quick conference to form a strategy, Rose just dipped the trailer in the water following Larry's directions while

Karl and Roxa nosed the boat into the cradle. They tied on quickly and Rose hauled it out.

The team spent extra days lingering in the area after the discovery of a broken trailer hitch forced a hunt for a repair shop. The crew tried several mechanics in Columbia, MO without any luck, but did receive a promising lead from a tire shop owner who recommended Merten's in Jefferson City. Karl made a call and secured an appointment for the following morning at 8:00 a.m., giving them the rest of the day to explore.

They walked the University of Missouri campus, but more interestingly, tried to track down author William Least Heat-Moon. (His *River Horse* was one of the books that Rose had read during trip preparation. It chronicled his voyage across America in a C-Dory.) Interested in the opportunity to meet a like-minded traveler, they took turns interrogating various merchants until they received directions to the Flat Branch Pub & Brewery, reportedly Will's favorite hangout. It turned out that no one had seen him in several weeks - the locals assumed he was away on a book tour - which wrecked the team's dream of swapping stories of snags and sandbars.

After the successful repair of the trailer hitch, they took two separate voyages on the Lake of the Ozarks, both of which offered interesting contrasts to the encounters thus far with blue-collar mariners. During the first excursion, the couples cruised the shoreline for several hours, marveling at the number and variety of powerboats zipping around, as well as the obvious commercialization of the lake; Karl likened it to Branson with its dedication to shameless self-promotion.

Even though it was late September and only a Thursday, an armada of ski and cigarette boats powered around the lake, each one equipped with at least one, 500 hp engine. *Acrosswater*'s sneaky acceleration surprised one of them during an impromptu drag race and the losing captain nodded in respect to the old duck boat at the finish line.

There also appeared to be a local regulation which required vessels to have a minimum of two co-eds wearing dental floss bikinis on board at all times. *Acrosswater*'s skipper idled over to one of the cruisers whose occupants observed the statute with notable enthusiasm and pulled alongside. "Permission to come aboard?!?" he hollered up to the wheelhouse. There was a pause.

"Permission denied!!"

Later that day, they also managed to avoid an altercation with the security personnel guarding an exclusive, Jack Nicklaus designed golf club. It had just been built and its signature hole protruded into one of the lake's eastern bends. The *Acrosswater* party had just finished the hike up from the lake to the fifteenth green when agents wearing blazers and mirrored sunglasses intercepted them.

Unsurprisingly, the wily captain not only sweet talked his way out of the predicament, but, with relative immediacy, had the sentries hustling off to fetch the entire crew some cold drinks. Refreshments in hand, the trespassers ambled back down the embankment to their boat and pushed away from shore.

Their second excursion on the lake included Rose's sister Chris and Chris' boyfriend John; they had driven from Chicago to St. Louis to indulge in the *Acrosswater* adventure. More specifically, they had made a ten-hour round trip (and stayed just one night), for the privilege of spending a few hours bouncing around on the deck of an aluminum, flat-bottomed jet boat. Either lunacy ran in the family or the wanderlust was catching.

Since the second run on the lake took place on a Saturday, even more watercraft filled the reservoir than had two days earlier. The team launched their boat alongside a sixty-five-foot, experimental racing vessel with twin, 650 hp engines and a sensational paint job. Once on the open water, the *Acrosswater* crew and guests found themselves on a bull ride of wake and chop kicked up by the countless motorboats roaring around the lake, but they fought their way to a secluded cove and found enough sanctuary to have a nice barbecue. Then it was back out into the chaos. By mid-afternoon, they had grown tired of dodging all the other boats and decided to pull out of the water.

The ladies elected to shop for antiques while Karl and John traded their life preservers for golf clubs. Larry attended the locally renowned Hillbilly Fair, which turned out to be a mild disappointment. It was suitably organized, served plenty of good food, had craft beers on tap, had rides for younger visitors and displayed a range of well-intentioned exhibits, but it had none of what the name implied.

Instead of a prettiest-sister pageant or a banjo-picking contest or a squirrel-skinning demonstration, Larry was dismayed to find only bingo, square dancing and the typical arts and crafts. He checked every stall among the food tents, but found no evidence of a hooch distillery or any pots of braised opossum. And every one of the booths were attended by people who had full sets of teeth to go with their brand new overalls. Clearly those folks were only *posing* as hillbillies.

The travelers said goodbye to Chris and John the next morning at 9:00 a.m. then returned to their adventure. During a routine inspection, the team discovered that the SUV and one of the rigs needed some maintenance so they moved their camp to St. Charles, MO. They had found a motor coach dealer in nearby Washington who could perform a satisfactory brake job and St. Charles, positioned between the Mississippi and Missouri rivers, gave them a centralized base of operations to complete the repairs and conduct some last minute prep before hitting the water again.

Most appealing to them was the thought that they would shortly be on the Mississippi to begin their southern run to New Orleans. They planned to launch into the Missouri and boat east to where the two great rivers converged. Then it would be less than twenty miles to St. Louis where they would conclude the Lewis and Clark portion of their journey. Like all past and future travelers, they would soon be reminded that, more often than not, the river dictated their agenda.

Chapter 9
Give our regards to Meriwether

*"Olympic medals: US = 50, China = 37
Australia = 36, Russia = 28"*

Karl's journal - September 23, 2000

The Sydney Olympics were in full swing.
Ever the competitor, the skipper had his
eye on how the U.S. was faring against the
rest of the world.

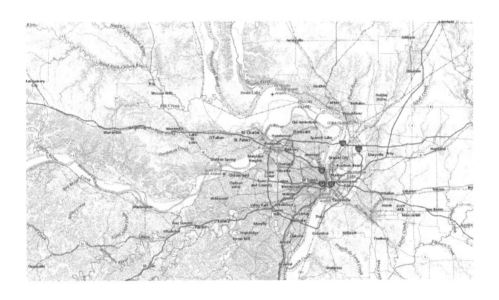

St. Louis and vicinity

WITH good reason, the most frequently mentioned water measurements by organizations like the USACE and the National Weather Service refer to high water. For those living along the rivers' edges, the risk of flood and the call to arms when levels approached flood stage necessitated tracking and observing water flow at all times. In his peerless book *Wicked River*, Lee Sandlin described the path altering power of the river when he wrote, "...the most dramatic erasures and remakings of the river course happened in the floods."

The *Acrosswater* team had already witnessed those types of transformations when it strolled through landmarks in regions that looked markedly different from previous years, where bends in the river had moved considerable distances from previous channels (Fort Union, the *Bertrand*, the *Arabia*, the Sergeant Floyd Memorial). When the foursome launched into the Missouri, they frequently did so at decrepit ramps and craggy pads not yet repaired since the last great flood in 1993. But water levels of a different sort hampered the *Acrosswater*'s journey in 2000. Without knowing or planning for it, they were exploring during a year that would ultimately have some of the lowest water flow on record.

People began tracking water activity throughout the Mississippi River Basin sometime in the mid-nineteenth century and they used a series of gages installed along both the smaller tributaries and main waterways. Some of the instruments measured crests of waves as water flowed down the rivers, some measured river depth and others recorded cubic feet per second. The most eye-popping measurements were, again, related to flood years and, regardless of the type of record, sent a shiver down the hardiest of spines. For example, the highest crest recorded on the Mississippi was 49.58 feet on August 1, 1993 (the river is effectively "full" at 43 feet). That same year, a gage in St. Louis pegged the water volume at over 1 million cubic feet per second; 500 miles south, in Vicksburg, the crest gage never dipped below 16 feet. Scientists who looked at those metrics, without setting foot on the ground, predicted catastrophe, knowing that the system could never absorb all that fluid without a breach or overflow of a levee.

Conversely, someone studying the measurements for the year of *Acrosswater*'s journey could tell that barely a drop was trickling in the river bed. Only two years in history recorded a crest lower than the measurements of 2000 and in Vicksburg, the high water mark checked in at twenty-nine feet all year; it bottomed out at five inches.

At St. Charles, from where the *Acrosswater* team planned to launch first into the Missouri and then jet to the Mississippi (so they could better savor a dramatic entry), the year 2000 was the only one listed twice in the top twenty for historically low water; September 20,

2000, the day before they tried to launch, was the sixteenth lowest ever recorded. They were setting afloat in some of the driest conditions for river travel ever and that first launch would be just a taste of the struggle to find water in the weeks to come.

They found a perfect ramp about one mile from their RV park. The concrete went just to the water's edge and then dropped abruptly, but after taking some measurements, the team thought the trailer had enough clearance for a successful launch. Just as the tandem axles passed the bottom end, however, the trailer high-centered and they could not pull it free, even with the SUV in low. With a call to AAA looking more and more probable, Larry suggested building a makeshift ramp out of the rocks exposed by the low water. He assembled a large collection of stones and then meticulously built a pile on either side of the ramp, slightly in front of the trailer tires. He theorized that they could pull the trailer forward just enough onto the stone piles to lift the center axle clear.

Sure enough, once Larry completed construction and gave the thumbs up, Karl hit the gas on the SUV and the trailer popped free. He shot to the top of the ramp and skidded to a stop, the rest of the group coughing their way through the dust to join him. As they were inspecting the integrity of the trailer and boat, a U.S. Fish and Game warden, Officer Guntle, emerged mysteriously from the haze and suggested to them that they should try a marina over on the Mississippi instead. He indicated that most of the boat ramps within twenty miles would not allow entry to the Missouri because the water was too low. They thanked him and, after a brief map consultation, drove eight miles north to a slough that had a choice of boat landings.

With surprisingly little fanfare considering the significance of the milestone (it was, after all, their first plunge into the Mississippi), the crew dropped in the water at the Heartland Marina. It took them some time to gather their bearings because the perspective at river level differed drastically from their maps and charts. Not only did the Missouri and Mississippi Rivers run parallel, but the Illinois River also converged in the same area so the captain struggled at first to fix a reference.

Once oriented, they motored upriver to Lock and Dam 25, the state of Missouri on their port side and the state of Illinois to starboard. Rather than locking through, they came about and cruised back downriver, eventually deciding to stop for lunch at Kinder's Restaurant, a local favorite first established in 1929 as a tavern adjoining the nearby ferry. The crew tied off at the dock out front and went inside to enjoy a meal and gather some local intelligence. As the plates were being cleared and they sat watching the Golden Eagle ferry as it shuttled cars and people, a mark on the wall of the restaurant caught the captain's eye. He stared at it for a minute and then confirmed with one of the servers its significance. Sure enough, it was the high water mark of the flood of 1993.

Some moments in time certainly have a more jarring effect than others on a person's consciousness. As Karl looked out at the boats on the river, then at the water mark and then back at the horizon beyond the ferry terminal on the other shoreline, he visualized, perhaps for the first time, the scale of the floods along the Mississippi. He tried to imagine everything before him inundated as the river first pushed up the sides of the bank and either overran the top or breached the levee. Had Karl tried to dine at Kinder's in 1993, he likely would have been pressed into sandbag duty instead, helping an army of people stem the tide of the rising water thirty feet above the normal path of the ferry. The skipper had read the list of tragedies and the statistics, but he had not seen a good, physical representation of those numbers until then.

Possibly even more striking was the attitude of the people living along the river. Construction of new homes was visible from the restaurant and Kinder's own motto - "On and Sometimes in the Mississippi" - confirmed that the community had a spirit of daring and steely acceptance of the risks at the water's edge. Much of the time they enjoyed the benefits the river provided like industry, recreation and scenic beauty, but they also understood that devastation and calamity were a way of life.

The party shoved off from Kinder's and cruised past their marina to where the Illinois River joined the Mississippi. They turned upstream and hummed along for twenty miles, then rode the current back down to the confluence of the two rivers, pulled into their marina and hauled *Acrosswater* back out. Aside from the brief delay at the first ramp, they truly had a terrific day of boating and had regained some confidence. With a better understanding of the access points in the area, they planned to put into the Mississippi near the Clark Bridge and then journey downstream to view the Gateway Arch in St. Louis from the water. The group turned in with high expectations for the itinerary in the morning.

Just three miles downriver from their initial launch on September 22, right at the exit point of the Melvin Price Lock and Dam, the company *Acrosswater* realized that it would be a struggle to survive along that stretch of the Mississippi. The wind, the chop, the current and the flotilla of tugs with barges made their jet boat seem extraordinarily tiny and insignificant. Still, they navigated downstream for several miles and took the Chain of Rocks Canal, which bypassed an impassable series of rapids in the river proper. After lock 27 at the end of the canal, they could see the famed Arch in the distance, but the captain and crew maintained their sense of vigilance because if anything, the commercial traffic seemed to increase; *Acrosswater* was the only pleasure boat on the water as she picked her way south.

They made it to their destination and took some photos from the river, each couple taking turns posing with the Arch framed in the background. They chose not to linger too long because of the water conditions and because they had a more detailed, land-based excursion planned for the next day. Besides, they failed to see any waterfront parks at which to tie off so instead, they buzzed over near the McDonald's restaurant floating in the shadow of the Arch; Karl stayed with the boat while the rest of the crew went ashore to buy food.

The captain struck up a conversation with a passerby and his two sons and the man turned out to be the general manager of Busch Stadium, the home of the St. Louis Cardinals. They had just eaten at McDonald's themselves and were intrigued by the sight of a fishing boat with a Harley secured to the deck. They wished Karl good luck and when Larry, Roxa and Rose returned with the burgers, the *Acrosswater* party alternately ate lunch and stared at the surroundings. It was all quite surreal. (The floating McDonald's closed shortly after their visit. Exact dates of the closing vary from November 6, 2000 to sometime in 2002, but either way, the captain and crew were some of the last people to buy food from the landmark. Old Busch Stadium was replaced by an updated version in 2006.)

Rather than press their luck any further amidst the tugs, they decided to go back upstream and soon pulled back into the Chain of Rocks Canal. They saw their first recreational craft since launching that morning when they encountered a kayak coming along the right, descending bank. Easing towards each other, the occupants of both boats expressed admiration for the other.

The fellow in the kayak had never seen a set up like *Acrosswater* before and the jet boat crew always respected other adventurers. The kayaker, with a cat tucked into the bow for companionship, turned out to have paddled from Kansas City and was concluding his trip in St. Louis. Both parties exchanged poses for the others' cameras and then the solo traveler floated off, leaving *Acrosswater* to wait for its turn to enter the lock. That's when the commander slightly misjudged the behavior of the water in the canal.

The wind roaring down the tunnel formed by the canal walls kept pushing *Acrosswater* off-center so, rather than fight the gusts, the captain idled over to the rocks on the leeward side of the canal and just put the nose of the boat on shore to hold the craft steady until the doors opened. He expected the water from the lock to flood the canal, allowing him to reverse off the rocks and cruise inside the lock to be raised up a level. From there, they would continue on their way upstream.

What actually happened was the water level instantly dropped two to three feet, leaving them stranded directly on the rocks. The captain had no choice but to throw himself on the mercy of the lock tender. He set the dial on the radio to channel 12 and toggled the mic. "Ah, come in lock 27, this is *Acrosswater*. Over?"

"This is lock 27. Go ahead *Acrosswater*. Over?"

"Yeah, 27...um...I'm on the rocks. Over?" There was silence for a minute and the crew felt the scorching gaze of the tender as he surveyed them through his binoculars. The radio crackled.

"*Acrosswater*, were you near shore when the doors opened?!? Over?"

"That's affirmative 27. We're from Oregon and still getting the hang of lock maneuvers on this river. Over?"

"*Acrosswater*, you should never, and I mean never, go close to shore near a lock. I'll let out some water but you'd better get the hang of this quick. Over?"

"Ah, roger that 27. I appreciate the advice and the water. Over and out."

The water came out as promised and *Acrosswater* floated free, but the captain could only limp into the lock. Adding injury to insult, debris had fouled one of the intakes during their outing on the rocks (which limited the amount of thrust), but after they had locked up, the jets had cleared (thankfully) and the boat ran without issue the rest of the way back to camp. By the time they cleaned up at HQ and arrived at their dining destination for the evening - the Alton Belle Casino - the episode at the lock had transitioned from being an embarrassment to just another critical lesson about life on the river. They managed to choke down a mediocre meal at the buffet and then reminisced about the day, deciding that, all in all, it was pretty special. To top it off, the skipper won $1000 at a slot machine on the way out the door.

In the evening of September 23, 1806, Meriwether Lewis finished writing a letter to President Jefferson, informing him of the safe return of the Corps to St. Louis and apologizing for not writing sooner. Lewis included a letter he had written for William Clark because Clark thought Lewis was much better with words. He also took care to mention each enlisted man, noting their personal impact on the expedition. The following day, because they had already missed the post in St. Louis for the week, the captains entrusted the priceless bundle of correspondence to the ever-reliable Drouillard, sending him across the Mississippi to Illinois where he caught the post and mailed the letters. Impossibly, the great odyssey was over. The planning, the physical and mental exertion, the weight of the nation, the uncertainty of what they might find in the miles ahead, the complex decisions, the camaraderie - all were behind them.

Fittingly - one might almost say inevitably - the day the *Acrosswater* party toured the Arch in St. Louis (a monument dedicated to President Jefferson and his vision for Westward Expansion) and walked through the Lewis and Clark museum, was September 23. The skipper left the Arch investigation to the other three and instead spent extra time at the museum, admiring the exhibits chronicling the Corps of Discovery. Having boated the same waters and seen the same landscapes, he appreciated that expedition's resilience all the more.

The next day, September 24, nearly 200 years after Lewis sent his report to Jefferson, Rose, Roxa and Larry went searching for a camp said to have been used by Lewis and Clark. As luck would have it, a reenactment was underway when they arrived. Little did the rest of the crowd know, but modern adventurers were among them, people who had literally walked the paths of Lewis and Clark.

As was their custom, the *Acrosswater* team befriended a local family also attending the production and at some point the conversation turned to finding Captain Clark's grave. The locals not only knew its exact location, but insisted on leading the field trip to the cemetery, claiming it would be impossible to find without clear directions. So it was that the three travelers found themselves surveying the commanding bust of William Clark at the site of his burial, on the same day of the month that he himself returned to the region. It was, without a doubt, a satisfying, equally inevitable coda to the first chapter of their trip.

For a novice group of adventurers with a vision to follow in the footsteps of America's greatest explorers, they would have been hard-pressed to improve on any of the experiences over the first half of their odyssey. Did they replicate exactly what the legendary Corps had done? Hardly. Were there obvious advantages to modern travel along the developed roads and waterways? Of course. Did they have to subsist on rotten fish, boiled dog or poisonous roots at any point along the way? Never. Yet, the achievements of the *Acrosswater* party were still remarkable.

They had traveled close to 4,000 circuitous miles, hopscotching their way from Astoria to St. Louis in just over two months. They never once saw any other travelers using the same strategy to navigate the route and in fact, a launch into or haul from the river rarely passed where they were not surrounded by onlookers who were intrigued by the sight of the Harley swinging precariously on its hoist.

They went through the same regions as Lewis and Clark and lingered at many of the sites where the Corps had undeniably been:

Sergeant Floyd's Memorial, Reunion Bay, Knife River, the Nez Perce territories, the Bitterroots and, of course, Fort Clatsop. And just as the expedition of 1804 had depended on so many of the people living along the trail, *Acrosswater* might still have been lodged on a sandbar on the upper Missouri or rattling down a dusty road looking for a place to launch were it not for all the local people the adventure of 2000 encountered along the way.

With those thoughts in their heads and a deep sense of accomplishment in their souls, the three travelers turned from Captain Clark's grave and headed for the SUV. They had to return to their camp and make preparations for the next day. The captain was back at HQ, already hard at work on an improvised plan and agonizing over the lack of water and accessible ramps. (He commemorated his angst poignantly in his journal with the elegant phrase, "No WATER! FUCK!") They still had at least 1200 miles to go before they would reach New Orleans.

Chapter 10
Southern flair

"We had heard about a little restaurant called the Pancake Pantry where Garth Brooks eats when he is in town..."

Roxa's Web journal - October 8, 2000

The expedition never missed a chance to taste regional fare, especially if recommended by a local.

Cairo flood walls
The high water mark of the flood of 1937
can be seen at shoulder level.

IT was December of 1810 and the *Tonquin*, under the command of Captain Jonathan Thorn, heaved to near the Falkland Islands. The seafaring branch of John Astor's fur expedition had already sailed 7,000 miles into its journey to the Pacific Northwest and fresh water was running perilously low. Because rough seas had also damaged parts of the ship, Thorn gave the order to shelter in one of the natural bays of the Falklands to allow the carpenter and sailmaker to perform much needed repairs. Stern, confrontational and authoritarian - as captains often needed to be - Thorn demanded respect and absolute obedience from those on his ships.

Unfortunately for him, the unruly collection of French trappers, business clerks and Scottish partners who accompanied him during the journey rarely agreed with his methods and thus served as constant, daily irritants to the regimented habits normally found on naval vessels. Thorn surmised that the disrespectful stowaways would be invaluable once the party arrived at the mouth of the Columbia, still almost 8,000 miles in the distance, but for the time being, they were little more than bees in his bonnet. Because of the combination of close quarters and wretched provisions found on the *Tonquin*, the pit stop could not have come at a better time.

For several days the crew repaired the ship, filled the fresh water cisterns, explored one of the islands and hunted birds. On the final day, Captain Thorn himself stepped ashore with his fowling piece to do a little hunting before they departed. That's when the simmering tension amongst the voyagers boiled over.

Some of the crewmen and trappers had spent most of their time on the island since arriving, grateful to be on land for even a short stay, and they were scattered over its craggy shores. A few were hunting, some were attending to a crude gravesite they had discovered and others were shuttling fresh water to the *Tonquin*.

At some point, Thorn spotted a goose and shot at it with his gun. When the bird did not fly away, he reloaded and shot again. Still it stayed put. Drawing nearer to the goose, he saw that someone had tethered the bird to the ground which had kept it from escaping. He noticed some of the men in the background snickering and, in a rage, stalked back to his rowboat and shoved off in the direction of the *Tonquin*. The crewman who had trussed the bird was only trying to have some simple, torturous fun with the creature and had no idea the captain would shoot at it, but it was too late. The laughter had lit Thorn's fuse.

Minutes later, one of the men looked up and saw the *Tonquin* at full sail, accelerating out of the harbor. Panicked, he signaled one of the others and sprinted towards their own dinghy. One of them fired a gun to draw the attention of the other men on the island and they all converged on the rowboat, pushed out into the surf and pulled at the oars for their lives. Truthfully, they had little chance to catch the ship outright, but they hoped to at least draw its attention, thinking that they had been forgotten.

It soon became clear that Thorn intended to leave them in the Falklands. Losing cause that it was, they continued to row, even as the ship pulled away from them until, miraculously, they saw the sails start to luff. The ship was stopping. Records later suggested that Thorn turned the *Tonquin* only after the nephew of one of the men struggling with the oars in the trailing dinghy held a loaded pistol to the captain's head.

Tension always occurs when people travel together. There are hurt feelings to navigate, differences of opinion on directions to take, a notable divide on what one person may find interesting and anxiety when plans do not proceed as expected. History is littered with examples like that of Captain Thorn and the grounded goose, with the ultimate divorce typically preceded by a minefield of disagreements. The *Acrosswater* expedition was no different and the members took pains to respect each others' spaces while staying on schedule.

Of note was a morning routine established by Rose and Roxa to signal that both parties were up and ready to tackle the day. Each woman had a pennant that coincided with their CB handles; Rose was Autumn Leaf and Roxa was Sunflower. The first one awake in the morning would hang her pennant and when the other hung hers, they would then connect on either channel twenty-two or twenty-five (using the appropriate handle) and review instructions for the day. The team regularly fleshed out a rough strategy prior to turning in the night before, but Rose and Roxa's system allowed the couples to maintain a semblance of privacy while staying on task. Those small acts of civility allowed the team to remain united, even when their plans required a total rewrite, like they did now that they had reached the Mississippi.

On paper, the original plan (post-Lewis and Clark) looked exceedingly simple: launch into the Mississippi in the morning, motor downstream until just after lunch, ride the Harley back to retrieve the campers, find a place to park, take in some historic sites and repeat until the champagne popped in New Orleans. They anticipated a few delays at locks and expected to have to avoid commercial vessels here and there, but otherwise the route would be a serpentine investigation of the most famous waterway in America.

When they discovered that the ramps south of St. Charles were dry and when subsequent discussions with tug captains confirmed that they could expect little water in the river all the way to the Gulf, they despaired over next steps. The skipper had little appetite to drive all the way to New Orleans when the whole point of the expedition was to ride the rivers and portage only when necessary. Their carefully prepared trip agenda had counted on the Mississippi being the only way south. There was no plan "B." Then, Karl thought about a benign discussion with a stranger.

The team's launch into the river near St. Louis had taken place at a marina near Clark Bridge and U.S. 67. The captain, as usual, struck up a conversation with the woman manning the counter at the dock, a conversation which, in retrospect, rescued the party from a sentence of rest stops and Cracker Barrels all the way to Louisiana. First, she offhandedly inquired if Karl was using *Quimby's* as a resource to find his way south. He had never heard of *Quimby's*. He assumed that the preferred method of navigation was to do what he did; order a shipping container of maps from the USACE and get to work with different colored high lighters. She pulled her last copy off the shelf and handed it to him.

It was as if someone had provided him a copy of a map that contained not only directions to the treasure, but thoughtfully included the names of all the native tribes along the trail, the languages those tribes spoke, the gifts to bring to secure the tribe's assistance, precautions to take so as not to insult the chief's wife, the location of all the booby traps along the way and the types of tools needed to excavate the gold. *Quimby's* listed river routes and their confluences, all the marinas and ramps along those rivers (with accompanying phone numbers), mile markers, distances, locks, fuel depots, repair facilities, site recommendations and hints for safe water travel.

Every page had a purpose, from the ads to the lined, blank spots for journaling. Many pages included "Captain's Notes," brief but invaluable remarks about a specific part of the river. For example, a note would urge a skipper to "...monitor VHF channel 13 coming out of the mouth of the Great Kanawha at mile 265.7 for tow traffic," details that would never exist in a publication produced by the U.S. Army Corps of Engineers. No more thumbing through the Yellow Pages to find a marina or trying to interpret what a USACE draftsman meant when he wrote, **"ABOVE O.H.E. EL. 36.7."** Karl could research all he needed in a manual designed specifically for travel along the river.

Second, the proprietress told him about the flotilla of yachts that always came down from Chicago that time of year when the weather turned cold. They migrated to warmer waters for the winter and never went the entire length of the Mississippi due to the excessive commercial traffic. Instead, they would cut over to the Tennessee-Tombigbee Waterway and travel down to Mobile. In doing so, they also shaved miles off the journey because the Tenn-Tom was essentially a straight path, not a serpentine one like the Mississippi.

Well, as the skipper poured over his maps the day the rest of the crew ventured out to search for the remains of Captain Clark, he reflected on his conversation at the marina and pulled out his newly acquired *Quimby's*. It was only 100 miles to Cape Girardeau. A little further south from there and they could take the Ohio to the Tennessee, and the Tennessee to the Tombigbee. It would not follow the original plan but it was certainly in the same spirit and it had the added benefit of saving some time (in theory). With October almost upon them, they had just over a month of travel left before they would need to turn for home. The captain spent the remainder of the day until the others returned sketching out a rough proposal of the route they could take to New Orleans. As always, the rest of the crew supported the plan wholeheartedly.

On September 26, they broke camp and headed south, eventually finding their way to the outskirts of Cape Girardeau. Without suitable accommodations for their rigs (the only RV park they found was built at the end of a long, tree-lined driveway that would have scraped their paint down to bare metal), they elected to dry camp in the parking lot of the Trail of Tears visitor center. The next morning, after moving their rigs away from the front entrance of the center but before driving to the only launch ramp available in the area, they ducked inside the museum to investigate the Trail of Tears. There, they considered the ordeal suffered by the Cherokee tribe in the mid-1800's, a transgression once described by John Quincy Adams as an "...eternal disgrace upon the country."

In his book *River Horse*, William Least Heat-Moon quoted remarks by Samuel Bowles that, shocking as they were, honestly revealed the mindset of the white settlers bent on occupying Native American lands. Stated in 1868 (years after the Trail of Tears), Bowles cut straight to the heart of what people like the Cherokee were up against:

>...let us hesitate no longer to avow it and act it to the Indian.
>Let us say to him, you are our ward, our child,
>the victim of our destiny,
>ours to displace, ours also to protect.
>We want your hunting-grounds to dig gold from,
>to raise grain on, and you must "move on."

Tragic, heartbreaking and painful to read, Bowles nonetheless captured a common sentiment that might be summed up today by saying, "It's not personal, it's business."

The Cherokee tribe was one of the eastern, indigenous powerhouses in terms of military strength and commercial enterprise. They tried to assimilate aspects of European culture into their own by writing a constitution, erecting schools, conducting regular trade and commerce and establishing relationships with men of influence within the U.S. government. If ever a tribe existed that was designed to live side by side with white settlers in the South, the Cherokee Nation was it. However, the tribe's wealth and land holdings made it a target of those espousing the ideology described by Samuel Bowles, all but guaranteeing an event like the Trail of Tears.

Following the Indian Removal Act of 1830, only the most resilient of the eastern tribes remained on ancestral lands, among them, the Cherokee. They held onto the belief that they would find protection through established treaties and the court system. In 1832, when they won an appeal to the Supreme Court and Chief Justice Marshall ruled the Cherokee Nation as a "...distinct community," they scored a rare judicial victory in an exceedingly unenlightened age.

Unfortunately, the Cherokee land coveted by white, Georgian settlers was too alluring and the Georgians enjoyed the favor of President Jackson, the man responsible for enforcing the Supreme Court's ruling. He ignored the decision and, along with his successor Martin Van Buren, encouraged the people in Georgia to continue pressuring the Cherokee to leave.

In 1835, several, prominent, Cherokee leaders signed the Treaty of Echota which, effectively, exchanged their developed and familiar homeland in the South for unsettled lands west of the Mississippi. (They had also signed their death warrant. Dissenting voices within the tribe were violently opposed to the treaty.) Many of the Cherokee accepted their fate and departed but, eventually, those that remained were removed by force. Between 1837 and 1839, under the direction of Winfield Scott, the U.S. Army escorted thousands of Cherokee to a reservation in what is now Oklahoma.

Poor sanitation, meager rations, drought, exposure and lawlessness contributed to a significant loss of life. Estimates vary, but between 4,000 and 8,000 Cherokee perished along the way. A missionary accompanying the indigenous migrants wrote in his journal, "It is mournful to see how reluctantly these people go away, even the stoutest hearts melt into tears when they turn their faces towards the setting sun."

The *Acrosswater* crew had heard about the Trail of Tears, but knew little of the details until they stepped inside the interpretive center. They spent a solemn hour walking through the displays and reflecting upon the tragedy, mostly in silence. They all thought back to their visit to the Blaine County Museum and the multi-media presentation about Chief Joseph. Some quick math and they realized that not much had changed in the fifty years between the Trail of Tears and the flight of the Nez Perce. Anglo populations continued to regard Native peoples with disdain and an abysmal lack of compassion or as, in the words of anthropologist James Mooney, "...an incumbrance (sic) to be cleared off, like the trees and the wolves." The *Acrosswater* journalists later recorded their sentiments using the terms "...unbelievable..." and "...harrowing." They had come to sincerely appreciate the eye-opening peeks into their nation's past, whether appalling or inspiring. This encounter fit squarely in the appalling category.

They moved their convoy across the river to East Cape Girardeau and the only true RV park in the area. They paid ten dollars to launch out of Honker's Marina and had a pleasant cruise around the area, lunching near the water side of the Trail of Tears Park and visiting white cliffs once climbed by Captain Lewis. The next day, they went east to start their newly modified push to the gulf; they scheduled it to originate from Paducah, KY where they had access to the Ohio, Tennessee and Cumberland Rivers, as well as the distinct, cultural flavor of the five, different states that converged in the area.

They uncovered another somber story when they made a quick stop in Cairo, the southernmost town in Illinois and a place that was struggling to survive flooding and societal strife. The *Acrosswater* visitors were struck by Cairo's notable decline in the form of boarded up businesses and flood walls covered in graffiti. When they visited again from the river side a few day's later, they were even more stunned by the water's isolating effect on the community.

Before tying off at the river's edge and walking up the embankment to the town, the captain noted that the river gage they had passed along the way read twenty feet. At the crest of the bank, just where the land leveled off and the flood walls came into view, he glanced down far below to where *Acrosswater* bobbed in the river. He then turned to look at the flood walls guarding the community and remembered the high water mark he had seen at Kinder's restaurant further upstream. Again, he tried to imagine the entire horizon under water, an impossibility during such a dry year. Had he been there just seven years earlier, when the river gage read nearly fifty feet and, even more ominously, water flow had registered 1,750,000 cubic feet per second, the town would have looked like a boat in distress, surrounded by open ocean.

Exploring Cairo, they struck up a conversation with a passing sheriff and learned that the community had never recovered from race riots that took place in the sixties and early seventies. Its population fell without pause, reaching just 3500 by the year 2000. A town ideally located to take advantage of river commerce, one that had once refused to float a loan to the city of Chicago and had run out of space to accommodate all the freight being unloaded on its docks, found itself in irreversible decline.

Shoulders slumped, the captain and crew retreated down the embankment to their boat. After successive stops in places where they punctuated their journals with the adjective "...miserable..." to describe what people endured, they were all in the mood for something upbeat. Somewhat surprisingly, Paducah, KY turned out to have just what they needed.

The first indication that they were in store for something a little more lighthearted presented itself immediately after they set up camp. They drove into town and discovered that the Best BBQ Contest was underway. Following a lunch and dinner during which the team devoured forty-three pounds of ribs and sixteen slices of Bundt cake, the depressing penury of Cairo was but a distant, hazy memory. Still nursing protein-induced hangovers the following day, the travelers opted for contrasting activities as a means of recovery.

While the crew invaded downtown Paducah to explore the antique shops, the skipper searched for the nearest golf course. He settled on the Edwin J. Paxton Municipal Course, walked on without a tee time and spent a few hours in the company of the club champion. After his round, he found the others, not at an antique bazaar, but at a famous, Paducah attraction (well, famous for Kentucky).

A guy could be forgiven if he assumed that a building with the sign National Quilt Museum over the entrance was filled with husbands napping on benches, but, in fact, it was nothing short of sensational. Open almost a decade, the museum had a collection of quilts that dated back over two centuries and contained brilliant examples of the art form. Several were sewn together at the time of the American Revolution and ingeniously used every spare scrap of fabric to create wonderful, bright tapestries.

One of the prettiest was made entirely of white cotton, but it had the most exquisite designs, some of which contained over 200 stitches per square inch. The whole party exited the museum in awe of the artists' creativity and resourcefulness. More importantly, they all felt like they were back in their exploration groove and ready to continue their adventure with renewed vigor.

On the last day of September, a Saturday, they shoved off into the Ohio River intent on spending a day on the water. They hit the ramp early in the morning to avoid any congestion caused by the ongoing barbecue festival and jetted upstream on the Tennessee River, eventually locking through Kentucky Lock & Dam into Kentucky Lake. They tied off at one of the marinas and had lunch at Patti's in the village of Grand Rivers, the northern most entrance to a narrow slip of terrain called the Land between the Lakes; the Land divided Kentucky Lake (created by a dam on the Tennessee River) and Lake Barkley (created by a dam on the Cumberland River).

After lunch, Rose and Roxa decided to walk off their meal and agreed to meet the men at the Green Turtle Bay Marina on the Cumberland River side of the Land between the Lakes. Karl and Larry took *Acrosswater* out of the marina and navigated the Barkley Canal, a free-flowing waterway that connected the two lakes and thus, the two rivers. They puttered down to Green Turtle Bay, retrieved the girls and, seeing that it was after 3:00 p.m., sailed over to the Barkley Lock & Dam to try to lock back through to the Ohio River. Then the fun began.

At the Barkley Lock, the captain tried for over an hour to raise the tender on the CB without receiving even an acknowledgment. They motored back through the Barkley Canal to the Kentucky Lake side where the lock master answered, but he informed them it would be two hours or more because of all the barge traffic heading upstream. The skipper finally understood why the Chicago yachts traveled in armadas, so they would have some measure of influence when they reached a lock.

With daylight seriously at risk, they had to find a way to set the motorcycle on shore so one of them (Karl) could ride back to Paducah and retrieve the boat trailer. Throwing caution to the wind, they decided to try the private, Grand Rivers Marina and had barely tied off at the dock when they were confronted by the manager, a smartly dressed woman used to handling personalities that ranged from dip-shit, drunken fishermen to over-starched, egotistical, ascot-wearing yachtsmen.

Interested in the design of *Acrosswater* - especially the Harley hoist - she agreed to allow them to offload the bike. She even volunteered to hold the gate open at the top of the gangway (a near vertical face), so that the daredevil-cum-captain would have a straight path onto dry land. Privately she hoped to see a Yankee plow into the pilings, but her sophisticated training did not allow her to be that forthcoming.

Acrosswater's seasoned support team expertly craned the bike from the boat to the dock and then the captain - wearing not his trademark leathers (or even the patriotic jumpsuit normally favored by stuntmen), but boat shoes, swim trunks, a tee shirt and helmet - mounted up and gunned the engine. Waving off pleas to be careful, as well as the salient point that he had nothing to use to load the bike onto the trailer because the ramp was on the boat, the skipper snapped down the helmet visor, tromped the gearshift into first and hit the gas. He shot up the incline and roared past the woman holding the gate, disappearing into the setting sun.

Thirty minutes later, he rumbled into the parking lot where the SUV and trailer were parked. Mercifully, most of the barbecue crowd had already left to nurse stomachaches of varying severity so the skipper had some room to maneuver, depending on the strategy he chose to load the bike. He thought about backing the trailer up to an embankment like he had done in Astoria, but there was not a hill to be seen.

Surveying the lot, he noticed an old Chevy parked close to the trailer, the kind of truck that typically had in its bed an array of junk that might serve as a ramp, things like a discarded board or the ammunition rack from a Sherman tank. Approaching the passenger side of the vehicle, Karl peeked in the bed to confirm his suspicions and then peered in through the open window. A handicap tag hung from the rear-view mirror. "Howdy," he said to the driver, "what's the tag for?" He rested his elbows on the open window frame of the truck.

"I had polio," the man in the truck answered, wiping his mouth.

"I'm Karl with a 'K.' You live nearby?"

"Yessir. I'm Jimmy with a 'J.' I'm just finishing up my supper." Jimmy's dirty blond hair trailed out from under his Schlitz baseball cap. He looked about fifty.

"Well, Jimmy, I'm hoping you can help me. I need to get my bike onto my trailer, but I don't have the ramp with me. Do you have a board or something I could use?"

"I might have something that'll work." He set his Big Mac down on the seat and opened his door. He limped around to the side of the truck and started to pick through the junk. "I went camping last weekend and still haven't cleaned up."

Karl saw a minimum of sixty-five, assorted, pull-tab beer cans, an old shovel, some short pieces of lumber, a tow chain, a rusty jack, a broken cane pole and a rotting clump of leaves. None of it looked suitable for a ramp and all of it had been there much longer than a week.

"I know," said Jimmy, "what if we use the tailgate of the truck? I set engines on it all the time." He hobbled to the back, lowered the gate and then lifted the hinges out of their sockets. He and Karl carried it over to the trailer and discovered that it was a perfect fit. The tailgate even had a groove running down its middle that was seemingly designed for the Harley tires. In less than five minutes, they loaded the bike and then returned the gate back to the truck.

"Well, Jimmy I gotta tell you," Karl said, reaching into the pocket of his swim trunks, "you're a real lifesaver." He pulled out his money clip.

"I can't take anything, Karl," Jimmy said, turning and limping back to the cab of his truck.

"What if I just buy your next supper?" the captain pleaded, holding out a couple of bills.

"Nope," Jimmy said, slamming the door and turning the key, "sometimes the Lord just works in mysterious ways." And with that, he folded up his Big Mac in its wrapper, put the truck in gear and drove off, beer cans bouncing onto the pavement.

Mechanical concerns hindered their progress over the next week. Karl had discovered a problem with the boat trailer hitch and braking system and wanted to repair them before traveling much further. The hitch called for a larger, 2 5/16" diameter ball, which many of the shops in the area did not carry. And Larry reported a failing water heater that left he and Roxa taking cold showers (and the Corps of Discovery thought they had it tough) as well as a lingering issue with one of the entry steps. That left the party debating if they should risk a side trip away from their water route while they fixed the equipment.

The skipper had contacted North River about the trailer and the manufacturer promised to overnight a new master cylinder, actuator and ball hitch, but Larry and Roxa still had to find someone to inspect their RV. The revised, travel plan called for the *Acrosswater* party to boat south from Paducah on the Tennessee River, but with the added delay, some of the crew members lobbied for a junket to Nashville - it was just over 100 miles east. Even though the captain calculated barely a month remaining before they needed to turn back west, he relented and agreed to a brief detour to Nashville.

The *Acrosswater* four hopscotched their way from Paducah to the outskirts of Nashville. Karl, Rose and Roxa took in a practice session at the golf course near the Opryland Hotel, but Larry remained behind at the RV park because he had convinced a handyman to drive over from Calvert City (also 100 miles) to help him fix the water heater on his rig.

Returning from golf and finding Larry still hard at work, Karl volunteered to go to a Ford warehouse to pick up some parts for Larry's camper. On the way back, he stopped at a barbershop to have his hair cut; they were going out that night and he felt he needed a trim. Stepping inside, he discovered that not only was he the only customer on site at the moment, but even more surprisingly, the barber was transitioning from a man to a woman. (Or that was the direction Karl assumed since she had a five o'clock shadow under her makeup, an Adam's apple and a voice like Barry White's, but she was wearing a floral-print dress. Oh, and she also had mountainous boobs.)

Before he knew what was happening, the skipper found himself parked in the barber chair where his hair was expertly coiffed with clippers swallowed up by hands the size of baseball mitts. The barber manhandled his head to-and-fro, shears blazing. After she dusted him liberally with talcum powder, she whipped off the cape like a magician completing a big reveal and yanked her client from the chair. Turning so he could examine all sides in the mirror, the captain murmured some words of thanks, offered a healthy tip and stepped back outside into the afternoon sun. Suffice to say, he had not expected that.

That night, the whole crew had dinner at a small diner just off Hillsboro Road, far from the Nashville city center. Larry had made enough progress on his rig to join the party so they all rode together to a joint recommended by another tenant at the RV park. Rose followed up on the suggestion and felt so convinced that the evening could be something special, she decided to make reservations for both the 6:30 p.m. and 9:00 p.m. shows. Were they all glad she did.

You would be hard pressed to find a more unremarkable setting in any field that had seen a larger list of dignitaries cross its stage than the Bluebird Cafe. Started in 1982 and hiding ever since amongst neighboring hair salons and dry cleaners (the captain drove by the place twice trying to find it), the tiny venue sported barely twenty tables yet it had attracted an exhaustive list of songwriters and musicians.

The pamphlet collected by the *Acrosswater* visitors in 2000 listed over 150 artists. Some, like Bob Mould, Bob DiPiero and David Kersh were unknown outside the industry whereas others like Garth Brooks, Carole King and Melissa Etheridge were musical titans. The Cafe dedicated itself to showcasing songwriters and undiscovered talent, holding open mike nights every week and accepting auditions for other performances from only those living within 100 miles of the Bluebird. Combined with the intimate atmosphere, that pipeline of talent made for one unforgettable performance after another.

The *Acrosswater* clan arrived in plenty of time for the 6:30 p.m. show. They took a table near the front, ordered the special from the menu and chatted with some of the other guests. Once the artists hit the stage, however, all talking ceased and they were entranced. They could not have picked any of the singers out of a lineup, but, boy, were the songs terrific.

All of the performers were writers and most had already been in the industry for many years, churning out songs that had been recorded by country royalty. Between them, they had written or co-written for the likes of Phil Vassar, Ronnie Milsap, Lorrie Morgan, Alison Krauss and Trisha Yearwood. Several of the singers tried out some new material that night and one of them described how golf haunts even sleeping players. ("I go to bed at night and dream of bunkers on my left, water on my right.") That number struck a chord, as it were, with the *Acrosswater* foursome.

During both shows, the musicians backed up each other on piano or guitar and the audience was impressed by the notable sense of community between the performers. It was like having a family of entertainers join you for dinner, but only if you agreed to let them take out their guitars and play for a while before bed. The travelers returned to camp after 1:00 a.m., exhausted, but smitten with their night out.

On Saturday, they attended the Grand Ole Opry, an institution in town and the cornerstone of Nashville's musical heritage. Launched in 1925 as the WSM (We Shield Millions) Barn Dance, the program had the financial backing of the National Life & Accident Insurance Co., the reach of a powerful radio station and the cultural appeal to the rural, farming population in all the surrounding counties.

The show acquired its more familiar name in 1927 when, just before going on air one evening, producer George D. Hay quipped that listeners would be treated to a "...grand ole opry...", a play on the word opera. (The Barn Dance filled a time slot that followed a classical music program.) The nickname resonated with the performers and fans alike and in the decades that followed, musicians considered membership in the Opry more than an honor; it was a prerequisite to a lasting career in country music. In many ways, the Opry drove the growth of the genre and at a minimum, was the foundation for modern, country music success.

For all the hype surrounding the venue, the show at the Opry House received, on average, muted reviews from captain and crew. Roxa, usually the most polite of the critics, remarked in her journal only that it was "...fun." Larry offered a play-by-play of the evening, including a list of the sponsors for each segment. (One of the sponsors was Folex Instant Carpet Spot Remover, a subtle indicator of the target demographic.) His favorite performer was Mandy Barnett, but he also made a passing reference to the "...greats..." of the Opry, without a doubt referring to Porter Wagoner, Charlie Walker, Skeeter Davis and Eddie Arnold. They had been performing from as far back as 1943 and had earned the admiration of countless audiences and radio listeners.

The skipper, clearly not an admirer, concluded that the older members of the show (and by that he meant all of them) should have retired years ago. He probably was not far off since four of the entertainers they saw that night died just a few years later. On the ride back to the campsite that night, they unanimously voted that the Bluebird was far more memorable, despite the greater fame of the Opry.

Regardless, before leaving Nashville two days later, they purchased tickets for a return engagement on October 14 when the old Barn Dance would be celebrating seventy-five years in the business. In all likelihood, captain and crew were drawn more by the historical uniqueness of the event and not necessarily the acts they expected to see on stage (though Roxa did mention Garth Brooks approximately thirty-six times over the course of two paragraphs).

They rounded out their side trip with a run down the Cumberland River and a chance to see Nashville from the water. It was cold enough that they had to fire up the on-board heater, but it was still clear and a fine day for boating. The Cumberland turned out to be a gem with exceptional navigation markers, a deep channel and clean water. They cruised into the city center and offloaded at a dock across from the Tennessee Titans stadium. They walked around town, toured the Ryman Theater (the Grand Ole Opry's home until 1974) and took a taxi to the Pancake Pantry for brunch. Then it was back to their ship where they had one of the best afternoons of boating since they had left the Missouri.

The air was crisp, the scenery was resplendent with foliage and limestone cliffs, there was no water traffic or current to speak of and they had zero risk of being impaled by a submerged stump. That run on the Cumberland reminded them of the joy they experienced being on the rivers and stoked their enthusiasm for the remainder of their journey to New Orleans They set their alarm clocks for an early start in the morning. They were going to Memphis.

Fall on the river

Chapter 11
The river bottom blues

"Made it, now we can legally bitch for the next four years."

Roxa's blog - November 3, 2000

"Now they're going thru <u>hand</u> recount! Gore, give it up!!!"

Karl's journal - November 13, 2000

The presidential election of 2000 was full of intrigue and introduced the term hanging-chad to the American people. Captain and crew voted by mail.

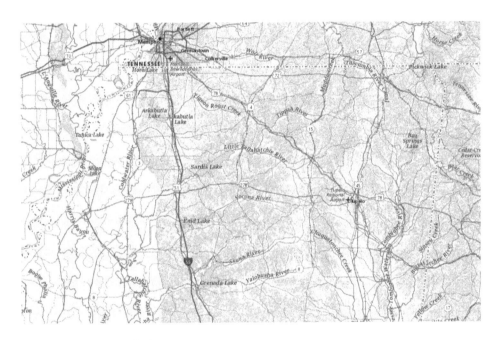

Mississippi and Tennessee

HERBERT Hoover, the second most famous resident to stay at the Peabody, moved into the hotel in April of 1927 to oversee the relief effort demanded by the Great Flood. He had already earned international acclaim for humanitarian work during World War One, when first he had managed the distribution of aid to the people of Belgium and then to the wider European populace. By the time of his arrival in Memphis, the unrelenting waters of the Mississippi and its tributaries had covered over 16 million acres and driven 500,000 people from their homes. Somehow, Hoover had to find a way to house and feed all those refugees in the midst of the growing crisis (the rivers would remain at flood stage through the summer) and accumulate resources to aid in the future rebuilding effort.

Even with the power of the federal government and the centralization of relief organizations under his control, the commerce secretary had his work cut out for him. He had selected

Memphis as his base of operations due to its access to the river, the railroads and the surrounding territories most affected by the disaster. The available high terrain in the city also meant he could work without fear of being flooded out himself. He selected the Peabody, presumably, because it was the swankiest hotel in town.

He did not choose the Peabody because of the *most* famous residents of the hotel. They moved in just a few years after Hoover departed and they swiftly enchanted visitors and staff alike. The story of the Peabody Ducks began one afternoon in the thirties when a couple of outdoorsmen (who had spent more time that day nipping off their hip flasks than hunting) turned loose some live decoys in the decorative fountain of the hotel lobby. The ducks and their ancestors stayed and by 1940, the hotel employed a full time Duckmaster who escorted the birds, via elevator and over red carpet, from their rooftop home to the fountain at 11:00 a.m. and back upstairs at 5:00 p.m.

Accordingly, guests and tourists planned their visits so they could line up in time to watch the parade. A front row seat was ideal. If someone just looked at a photo of the mallards on the march, he might be fooled into thinking they strutted along like cartoon ducks in a military procession, each webbed foot stepping in time. In fact, they hustled out of the elevator and ran to the fountain as quickly as possible, as if hurrying across a busy street. Anyone arriving late or standing in the back would certainly miss the show.

Larry had noted the duck parade as a point of interest when helping craft the original itinerary and the *Acrosswater* corps left Nashville in plenty of time to catch the afternoon viewing. The 240 mile commute took them five hours and they were hooked up at their campsite on the Arkansas side of the Mississippi River by 4:00 p.m.

With metronomic precision over the next hour, they made an appointment at a service center in Marion to fix the tire of the SUV, called tech support about Roxa's laptop, drove into Memphis to the Peabody, asked the concierge for a hairdresser recommendation and still were in the queue in time to watch the ducks at 5:00 p.m. Being the U of O alumnus that he was, Karl purchased a duck carved out of a century-old, cedar fence-post as a souvenir. They topped off their initial inspection of the city with a walk down Beale Street and a meal of Memphis barbecue at the Blues City Cafe.

As had become a regular occurrence, the group mixed maintenance with pleasure the next day. Karl replaced the actuator on the boat trailer and had the tire on the SUV repaired before he and Larry dropped off the girls downtown. Rose and Roxa had appointments at the concierge-recommended stylist plus they both needed pedicures and wanted to do some light shopping.

Meanwhile, the men searched for a good spot to launch the boat later that day. They first tried the Memphis Yacht Club near Harbor Town, but were politely informed that it would be a cold day in hell before a Memphis institution like the Yacht Club would allow its waters to be sullied by the likes of an aluminum fishing skiff, especially one with North in the name of its manufacturer. The guys were starting to sense that people in the South still nursed a grudge of some kind against their northern neighbors.

They found a suitable ramp on Mud Island (on the island's northern end, appropriately) and then set off to find a supplement to their *Quimby's* river guide. They tried the U.S. Coast Guard office without success and then spent nearly two hours downtown at the Memphis bureau of the USACE, but all they came away with was a used book entitled *Historic Names and Places on the Lower Mississippi River*. By mid-afternoon they realized that they had better get on the water while they had the chance so they picked up the boat back at camp, retrieved their wives and hurried over to the ramp.

They launched without issue, but their ride ended up being more symbolic than pleasant. Instead of having a relaxing cruise on a historic stretch of the greatest, American river, the team spent an hour dodging tugs and barges and grabbing fretful peeks of the city in between floating convoys. They gave up and pulled back into the Mud Island slough in time to make a mad dash back to the Peabody to watch the ducks again. Roxa talked her way into a ride up the elevator to the roof with the birds and captured some nice photos for her on-line journal.

On their last day before driving back towards Nashville, the couples spent time at the more famous attractions in the Memphis area. Their first stop was Graceland. Garish, dated and commercialized, the former home of Elvis fascinated them nonetheless. From the sequined jumpsuits to the gold records to the furry eccentricity of the Jungle Room, the captain and crew could not take their eyes off the crazy excess of the mansion. (Coincidentally, Rose had purchased a sweater the day before from Elvis' tailor, Bernard Lansky. Historical records are unclear if hers came with sequins or not.)

Next, they drove back into downtown Memphis and paid a visit to the National Civil Rights Museum, housed in the former Lorraine Motel, the site of Dr. Martin Luther King Jr.'s murder. The outside of the building was frozen in time, familiar to anyone who had seen photos of the assassination, with the curtains slightly askew, a dated color scheme on the doors and vintage Cadillacs parked in front. One could easily imagine ghostly bystanders still pointing in the direction of the boarding house across the street from where the shots were fired.

Inside, the exhibits traced how black Americans struggled for civil rights, beginning in 1619 (when the first slaves were brought west) through the Jim Crow era and into the marches of the 1960's. Open since 1991, the displays ranged from horrifying (ledgers with lists of slaves) to inspiring (the story of Rosa Parks) and stirred the *Acrosswater* visitors similarly to their stop at the Trail of Tears museum.

From the Lorraine, they headed back to the river to more thoroughly investigate Mud Island. They opted for the tram that shuttled visitors over from the mainland, rather than the long walk on the pedestrian bridge. Their favorite attraction on Mud Island was the concrete model of the lower Mississippi River. It was the length of five city blocks, was constructed to scale (every inch equaled eight topographical miles) and its channel sloped from top to bottom so that tiny Cairo at the beginning was five feet higher than the pool representing the Gulf of Mexico at the end. Combined with the thoughtful displays around the perimeter which tied in tributaries like the Missouri, the replica helped put into context for the *Acrosswater* trekkers the ambitious scope of their journey; even at 1/30th of the actual dimensions, they felt a swell of pride in seeing how far they had come.

They topped off their tour around the city with one more slog through racks of ribs at The Rendezvous, another legendary restaurant dedicated to Memphis barbecue. Though the team agreed that Blues City was better, the glistening piles of bones left on the table suggested that the Rendezvous chef knew his way around a smoker. Sated both physically and culturally from the events of the day, they felt better prepared to return to Nashville and reluctantly turned their backs on the Mississippi until their planned terminus in New Orleans.

On a crisp morning in early April of 1862, two young men stood quietly in a thinly wooded forest. The sky overhead was starting to show the first sign of dawn and they could see their breath. One of them noticed some wild violets growing at their feet and pointed them out to his companion. He bent down and picked a few, arranging them in his cap. He was seventeen-years-old.

The other fellow was Henry Stanley who, ten years later, would find notoriety when he located missionary David Livingstone in Africa, but who, in 1862, was serving as an infantryman in the Confederate Army. The two men were assigned to a brigade under the command of General William Hardee and along with more than 44,000 other soldiers, were mustering for an attack against the unsuspecting Federal forces gathered near Pittsburgh Landing along the Tennessee River. It was a quiet Sunday morning and Stanley himself later wrote, "...the woods would have been a grand place for a picnic." Instead, the forest and fields were soon transformed into the arena for one of the bloodiest, most ferocious fights of the Civil War. Historians later named the battle after a church that was used as a mustering point by both armies. It was called Shiloh.

For the next two days, the opposing armies fought desperately over strategic points like the Bloody Pond and the Hornet's Nest. The future explorer and his young friend - boys really - hurled themselves at the Union lines for most of Sunday, helping to force the Federals backward until they were pinned against the Tennessee River. Had Union Generals Wallace and Buell not arrived late in the afternoon to reinforce the Federal lines, the Confederates almost certainly would have captured Pittsburgh Landing. Instead, the Union Army regrouped and stopped the enemy advance.

The following day, with the support of gunboats on the river, the Yankees pushed the Rebel forces back over all the terrain the South had gained on Sunday. Confederate General P.G.T Beauregard ordered a full retreat and at the end of the two days, nearly 3500 men were killed and more than 16,000 were wounded. Stanley survived. His companion did not, cut down by a bullet during one of their charges.

The *Acrosswater* party stopped at Shiloh on its way back to Nashville. Though they had seen the site of the Battle of the Hemp Bales on their way south, they had not yet visited any large battlefields of the Civil War. They entered from State Route 22, which skirts Shiloh's western edge, and drove east to the visitor center, a simple building sitting next to a National Military Cemetery on the property. After perusing the museum and viewing a film about the conflict, they made a run to the historic Catfish Hotel Restaurant for lunch and then hurried back to the center in time to join a tour of the battlefield.

Much like Henry Stanley 140 years earlier, the four travelers could not square the savagery and gore of the fight with the pastoral splendor of the park. Shiloh was indeed the perfect venue for a Sunday picnic, with over twelve miles of scenic roads and trails winding through semi-manicured fields and lightly-maintained woods. The Tennessee River formed the eastern boundary and was painfully picturesque, especially when viewed from some of the higher vantage points in the park; the area was also the site of an indigenous community in the distant past, so ancient mounds near the river invited exploration. And yet, at nearly every turn the *Acrosswater* team was reminded of the terrible campaign that had happened there so many years ago.

Their tour took them past batteries of cannon, most of which had actually been used during the battle and were arrayed as if the fight was still in progress. Historian Winston Groom, in his spellbinding account of the contest, estimated that as many as 100,000 projectiles per minute - bullets, grape, cannonballs - may have filled the air when the clash reached its peak intensity. The captain and crew thought back to the recovered munitions they had viewed at the museum and shivered at the thought of them tearing into the lines of men only paces away.

Many monuments were dedicated to specific combatants from each side and were named for rivers, not states (i.e. the Army of Tennessee). Each had a unique design, but all tried to capture the valor and sacrifice of the participants.

The *Acrosswater* visitors came upon a Union field hospital, one of the first of its kind used during the war. Immediate death was oftentimes preferable to injury. Due to poor sanitation and the absence of antibiotics, injured soldiers could suffer for weeks before finally succumbing. Accounts from other, longer skirmishes (like the siege of Vicksburg or Port Hudson) told of wounded men moaning for days as they lay in no-man's-land between enemy lines. Surgeons performed amputations as a primary means of treatment instead of risking the inevitable infections associated with wounds. At Shiloh, with over 8400 maimed men on the Union side alone, the field hospital was a crude but effective triage, regardless of how the piles of amputated limbs accumulating outside the tents may have looked.

Particularly moving to the visitors were the Confederate burial sites. After the Rebel retreat, the Federals buried their dead foes in deep trenches, one man stacked on the other. The sites were marked simply, some in wooded turnouts, others on the main route with the largest said to contain over 700 men. At one stop, after their tour guide described what they were seeing, the pilgrims stood in silent contemplation for many minutes, clearly touched by the moment.

Throughout their journey, the effect a place or experience had on the captain and crew was often reflected in the length and detail of their journal entries. This one garnered a full paragraph from Roxa (remember that her space was precious, given the limited sophistication of Web publishing at that time) and Karl dedicated two full pages - including the margins - of tight script. They would not soon forget Shiloh.

The *Acrosswater* company pursued slightly less melancholy diversions over the next week. The day after Shiloh, their primary goal was to reach Nashville in time for the 75th Anniversary of the Grand Ole Opry. It was a simple two hour drive north from their camp in Pickwick, however, as they were wont to do, the foursome chose to wring as much cultural immersion out of the commute as they could. Conveniently, the most direct path to Nashville was the Natchez Trace Parkway, a place the travelers would have never known about had they not started their journey so many months ago and exactly the type of discovery they loved to find.

The Trace likely started as a game trail centuries before evolving into a path used regularly by the native tribes in the region. As the European settlers dared venture over the mountains into the old Southwest (an area *east* of the Mississippi), the path morphed into a primary route for travelers. It was named a postal road by President Jefferson and soon stretched over 400 miles from Natchez to Nashville. The old road came under National Park purview in 1938 and remains one of the prettiest drives in the country with miles of pristine wooded hills, rural communities and camera-worthy overlooks at every turn.

The Trace has a number of historic stops, most notably a memorial dedicated to and the burial site of Meriwether Lewis, *Acrosswater*'s old friend from earlier in the trip. Lewis had died in the nearby Grinder House under mysterious circumstances in 1809 and was buried adjacent the property by legislative proclamation in 1848. His obelisk took the form of a broken shaft, representing a life cut tragically short. A stop at the Lewis monument, combined with a charming stretch of historic, American roadway, made for a perfect drive up to Nashville and the Opry.

Or it would have had the part of the park surrounding the memorial not been swarming with insufferable fairgoers. Unbeknown to our protagonists, a craft fair in that section of the Trace had been planned for months. Music, hippies, bumpkins, hicks, redneck wannabes, kids with musket-shaped cap guns, barbecue fragrances and other, smoky plumes of suspicious origin filled the woods, deterring the foursome. Not that the proceedings were beneath them. Quite the contrary. They would have happily investigated the event under different circumstances, likely making several new friends and perhaps choking down some varmint stew. For sure they would have bought a frontier soap dish or pioneer rag doll or artificial, coonskin cap, and dutifully carted it back home to be secreted away for exhumation years later.

But on that day, Garth was calling them from Nashville so they rolled up the windows and locked the doors on the SUV and kept moving. They arrived at the Opry just in time to catch the headliners for the evening's program parading into the venue on the red carpet. The concertgoers found the show much more enjoyable than the previous week - even the skipper rated it "...great..."- mostly because the

Opry leaned on current country stars like Garth, Vince Gill and Trisha Yearwood and left the more cadaverous performers backstage. After the final ovation, the team grabbed a cup of coffee at the Opryland Hotel and then cruised back to camp, finally turning out the lights at 2:00 a.m.

Two days later, *Acrosswater* felt water again on her hull. The party had recuperated in camp the morning immediately following the outing in Nashville and had also sneaked in a round at Shiloh Falls golf course, but a turn on the lake was what they needed. They dropped the old jet boat into Pickwick Lake, a reservoir on the Tennessee River created by the Pickwick and Wilson dams, and motored along the shoreline, stopping every so often to explore a cove.

Along the way, they noticed a gorgeous home tucked up in the trees. They had a habit of rating eye-catching homes during their cruises and up until then, they had spied the most engaging on Lake of the Ozarks. That home on Pickwick really caught their attention - possibly because they had cabin fever after living in the limited confines of their campers for the last four months - and they all rated the property a ten-plus. Karl was especially drawn to the J/92 sailboat nestled in a cradle on a track that allowed the owner to launch and remove the boat from the water with ease.

The couple who owned the home was near the shoreline, the missus fussing with something along the beach and her husband pretending to work but really just tooling about on his Kabota tractor. The travelers could not resist idling over to strike up a conversation and were immediately treated to a tour. The owners had retired from a Cummins dealership and had additional properties in Memphis, Vail and Florida. They were delighted to show the *Acrosswater* crew around and even suggested the ideal spot for a picnic lunch in a tranquil cove just a short distance away. The explorers took the advice and found the location as lovely as advertised.

That same night, they had dinner at the Pickwick Lodge and used the upstairs lounge to spread out all of their maps and charts to finalize the remaining part of their journey. Truth be told, the forced detour away from the Mississippi had sapped some of their passion for the trip. The Tenn-Tom Waterway, the Black Warrior River and the Tennessee were all fine alternatives - actually shorter and safer, as previously noted - but they were sorely absent the allure of the Mississippi. The commodore lamented as much as he journaled one morning. He looked out the window, espied *Acrosswater* sitting alone in her trailer and wrote, "Now we're wandering, looking for day excursions on the water, antique malls and golf courses." Through no fault of their own, their adventure had become less grand expedition through America's heartland and more retiree road trip.

So, the team settled into the couches of the lounge, consulted its maps and listed what each member thought should be the group's remaining priorities. First, the skipper insisted they stay on task and commit to a return date. Detours and unscripted sightseeing were part of the original plan, but winter was fast approaching so they had to adhere to a schedule. Next, both couples had connected with other family members in recent days so the parties agreed to separate, side trips. After all, even Lewis and Clark split up briefly during their trek. A variety of people they encountered all mentioned stretches of the Black Warrior and Tennessee Rivers as must-sees, especially in the fall when the foliage was nothing short of spectacular, so they penciled those onto the itinerary.

Lastly, they believed they could risk one launch into the Mississippi once they reached New Orleans. Even if it took them all day at the final lock, just dipping the nose of the boat into the river would be a fitting end to their remarkable adventure. They expected to round out their remaining time on the road with as much Civil War history as they could handle plus the requisite rounds of golf. They wrapped the Pickwick conference with a streamlined list of achievable goals that would see them through their final days on the road until they at last turned for home.

Searching for a launch site

Chapter 12

To the Bayou and back

"Heard that a suicide boat rammed a US Navy Ship in the Persian Gulf area; 6 sailors dead, 12 missing."

Karl's journal - October 12, 2000

The skipper recorded the attack on the *USS Cole.*

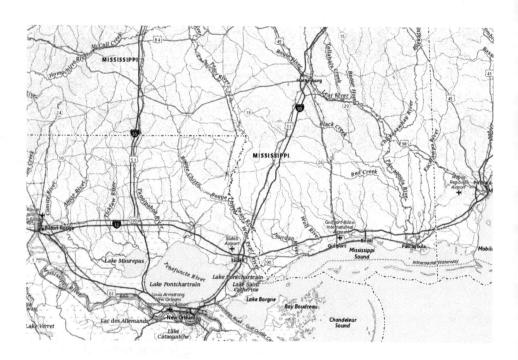

New Orleans and vicinity

AFTER restructuring the itinerary, they moved further east to Chattanooga. With some time to kill before they separated to meet up with family, the foursome hoped Chattanooga would have attractions diverse enough to suit all their interests. Having abandoned their original plan (the one that had taken months to prepare) they felt a bit unsettled to be improvising to such a degree and as such went into Chattanooga with a touch of apprehension. They were delighted to find the little city flush with hidden gems.

They had of course heard of the famous railroad terminal indelibly linked to the town and dutifully paid their respects to the refurbished locomotives and Pullman cars. They did not expect to find one of the finest, freshwater aquariums in the nation in southeast Tennessee, however, but so they did. They passed an enjoyable three or four hours walking the gentle slopes of the building. All members of the corps described it as either sensational or amazing.

Since clouds and drizzle lingered for much of that first day in the region, the team chose to stay mostly indoors and lazily took in both an IMAX and conventional film, perused the less memorable, International Towing Museum and searched for a decent launch for the next day, when they planned to hit the Tennessee River.

They had already seen stretches of the Tennessee, but a part of the river called the Nickajack had come highly recommended by their friends on Pickwick Lake. (They had referred to it as the Grand Canyon of the Tennessee.) Even with overcast, hazy skies, the captain and crew found the ride on the river spellbinding. They took their time puttering along the waterway as it snaked through the town and then jetted slowly all the way to the the Chickamauga Lock and Dam, using care to minimize their wake around other boats of any type, pleasure or commercial.

The foliage in the trees was breathtaking and they chanced upon the regional Fall Colors Festival, which gave them an opportunity to hear local music, eat local food and look over local crafts. The pace of the day was pleasantly unhurried, particularly the time on the water. None of them wanted it to end.

They spent their last day before splitting up at the Civil War battlefields of Chickamauga and Chattanooga. Opening in 1895, Chickamauga and Chattanooga was the first of the four, original, national battlefields to be established (the others being Shiloh, Gettysburg and Vicksburg) when veterans, local communities and the War Department of the federal government collaborated to preserve significant sites of the Civil War.

Roughly 15,000 veterans attended the opening ceremony and the battlefields almost instantly became the model by which future efforts would be measured. Paying tribute to the nearly 35,000 combined casualties from the battle, the area provided a classroom for both historians and tactical war analysts due to its unique blend of terrain. The *Acrosswater* adventurers visited all the monuments on the property they could, even taking the Incline Railway (at more than seventy-two degrees, the steepest in the world) to the top of Lookout Mountain and its view of the Tennessee River. None of them could fathom how any army could advance up that grade in the face of enemy fire.

Just as Lewis and Clark had contrasting experiences when apart, the *Acrosswater* family interludes were wildly different. Larry and Roxa drove about 100 miles south from Chattanooga to Athens, GA to visit a dear friend, Jacque, who was completing her PhD at the University of Georgia. They toured the campus, took numerous hikes within Athens and in surrounding communities, played golf, lingered in antique shops, visited a pottery studio, watched an iron pour (the process artisans use to cast shapes by filling molds with molten metal) and viewed some of the fine antebellum homes in the area. Sticking mostly with a quiet, holistic regimen, their travel recess was like a spiritual retreat.

Karl and Rose, on the other hand, drove over 300 miles north to Louisville to meet up with a host of family members: their daughter Christy, Rose's sister Chris, Chris's boyfriend John, their niece Karley and, the coup de grace, their niece Cori who was escorting a clutch of students from Saipan to Louisville to attend the National FFA Convention. So, while Larry and Roxa were meditating in quiet reflection, taking strolls along leafy trails and consuming cups of herbal tea, Karl and Rose were welcoming in kids at 2:00 a.m., helping track down lost luggage, wondering if they had enough life jackets for everyone to go on the boat and trying to keep up with all the conversations flying around during supper.

Even the trip up to Kentucky kept them on their toes. Rose drove the SUV and Karl the Bus with *Acrosswater* in tow. All was fine until they encountered some construction which shrunk the lanes to twelve feet, leaving just inches of clearance on either side of the Bus. The skipper held his breath until he had cleared the roadwork, expecting to hear the crunch of a lane marker the entire way.

They treated their family and friends to runs on the Ohio (they did have enough preservers for everyone) and they were able to catch downtown Louisville from the river, but the real thrill for the seasoned boaters was watching the joy on the faces of the visitors as they road in *Acrosswater*. The whirlwind sidebar through Louisville had them boating from morning until evening and then racing back to the convention center to join 15,000 screaming, FFA teenagers at a Toby Keith concert. It was worth every nerve-jangling second.

Tuscaloosa, AL provided the setting for the *Acrosswater* version of Reunion Bay. The two couples reunited on Halloween night of 2000, pulling into town at the same time. After check-in and while setting up camp, Larry noticed liquid pooling near one of his levelers; it was the hydraulic fluid from his leveling system. He contacted the manufacturer and was reassured he could still drive his rig even with all of the hydraulic fluid drained.

The next day, November 1, everyone except Rose (who stayed behind to pay bills and complete other administrative tasks) ventured into town to have the Sportscoach repaired. They dropped off the camper and upon hearing that the repair could take up to five hours, toured the town (which included the University of Alabama) and grocery shopped. During the exploration, the skipper noticed a sign for the Northriver Yacht and Country Club. A club with the same name as *Acrosswater*'s manufacturer could not have been a coincidence. He decided to investigate.

Over the length of their pilgrimage, they had already played several outstanding golf courses including Red Mike's in Williston, Osage National in Lake of the Ozarks, Springhouse in Nashville and The Bear Trace in Harrison. There were several duds in the rotation as well. Tracks like Rocky Knolls and Point Mallard barely scored one star from the players, but then again their names did not exactly suggest that golfers could expect manicured greens and raked traps. Pulling onto the grounds of Northriver, the captain could tell immediately that it was not the average municipal course. He ignored the small sign that read MEMBERS ONLY and went into the clubhouse.

"Hi there, do you have room for a foursome tomorrow?" He walked up to a young man who was polishing an assortment of silver, golf tees.

"Certainly, sir. May I have your name or membership number?" He carefully folded his polishing cloth and put it in his back pocket.

"Well, we're from out of town, but we're part of the North River family." The captain smiled warmly.

"The North River family? This property is exclusive to Tuscaloosa so I'm not sure what you mean."

"North River. The manufacturer that made my boat." He fished into his pocket and pulled out his money clip, looking for some snapshots.

"Ahh." Now seeing what he was dealing with, the man's expression changed from polite curiosity to tactful condescension. "I truly am sorry, sir, but this is a private club. You cannot play if you are not a member." He started to gently shoo Karl out of the room.

Desperate now, and with the attendant tugging at his elbow, the captain noticed a picture of Robert Cupp on the wall. Cupp had designed Karl's home course back in Oregon. "Wait! This is a Bob Cupp course? He built the one I live on back home!"

"Not today, sir," the attendant replied, a touch more insistently. He tightened his grip on Karl's arm.

"But, that means we have reciprocal privileges!" The skipper's voice cracked slightly. He tried to pull a putter out of a display as he was dragged past, but the young man had a grip of steel.

"I really am sorry sir." He pried Karl's fingers off the door jam. "Please call our office in the morning if you would like to inquire about becoming a member." He firmly shut the door.

"Can you at least have the golf director call me?" Karl slid his personal business card under the door. "I want to swap notes on Bob!" The captain heard some muffled platitudes from the other side. He concluded that a round at Northriver was probably not in their future.

So imagine his surprise the next day when they returned from a boat outing and he found that he had a phone message from David, the head golf pro at Northriver. Karl called back and they chatted for some time about Cupp designed courses. Bob Cupp's brother, a photographer, had just visited Northriver and had in his portfolio an extensive collection of pictures taken at Karl's home course. David was happy to give them a tee time for the following day.

And what a day it was. Not only did they play a round of

eighteen holes, they received a tour of the clubhouse and its surroundings from David. The owner of the club had filled the property with paintings, photographs, sculptures, historical artifacts, tapestries, rugs and more. Genuine Civil War cannons bristled on hillsides. A full sized, bronze, African elephant, ears flared and trunk raised, guarded one of the entrances. There were portraits on the walls and guns from every conflict involving the U.S. on display.

Without question, it was the fanciest, most opulent clubhouse any of the them had seen. They were not allowed to go to the yacht club nor the lodge (Southern hospitality only extended so far), but they could tell from the outside those were equally spectacular. The course itself was groomed like Augusta National and nearly as hilly. Still, nothing was going to ruin their outing and they delighted in every shanked wedge and hoseled drive. Upon departure, they smothered David in thanks for giving them such an unexpected, unforgettable day on the course.

The group's finest day on the water in those remaining weeks was found on the Black Warrior River and it rivaled many of the most notable outings throughout the rest of the journey. The captain's log reflected as much and the entry for the day harked back to the start of the trip when every detail about mile markers, lock names and precise time tables filled its pages.

They pushed off early out of Deerlick Park near Tuscaloosa onto water like glass and motored over to the first lock, John Hollis Bankhead. As *Acrosswater* approached, the crew saw a tug and barge ahead of them and figured they were out of luck for the moment. The captain radioed in to the lock master anyway, who in turn called the tug skipper. The pilot gave his approval (perhaps curious to find out what in the world a Hog was doing on a boat) and *Acrosswater* idled into the lock.

The skipper at the helm of the *Mauville* (her home port was Mobile) turned out to be one of the friendliest they had met on the trip and he chatted with them the whole time the boats were side by side. The team also tried a new technique while locking up, using only the center winch to tie off and throwing bollards fore and aft. That allowed the boat to flex with the motion of the water as the lock flooded. It proved effective and they wished they had tried it earlier in the expedition.

They were on the river for almost eight hours that day and relished every moment. Roxa fished for part of the return trip while Rose guided the boat with the little Honda motor. The Black Warrior had stunning, limestone cliffs and lovely foliage all along its length. They did not have to wait at the lock on the return, but instead pulled in and descended right at two o'clock as scheduled. It was a fantastic day.

Acrosswater also felt Southern water on her hull when the adventurers motored around Demopolis Lake, the largest impound on the Black Warrior - Tombigbee system. The captain heeded warning signs regarding the submerged dam that was a half mile downstream from their launch site and steered the boat upstream instead.

They did not find the area particularly charming, but they did espy an old cemetery back in the trees, floating wraith-like, and chose to investigate. Stepping onto the ancient soil still damp from an early morning rain shower and flecked with limestone, the explorers alighted from *Acrosswater* and found themselves surrounded by mausoleums, family plots guarded by impressive ironworks and huge headstones dating back to the early 1800's. It was eerie and beautiful.

They had one last water outing planned and that was in New Orleans. Less than three hundred miles from Tuscaloosa, the team could have driven directly there in less than five hours, but the resourceful travelers had found some sites of interest to visit if they detoured through Mobile so they stretched the journey out over three days.

The initial goal was to keep to the more scenic, coastal roads and dip into communities along the way, but poor weather (along with a strong recommendation from a county sheriff) forced them to stay on the elevated interstate and explore via offramp. Pesky winds also blew in a colony of sugar ants that infested their campers; the pests hitchhiked with them for the next several states.

Biblical plagues aside, captain and crew documented some noteworthy memories before they arrived in New Orleans. On Avery Island, the whole team visited the Tabasco compound. There, they took a limited tour (it was Friday and the bottling lines only ran Monday through Thursday) and learned about how the company crafted its renowned sauce. The three year process saw the seeds collected on the property, then exported to Central and South America to be cultivated into mature peppers. From there, they were harvested, mixed with vinegar, fermented and, finally, bottled.

After leaving Avery Island, the three amigos lobbied for a visit to an antebellum home they had discovered. The captain agreed to stop, but only if they dropped him at the Squirrel Run golf course. Had he known that the club had recently dressed the greens, he might have opted to join the others; upon hearing their report, he definitely regretted his decision.

Rose, Larry and Roxa found The Shadows a remarkable peek at life in the deep South. The home predated the Civil War and had remained in the same family for four generations. Eventually donated to the state of Louisiana, the property had over forty trunks of financial records, diaries, period clothing and dishes, among much else. It all offered a historical, unvarnished description of the enterprise of a Southern family, including the name of every slave who had lived on the property.

Their finale in New Orleans certainly did not follow the same route nor grand entrance they had imagined, but it was special just the same. They drove into the city on a Saturday by following U.S. 90 from New Iberia. Their quarters for the next two nights were found in an RV park located under an overpass in a highly industrialized area. It had none of the wooded charm they had come to expect, but it served its purpose and was ideally located for the launch the next day. They had dinner, hit the casinos and then went to the airport to pick up Marilee, Karl and Rose's oldest daughter. She had flown in from the West coast for the occasion.

They launched at 9:30 a.m. on Sunday, November 12 into Lake Pontchartrain. The only ramp they could find was narrow and it had little room to maneuver due to a concrete divider running its length, but Rose backed in the trailer on the first pass. They secured the SUV and scrambled aboard *Acrosswater* for her final voyage. From Pontchartrain, they motored down the Inner Harbor

Navigation Canal and passed under two railroad and three highway draw bridges along the way. They locked down with a tug near the St. Claude Avenue bridge and the next thing they knew, they were there. The mighty Mississippi.

Immediately, everyone on the boat could tell they had made the right decision by diverting around the river on the way south. The commercial traffic they merged into in New Orleans dwarfed anything they had seen in St. Louis or Memphis. *Acrosswater*'s depth finder pegged the primary channel at 120 feet and everywhere they looked they saw scores of freighters, barges, ferries, stern-wheelers and a surprising number of cruise ships. The river was entirely absent of other recreational craft their size.

Still, they navigated with relative ease upriver to view the city from the water. All of the practice since they began the journey many months ago allowed them to comfortably negotiate the fleet of much larger craft. Their actual cruise on the river lasted for only a short time, but they marveled at the cityscape and soaked in all of the sights, sounds and smells they could. Passengers on nearby ships snapped around to stare at them, likely wondering why a motorcycle was parked on the deck of a jet boat. It had happened almost every time they ventured in sight of other people yet they never grew tired of it. They felt so lucky and proud. The sun shone warmly on them and *Acrosswater*'s engine purred like new. The two couples looked at each other. They made it. They had actually made it. Marilee summed it up when she said, "Wow! You guys get to do this every day?"

After a lay day in New Orleans, when they had some fine Creole food, visited a Mardi Gras museum and waited for Marilee to meet with a Voodoo priestess, the crew turned west for good. The leaves were falling up north, they all had chores to tend and Larry and Roxa had an appointment in Prescott, AZ to have the windshield of their camper repaired. (They had taken a windblown, Igloo cooler off the glass as they drove across Alabama and the service center in Arizona was the closest facility that could order the parts.) Still, they made time for one last tour in the town of Vicksburg, before they considered the trip finished.

They hired a guide, a woman named Nancy who was in her mid-sixties and a native of Mississippi. She knew every intimate detail about the siege of the city, a torturous affair that lasted over a month. The Confederacy dug a line between the Union Army and Vicksburg so as a matter of strategic necessity, General Grant on the Federal side cut off all supplies to the Rebels. Union ships on the Mississippi shelled the city and its inhabitants without remorse. Formerly a hub of commerce and southern sophistication, Vicksburg became a ruin in less than a month. When reinforcements failed to arrive to put pressure on the rear of the Union army, General John Pemberton, commander at Vicksburg, had no choice but to surrender. On July 4, 1863, the Confederate forces filed out and the Yankees marched into the town. Since then, the residents there have celebrated Independence Day only once.

Nancy had probably heard stories of the siege. Born in the 1930's, she might have even sat at the knee of a relative who had fought in the war. For certain, she had seen evidence of the destruction brought upon the region by the Federal army. During the advance on Vicksburg, Grant had extended his supply lines to dangerous lengths, but, instead of slowing the push of his army, he ordered his men to forage from the residents in the area. The Federal quartermasters even used the residents' own wagons and buckboards to collect the supplies. Soon, convoys of flour, sugar, molasses, cornmeal, cheese, ham and fresh vegetables were pouring into the Union camps. The size of the haul surprised even Grant.

Even worse than the indignity of supplying the very enemy on its doorstep, that region of the South endured the first iteration of General Sherman's scorched earth policy. His philosophy culminated with the infamous March to the Sea in 1864, when his troops burned their way from Atlanta to Savannah, but as early as the Vicksburg siege, Sherman already believed strongly that the best way to end a war was to make life hell for the citizenry. During the siege, he led a detachment to the nearby Big Black River and set up a defensive front in anticipation of Rebel reinforcements arriving. As they went, his troops caused considerable distress for the Southerners living nearby. Sherman later wrote in a letter to General Henry Halleck, "I would... make them so sick & tired of war that Generations would pass before they would ever again appeal to it."

Well, as Nancy led the *Acrosswater* group through those hallowed grounds, even though she was at least two generations past the war, she clearly still felt like the Yankee troops had marched into the city only yesterday. At the conclusion of their tour, Karl (in his natural, good-natured manner) told the guide that they (Rose, Larry, Roxa and he) "...held no grudge." Instantly, the air turned to ice and the woman went from being a kindly, middle-aged chaperon to the conduit for all the rage, embarrassment and indignation felt by an entire region. "We do," Nancy said, with narrowed eyes and clenched teeth.

Captain and crew were taken aback. Their route had taken them through some of the most patriotic, purely American parts of the country. They had seen a genuine powwow, stood near the grave of one of the most revered explorers in the nation, sat with salt-of-the-earth, rural farmers and felt their hearts bursting with pride as they watched the light show at Mount Rushmore. And yet, here was someone, just as authentically American as they were, who held a completely different opinion of their great country. She stood for all those who referred to the Civil War as the Northern Aggression and who viewed Abraham Lincoln as a murderer and a despot, not the greatest president in American history. Even an innocent remark was an affront to her Southern heritage. It was a shocking end to an otherwise fascinating day and a microcosm of the entire *Acrosswater* campaign.

They had started with a vision to travel from the Pacific to the Gulf, roughly adhering to the course used by Lewis and Clark at the outset, and exploring by following as many of the backroads and waterways as they could. Along the way, they anticipated discovering slices of America that they never knew existed and seeing in person places they had only read about. Their day in Vicksburg exemplified why they dared to begin the journey in the first place. They had heard of Vicksburg, but none of them had seriously investigated it, and so they were amazed at the valor and heartbreak of the people involved. And despite the uncomfortable conclusion to the tour, they had an irreplaceable, authentic experience that none of them would ever forget.

By the end of the trip, they had driven their campers nearly 10,000 miles, ridden the motorcycle over 1200 miles and piloted

Acrosswater over 2400 miles (a watery route longer than either the Missouri or the Mississippi). They had made countless new friends, seen unforgettable places and been reminded time and again that their elected mode of travel was unheard of. And they had enjoyed an incredible run of good fortune. Not only had *Acrosswater* performed admirably the entire way, but they never had one breakdown with the motorcycle and outside of the faulty electrical system and hydraulics on Larry and Roxa's RV, both campers were steady and reliable.

Health wise, they all survived virtually unscathed. On most expeditions of that length, someone inevitably suffered a serious injury. Explorers were forever blowing off their faces while cleaning muskets or enduring some weird disease. When Zebulon Pike traversed the Rockies, his team had to carry him the last half of the journey because he was so debilitated by trench foot. And that was after he had threatened them with execution because they were grumbling about starving. The closest call the *Acrosswater* party dodged happened during their chance investigation of the ancient cemetery on the shores of Lake Demopolis. While on land, Rose slipped on some wet limestone and fell on her back, hitting her head in the process. She suffered bruising and a serious headache, but it could have been much worse.

By the end of the five months they were on the road, the expedition had made such an indelible stamp on them that for the first few weeks upon their return to the Northwest, the couples would spend hours on end in darkened rooms watching movies to try and avoid the effects of post-journey depression. They constantly thought about where they had been and the people they had met: the Longs, Sam Duvall, Jimmy in Paducah, innumerable sheriffs, the family who insisted on escorting them to the Clark gravesite, Nancy (the guide at Vicksburg). They closed their eyes at night and were instantly transported back to the Badlands or the Bluebird or the *Bertrand*.

After a time, their lives began to more closely resemble those of the average retiree as they filled their days with golf, time with kids, holiday dinners, doctors' appointments and hobbies. But the call of the water never went away and eventually, Karl hinted, first to Rose and then to the others, at his dream of being back out on the rivers to finish what they started. It would take more than a year but in due course, they started to plan a sequel to their first trip.

They called it *Acrosswater* II.

Part ll

Chapter 13
Those wandering Jones

"Took 3 rolls of film in to be developed - ready Tomorrow!"

Karl's journal - September 4, 2002

Note the emphasis that the pictures would be done the next day. Though not in the dark ages, the early 2000's were severely limited, technologically. A cutting edge digital camera made by Olympus came with 8 MB of storage, a huge selling point at the time.

CONSIDER for a moment seaman Juan Rodriguez. Born around 1474, few details exist about his childhood or his life as a young man. Historical records fail to mention his education, how he made a living for much of his existence, whom he married, how many (if any) children he sired or how he died. In fact, only two details about Mr. Rodriguez's life are known for certain; he was deaf and, between 1519 and 1522, he suffered through three years of truly, appalling circumstances.

Juan had signed on with Ferdinand Magellan's ambitious expedition to find the Spice Islands and he, along with the rest of the party, left Seville in September of 1519. Promises of riches from the sale of priceless cloves collected in the Islands quickly gave way to misery and woe as the armada bobbed its way across the Atlantic, through the Magellan Strait and out into the endless Pacific.

The sailors rode out colossal storms, mutinous disagreements, weevil filled provisions, cramped conditions, scurvy and punishing isolation. They encountered indigenous people from Patagonia to the Philippines, tribes with customs, languages and dining habits much different from their own. Juan watched in horror with the rest of the crew as Magellan perished at the hands of native Filipinos who took offense to the Captain General burning their village.

When the surviving crew members split up between two ships - there were not enough men to sail any more boats than that - seaman Rodriguez found himself on the flagship *Trinidad* under the new command of Gonzalo Gomez de Espinosa, Magellan's master-at-arms. Espinosa had proven himself capable as a soldier, but as a navigator he was tragically ill suited. The *Trinidad* blundered around the Philippine Sea for several months and made it as far north as Japan before giving up and sailing back to Tidore near the Indonesian archipelago.

Unfortunately for Espinosa and crew, a task force from Portugal had been in search of Magellan's fleet for over two years. So, when the former flagship sailed back into the Spice Islands with the intent of securing provisions and making overdue repairs, an armed party out of Lisbon was waiting. A Portuguese detachment rowed over to the *Trinidad*, weapons ready, and boarded the vessel, expecting firm, determined resistance. Instead, the soldiers were driven back overboard by the unholy stench of dying men, sailors who had subsisted on starvation rations of rats, foul water, putrid hardtack and softened leather for weeks. The Spanish survivors could not have repelled the enemy any better had they fired every cannon on board.

The Portuguese fleet eventually overcame its revulsion, took captive the surviving crew, removed any usable rigging and supplies from *Trinidad* and then set her loose to be battered to pieces by the waves and the wind. Seaman Rodriguez, after a short stint in irons, stowed away on a Portuguese vessel on its way back to Europe and became one of four men from the *Trinidad* who returned to Seville. After he was jailed briefly for reasons unclear, Juan Rodriguez, deaf, middle-aged and extraordinarily lucky to have survived his first trip around the globe, received word that another expedition heading for the Spice Islands needed sailors. He signed up immediately.

Just to recap, Rodriguez was not a naive, uninformed teenager tricked into pursuing a life of adventure on the open seas. He knew full well that days after leaving port, all the fresh food on board would be gone and he would be resigned to months of spoiled, heavily salted meat and rock-hard biscuits. He realized that many of the tribes he would encounter embraced cannibalism, so he risked spending his remaining hours on earth simmering in a kettle. Not that it mattered in those days, but he understood that hygiene would be nonexistent and that his best defense against a hostile boarding party could very well be his own foul odor and that of his mates. Finally, he knew that as a seaman, he was just one rung or so above a page and therefore was doomed to the least desirable chores all along the way. He knew all this and yet, when the call went out, he raised his hand and said, "Here am I. Send me!" Either life on land in Seville was unimaginably worse for him or Juan Rodriguez's very nature, the DNA that filled every cell in his body, compelled him to hit the open water every chance he could.

That curious, unexplainable, traveling compulsion that consumed the ancient Spaniard was most certainly the driving force behind the *Acrosswater* team considering a return to the rivers and the open road. Karl's documented lineage certainly had more than one mariner in its midst, a character trait that he had embraced his whole life. Mixed in with his Nordic bloodlines were hints of Western Europe, a hereditary concoction that all but guaranteed him a life of marauding and restless exploration. For all he knew, the genes of Seaman Rodriguez were swimming in his veins.

His bride, even from a very young age, proved that she found the thrill of investigating the other side of a distant hill far outweighed any punishment earned by breaking some arbitrary rule. When her grandparents moved from their original homestead in eastern Montana to a larger property in another part of the state, Rose visited every chance she could. It was a working ranch so Grandma Schaak woke up every morning at 3:00 a.m. to cook breakfast for the ranch hands, a chore that necessitated a daily nap before she started preparing supper.

Rose waited until just after the old woman was asleep before she saddled up a horse and galloped out over the range. She stayed out until she saw the dust cloud from her grandfather's pick up approaching across the prairie, at which time she reined in her horse and waited. He would skid to a dusty halt, jump out of the cab and, in his thick accent, shout, "Wosemawy! You goin' to give you gwandmotha a hawt attack!" Back to the ranch they went, but when the next day's nap arrived, Rose would begin her adventure all over again.

Roxa shared her cousin's rebellious, inquisitive nature. The two of them had been partners in crime on many occasions and Roxa had even stirred up some trouble at the ranch in Montana.

When the first *Acrosswater* expedition hit the trail in 2000, Roxa embraced the experience with wholehearted abandon and was tickled by the simplest activity – meeting a lifelong resident of a small town, finding an historic marker lost in the weeds, enjoying a meal found only in a specific part of the country – so she needed zero convincing to embark on another journey.

And Larry, with his Germanic heritage, had proved exceedingly resourceful over the course of the first excursion. He possessed a more understated curiosity than the others, but it was a dominant trait nonetheless. Besides, in addition to the obvious worth inherent in his willingness to plunge into a freezing river to ferry half a ham sandwich to the skipper waiting hungrily on a sandbar, or his ability to trek across the bleakest terrain to find help, he had an uncanny gift for discovering obscure, interesting attractions in the tiniest communities. As with most Germans, he had territorial tendencies and had to be watched closely for signs he might try to annex a neighboring RV site, but otherwise, his enthusiastic participation was assured.

So over the winter of 2002, when the gray, dreary days of the Pacific Northwest ran together for what seemed like months instead of days and years instead of months, Karl looked out at the rain and the mist one day and hinted to Rose that the four of them had unfinished business on the rivers of America. Rose immediately phoned her cousin and discovered that Roxa and Larry had the camper idling in the driveway and simply needed instructions on when and where to meet. After a staggered exchange of calls, the foursome gathered at Karl and Rose's home and began to seriously plan the second phase of their adventure.

Their yearlong hiatus had found them completing a laundry list of tasks common in retirement. They had attended weddings, thrown birthday parties and lowered their handicaps; it seemed the assembly line of distractions never ceased. There were always more delphiniums to plant, more colons to scope, more cataracts to laser and more gall bladders to remove. They had an endless parade of visitors to entertain, people who assumed that, just because their hosts were retired, they had nothing better to do then to treat distant relatives to rounds of golf or teach acquaintances' children to ski. The upshot was when they met over dinner in early February, they all felt a familiar, bubbling excitement to leave behind the common trappings of daily life and explore the mystery of new horizons.

The first meeting focused on a rough route and time line for part two of the *Acrosswater* journey. Whereas the theme for the trip in 2000 varied between Lewis and Clark, the Civil War and regional landmarks, the focal point of the next leg was without question a cruise down the Erie Canal. Burned into Karl's memory since his visit as a young boy, a return to the Canal was two parts quest, one part inevitability. With that as the hub, they foresaw the beginning component of their journey as a meandering trek to the shores of Lake Erie and the start of the famed waterway and the conclusion as a celebratory trip down the Hudson to see Lady Liberty and Ellis Island. They expected to sprinkle in golf, historical landmarks and the ubiquitous antique shops, but all roads led to the Canal.

The preliminary draft of their route suggested a shorter journey than the expedition in 2000. The terrain they planned to travel was much different in both scale and substance with the land area of the three largest states combined - Ohio, Pennsylvania and New York - nearly 15,000 square miles less than Montana alone. In addition to the well designed Erie Canal, the rivers they planned to explore had markers, channels and other, clearer navigational aids so they expected far fewer days marooned on sandbars. And the importance of discovering the *Quimby's* guide cannot be overstated. Instead of a fifty-three foot trailer full of USACE maps and survey charts, the captain just ordered the 2002 edition of *Quimby's* and poured over it, making his usual, meticulous notes to direct their progress.

By early spring, Karl had mapped out a course that followed the Ohio River all the way to Pittsburgh, then turned north and used the available rivers (like the Allegheny) to reach Lake Erie and the entrance to the Canal. From there, the trip essentially planned itself as the Canal dumped into the Hudson River and, ultimately, New York City Harbor. He realized they would still need to portage at times so he built the itinerary to be flexible and, keeping with the trend of their first expedition, he foresaw river-based entrances into classic, American cities like Cincinnati, Pittsburgh, Buffalo and, of course, New York.

For the most part, they had all the confidence in the world in their gear. Their only concern fell on the Sportscoach, which had limped to the finish line in 2000. It was two years older and the mysterious, electrical ailments that had plagued the travelers the first time had not been fully resolved. Technicians had suggested a range of cures for the RV's uneven power generation, but none seemed to fix all its mechanical woes definitively. The team hoped that the shorter, less punishing journey would offset some of the risk.

Aside from the technical aspects of the trip, the team planned other, minor changes to improve the *Acrosswater* II experience. The captain installed an all-in-one gym in one of the bays of his rig and the foursome developed an exercise regimen that they all pledged to follow. Despite all the walking during the first trip, they had gained weight and none of them wanted a repeat performance. Rose asked her sister (an accomplished cook) to provide menus of healthy, simple recipes that would translate to the road. Like during the first journey, they expected to sample local fare from the towns they visited, but they hoped that the combination of exercise, nutritious staples and the absence of tempting delicacies like Memphis barbecue or Southern-fried catfish would keep the unwanted pounds at bay.

They knew for certain that this trip would be different. It was hard enough to replicate the magic of a transformational experience, but additionally, the world had changed since their first trip. Journal entries from September 11, 2000 included descriptions of a stifling, muggy day and a fantastic thunderstorm, but certainly no inkling of what would unfold just one year later. The events in New York City were still raw during that first meeting and the members of *Acrosswater* II knew that a tour of Ground Zero, a closeup of The Statue of Liberty and a visit to Ellis Island would be emotionally stirring. Still, they were all eager to be on the road once again and by late spring, each of them had circled July 6 on their calendars. They felt like children waiting for Christmas.

Chapter 14

Just like riding a bike

"Hello to all our family and friends, and welcome to our renewed web site."

Roxa's Web journal - July 6, 2002

Roxa fought with Internet access and computer challenges on both legs of the adventure, but her persistence brought the joy of the expedition to a wide audience of adoring fans.

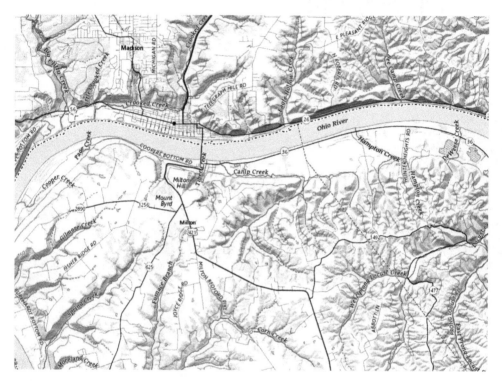

Madison and vicinity

RARELY do adventures proceed smoothly right from the start, regardless of how robust the spending or how detailed the planning. For instance, when the Philosophical Institute of Victoria's expedition set off from Melbourne in the spring of 1860 to try to reach the Gulf of Carpentaria at the opposite, northern end of the Australian continent, some 1800 miles distant, it did so with the full backing and confidence of the British Empire. Famously unexplored, the Outback was represented on maps of the time by empty, white space. Beyond the settled fringes of the coast, nobody knew what existed out there so explorers needed to prepare for anything; the expedition spared no expense, purchasing an exhaustive list of supplies for the trek.

Almost immediately the party ran into trouble. Even with a giant mound of provisions, the mission still required meticulous preparation, a lot of luck and a leader who was poised, experienced and resourceful, someone who could tactfully govern the corps with wisdom and diplomacy.

Unfortunately, the Victorian government had appointed Robert Burke as head of the undertaking, a man whose sole qualifications seemed to be charm and optimism, not exactly the characteristics needed to navigate a punishing wasteland. Before they had even left the inhabited settlements of southern Australia (they were essentially in the suburbs), the team's second-in-command and the person responsible for tending the expeditionary camels submitted his resignation following a squabble with Burke over the use of rum to treat the animals.

Discarding team members and useless supplies in equal measure as they went, Burke and his dwindling band slogged their way to Menindee, the last outpost before the Australian interior. After a few days of recuperation and resupply, and with perhaps a wave of sad resignation, the grand, exploratory endeavor shoved off. Robert Burke was never seen alive again.

Though certainly not as ominous as the shaky beginnings of the Burke expedition, *Acrosswater* II suffered some minor, annoying setbacks in the first days of its return to the road. The team members rendezvoused on July 6 near Hermiston after tying up a few personal, loose ends; from there, they planned to dead head for Madison, IN where they would begin leapfrogging their way along river and road to the Erie Canal.

Given they had to journey over 2000 miles to reach their starting point on the Ohio River, they scheduled only one, modest side trip along the way to visit the Custer Battlefield. The convoy fell into its usual procession with Karl and Rose leading in the Bus and hauling *Acrosswater* and Larry and Roxa following in the Sportscoach towing the SUV.

The first problem arose on day two when a vent on the Sportscoach became stuck in the open position during a rain storm. They feared that it was a continuation of the vexing issues that had plagued Larry and Roxa's rig at the tail end of their travels in 2000, but, fortunately, they were able to resolve the problem that same day when they discovered an RV repair shop less than a mile from their camp site in Missoula. The technicians at the shop had a replacement installed in less than an hour and that gave the group plenty of time to explore the town before calling it a day, as well as a touch of hope that they had already checked off the only annoying hurdle on their way east. Then they ate dinner.

For all the attention to proper nutrition and everyone's wholehearted commitment to eating right, they curiously ignored their pledges and accepted a recommendation from Ma Porter on a good place to dine when they stopped for the night in Missoula. They all knew that her suggestions needed to be considered with a healthy dose of skepticism, for she was a woman raised on the hardscrabble plains of a Montana homestead. She had lived through four wars and a depression and before retiring, she had prided herself on making do with the dented cans and semi-spoiled produce brought home from the grocery store she owned with her husband. And who could blame her? Why discard that tin of clams *just* past its expiration date when a nice chowder was in the offing? Her steely intestinal tract could endure far more than the average person. The upshot was the poor commander spent the next day curled up in the sleeping quarters with crippling cramps while his bride piloted the Bus from Missoula to Hardin.

On day four, while barreling over the plains, the group ran into a thunderstorm so ferocious that it damaged the canopy on the boat. In the design phase during the run-up to the first expedition, the skipper and North River had determined that a soft cover would best suit the travel strategy of the trip. Every time the hoist was deployed, the team first collapsed the canopy to make room for the upright stanchion and the boom. A hardtop would have been patently impossible to remove so frequently. The soft top had endured over two years of punishing wear and tear without incident, until then.

They cobbled together a splint comprised of a hammer, screwdriver and duct tape to hold the canopy in place until they reached Illinois and a dealer with the hardware and wherewithal to perform a proper repair. While in the same town but at another nearby shop, Karl also bought a new pigtail that connected the running lights of the trailer to the Bus. He had generously given his to a fellow traveler at a rest stop under the mistaken assumption that he had a spare.

Two final complications arose during their drive to Madison. One involved the communication gear; the CB on the Bus stopped operating properly somewhere in South Dakota. Though Karl and Rose could hear transmissions loud and clear, Larry and Roxa received only static on their end. To solve the issue until they found a permanent solution, the duo in the Sportscoach restricted themselves to asking only "yes" or "no" questions, which allowed for a tail-light flash response. While visiting family in Chicago and before they turned south for Madison, they bought long-range, two-way radios which had the added benefit of greater mobility than the CB.

Lastly, and also in Chicago, the windscreen on the tow rig developed a crack when Karl and Larry ran it through a car wash. After inspection, they concluded that unless the glass failed completely, any repair could wait until after they finished the trip. All in all, they arrived at their launch point with their equipment intact and their spirits high. They encountered some minor obstacles to their progress, but the second-in-command never stormed off in a huff and nobody had to endure starvation rations. They rolled into the City of Madison RV Park on July 15, eager to be back on the water.

At first glance, Madison might have seemed an odd choice to continue the *Acrosswater* adventure, but really, no place outside of Louisville would have been a better one. Captain and crew had ventured within fifty miles of Madison when they stopped in Louisville in 2000. After the low water on the Mississippi had forced them up the Ohio River, they had found the Ohio far more navigable. The lowest recorded levels on the Ohio in both 2000 and 2002 were identical (26.1 feet) versus the woefully dry conditions on the Mississippi. As an added bonus, the team thought that the reduced commercial traffic on the Ohio, then as now, made for a much more relaxed journey. Madison was, in fact, the perfect place to resume their cross-country expedition.

So the calendar turned to July 16 and day one of their return seemed scripted, containing every component of why they found their chosen method of traveling so magical. It started (early as usual) with the captain taking his morning walk before the others awoke. The skipper had a habit of running into colorful characters who willingly confessed all kinds of intimate details about themselves and just half a mile into his circuit, he encountered a man named Vince. Whether Karl or Vince initiated the discussion is ambiguous in the record, but what is crystal clear is that Vince had a catalog of improbable stories to tell and God help the man that got him going. After a brief greeting, he leaned in towards the skipper and asked in a hushed voice, "Have you ever killed a man?"

Karl, rarely at a loss for words, managed to stammer he had not.

"I killed three men in Jamaica," said Vince, giving his eyebrows a bounce. "You see this scar on my neck here? It's six inches." He pulled down his collar for emphasis. "The first guy come at me from behind, see, aiming to slash my jugular, but I saw him out of the corner of my eye. He got me good, but I got him even better. Killed him with a *Nukite* - that's Jap, it means spear hand - broke his neck. KIAI!!"

The captain jumped as Vince made a slashing motion. "That's so interesting," Karl sputtered, "well, listen Vince, I gotta…"

"Then his buddy come at me with a knife and it was a long one - like one a them David Bowie knives. Last thing he ever did. I grabbed the blade just as he was aiming for my guts - see this scar on my palm? It's seven inches." He held his hand up to Karl's face until it almost touched. "I dropped him with a *Teisho*. Drove his nose bones into his brain. THWACK!"

"Oh man, you have the best storie…"

"Then I whirled around to take the last one." Vince performed a delicate pirouette and continued, "WHAP he kicks me right in the nuts. It stunned me for a second." He dreamily looked off into the distance and then snapped his head around to stare at the bewildered captain. "But I got 'em too. Think I use a snap kick. And you want to hear the crazy part?" He looked at Karl, his eyes narrowed to slits.

The skipper stared back, unblinking. "There's a crazy part?"

"That kick changed my life forever," Vince declared. "Hold your middle three fingers out like this." He extended the fingers on his left hand and displayed them in front of his audience. "See that? A normal penis has those three veins that run straight, but because of that kick, mine has a varicose in the middle which gives my dick a bend at the end when I get a hard on - like this." He flexed the tips of his fingers. "The ladies just love it." He gave Karl a nudge to the ribs and a come-hither wink. "I've slept with over 3,000 women and every one…" he continued, lost in his own world.

Karl listened in stunned silence as Vince carried on for the better part of an hour. In between thoughtful nods, he passed the time thinking of creative ways to politely excuse himself and deciding which of the many stories was more unlikely. In the end, he concluded that Vince might very well have been a competent fighter at some point in the distant past, but found it impossible to believe that a man whose appearance closely aligned with that of a Magellan sailor after 200 days at sea - skeletal, hairy, toothless, malodorous - could ever convince 3,000 women to even look at his crooked boner, let alone touch it.

The skipper made his way back to the RV park and after breakfast, he and the team prepared to launch into the Ohio. They were beside themselves with excitement. As they prepped down by the docks, the owner of the camp, Bill, and another friend, Chuck, ambled over and struck up a conversation. Once the captain felt reasonably confident that the discussion would not detour towards martial arts or male enhancements, he learned that Chuck set up the course every year for the H1 Unlimited hydroplane event held in the city, a happy coincidence if ever there was one.

Unlimited hydroplanes were more akin to rocket ships than boats. The official H1 rulebook included quaint lists of restrictions and requirements (things like restraint harnesses, emergency oxygen, Kevlar shields and single prop design) that every entrant must meet, but at the end of the day, the engines still churned at 15,000 RPM's, the racers regularly exceeded 150 mph and the drivers sat in enclosed cockpits. Competitions nearly always included moments of mayhem when a boat became airborne or cartwheeled spectacularly going around a corner. The city of Madison held the distinction of sponsoring the only community-owned boat on the H1 circuit - aptly named *Miss Madison* - and the yearly race held on the river drew enormous crowds. Chuck said that 65,000 spectators was the norm.

Since the team rarely missed a unique opportunity to mingle with the locals, and after hearing Chuck describe so intimately the layout, the two parties agreed that the best way to formally launch the expedition of 2002 would be to run the old jet boat through the course. A few minutes later, after giving the engine some time to warm up, *Acrosswater* was roaring around every turn in a hang-onto-your-hats fashion, not quite as fast *Miss Madison* did, but still at a respectable forty knots.

They dropped their two new friends back off at the camp and then cruised upstream to the Rising Sun Casino Resort, a distance of some fifty river miles. They had to lock through at the

Markland Lock and Dam on the Kentucky side of the river which gave them all a chance to knock some of the rust off their respective assignments. The tender had them into the lock within five minutes of the captain's hail on the radio and the crew performed as well as could have been expected after a two year hiatus. The rest of the run up to Rising Sun was serene and uneventful, a picturesque cruise at 3200 RPMs.

They pulled up to the ramp at the resort and quickly discovered that the resort fathers had not included any means to tie off near the apron. Karl spotted some men watching them through binoculars from the levee above the parking lot and walked up to find out if they had any ideas. They were only too happy to help, given their curiosity at seeing a Harley on the boat. One of them remarked that a man and a mule had passed through town a week ago (that duo was on a seventeen year quest to circle the globe), but seeing the motorcycle and jet boat combination was even more intriguing.

Two of the observers backed their trucks near the water to allow the crew to cinch the boat tight and offload the bike. It was an expression of helpful kindness that remained a source of gratitude and wonder to the team, no matter how often it happened. After thanking them for their trouble, the team docked *Acrosswater* and Karl and Rose drove back to the RV park to retrieve the campers while Larry and Roxa took first watch and scrubbed the boat.

They finished off their day at the casino and unanimously agreed that their reboot could not have gone any better. There was a risk trying to replicate the old magic. The first trip had such a profound, life changing effect on the foursome that, upon returning home, Karl had sent a letter to Larry and Roxa in December of 2000 in which he wrote, "This has been the hardest trip to come down from that either Rose or I have ever faced." Just a few sentences later he lamented, "Quite frankly, I'm not happy with this sitting around business."

Throw in the draw of a journey along the Erie Canal and a return to the trail was all but inevitable. What was not inevitable was a positive response in their spirits and their psyches, but if day one was any indication, *Acrosswater* II promised to create just as many heartfelt memories as the original had. They all went to bed that night feeling like they had returned to where they were supposed to be. They were back exploring the world at ground level, feeling the wind in their faces, meeting wonderful, curious people and happily toiling through exhausting, sixteen hour days which wore them out so much, that they immediately fell asleep upon hitting the pillow, free to dream of rivers, canals and myriad other things with bends.

Chapter 15
Rivers of the Rustbelt

"I went back to Ohio, but my pretty countryside,
Had been paved down the middle, by a government that had no pride."

My City Was Gone
By The Pretenders

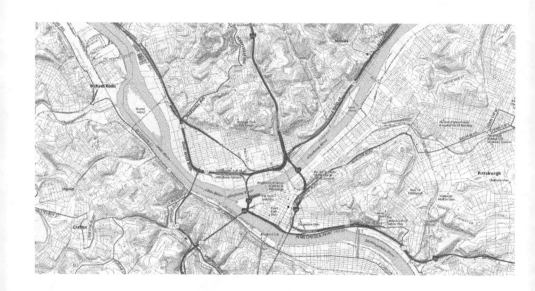

Pittsburgh

JUST west of the Colosseum in Rome, a narrow, ancient road - Via Sacra - leads straight from the famed arena to the ruins of the old city center. Visitors can queue at the Arco di Tito and purchase tickets to gain entry onto the grounds where they can walk the dusty cobblestones amidst famous sites like the Forum and Domus Flavia. Most tourists do just that, but a lucky few - less than ten percent of all the people who visit Rome - turn left before reaching the turnstiles and follow a steep, winding path that dead-ends at the Chiesa di San Bonaventura al Palatino. There, at select times of the day, volunteers lead small groups on a tour of the still active, Franciscan monastery.

Inside the unassuming building, astonished guests find stunning, hidden works of art, masterpieces like a large, stained glass window not noticeable from the outside, an arched, smooth ceiling cleverly painted to appear three dimensional and a room whose walls seem entirely paneled in wood but which, much like the ceiling, are partly painted to just look like wood. Only close inspection reveals the truth.

The tour terminates on an outdoor terrace with a unique view from the top of Palatine Hill that overlooks the Colosseum and a promise from the guide of one last indulgence before the exit and the tiring walk back down to the sweaty crowds below. Curious visitors find themselves led to a small fountain in the middle of the monastic garden from which everyone in attendance is invited to drink and fill their canteens or water bottles. Sourced from a centuries old aquifer, the water is cool and sweet, a welcome gift on a hot, Roman summer day, but an experience not usually considered notable or particularly special.

It really should not take a pilgrimage to an Italian monastery for someone to realize just how precious is a cold drink of water. Though the surface of the Earth is mostly water, over 95% of it is found in the seas and oceans and the bit of freshwater that does exist is mainly tied up in the ice caps. In fact, rivers, lakes, ponds, streams and reservoirs comprise a scant .03% of the water on the planet, a resource that, despite being a commodity that no human being can live without, has been carelessly treated as infinite.

Human beings have used it to ferry sewage away from city centers, to cool nuclear reactors and sluice radioactive chambers and to casually dispose of some of most lethal substances in creation. People have regarded its protection as a regulatory inconvenience and considered commonsense objections - like limiting coal mine runoff - as whiny liberalism. Rather than prohibit the dumping of pollutants entirely, regulators published levels of toxins like lead, arsenic and mercury that were acceptable in the water. And folks in communities went along with it.

The late sixties and early seventies were possibly the nadir in the U.S. for water pollution awareness. At that time, it was estimated that fully two-thirds of the rivers and lakes in the country were unsafe and, outside of select municipalities, few legal barriers stood in the way of further degradation. A spokesperson for a steel company once pointed out that his manufacturing plant was abiding by the law of the land every time it dumped industrial waste into a stream, because there was no statute against it.

Then debris on the Cuyahoga River caught fire in 1969. It was not a new phenomenon - the Cuyahoga had burned many times, so often in fact that when nobody took a picture in 1969, publishers just dipped into the archives and used a photo from 1952 - but for some reason, the nation at large took notice. Three years later, the Clean Water Act passed into law after clearing the Senate by a vote of eighty-six to zero and sailing through the House. Support for the bill was so unanimous amongst both parties that Congress even overrode a Nixon veto.

It attacked the problem from a slightly different angle. Rather than using a quality standard that applied to a reservoir, lake or stream, the new law placed restrictions on what companies and people could dump into the water. By focusing on the source of the pollutants instead of the body of water being polluted, the statute more effectively enforced discharge standards. It also gave the general public a legal framework on which to ground its newly discovered activism.

The Act was not perfect by any means and certainly did not come close to its desired goal of making all water clean throughout the country. How could it? Pollution already had a massive head start in terms of quantity and governing processes. On the Columbia, technicians at the Hanford nuclear site had been merrily dumping toxins for years, an amount estimated in the trillions of gallons. (For context, it would take the Columbia at normal discharge more than seventy days to convey the same volume of fluid.) Down in the Gulf of Mexico and starting in roughly 1995, researchers tracked an annual algae bloom caused by fertilizer runoff. The algae sucked up all the oxygen in the water and created massive dead zones (some as large as a medium-sized, New England state) in which no other marine life could survive.

Further upstream, that same runoff - particularly in the spring when farmers applied fertilizer to their fields - triggered warnings to people living in some communities in Iowa, telling those residents to refrain from drinking water from the tap. Nitrogen levels could be so high that they could impair the movement of oxygen in the blood stream, especially in children. And along the East Coast, hog farmers either did their best to keep their manure lagoons intact during hurricane season or simply took it for granted that some contamination was inevitable. After a breach caused by Hurricane Florence in 2018, one pork spokesman suggested to the Duke Chronicle that, though the release was regrettable, at least the rainwater "...diluted..." the manure levels in the runoff. Those are the words of a man who does not sip from a water supply that has been lightly seasoned with a million of gallons of pig shit.

Still, the clean water initiatives launched by that burning river in Ohio had some positive effects as governments and communities tried to find the tricky balance between safe, available water and business interests that employed the populace. By 2014, the number of unsafe lakes and rivers in the country had been halved from the estimates calculated in 1972. Companies like Intel and Coors actively pursued ways to reduce their water usage and improve their corporate stewardship. In the case of Intel, the company, in partnership with an Arizona community, built a water treatment plant on the site of one of its campuses and turned the operation of the plant over to the city itself. And the beleaguered Cuyahoga supported fish again in its troubled waters as the laws took effect and the flow of pollutants was choked off.

Even with the improvements to water quality spurred on by legislation and activism, by the time *Acrosswater* arrived on the scene in July of 2002 and started heading east, they were chugging up a river that had just started its decade-long run of being ranked the most polluted in the country. Though they had left their water test kits at home, the industrial surroundings noted in the area by the crew hinted at a vastly different cruise than the untamed wilds of the upper Missouri. Nonetheless, they departed the Rising Sun optimistic as ever and meandered upriver. The three primary diarists all noted the abundance of industry along the way and they tallied three, coal-fired power plants before they had even reached Cincinnati.

Just as they had during the first leg of the trip in 2000, the group found water based arrivals into large cities especially appealing and were delighted to discover that Cincinnati had poured resources into sprucing up its waterfront, even allowing travelers to tie off at the park between the football stadium and baseball field. They explored the area near the docks for a time and, considering the preponderance of the name, concluded that the Lytle family was of some importance to the history of the city. (They would later find out that the Lytles had contributed territory in the area at the time of the American Revolution and members of the clan had fought in all the early wars. One of them,

General William Haines Lytle, died during the battle of Chickamauga and Chattanooga and was so highly regarded by both sides of the conflict, that a temporary truce was called to allow his body to be escorted back to its hometown.)

They exhausted their interests in Cincinnati and ducked across the river to Newport, KY for lunch. Once tied off at the dock, they were immediately quizzed by a curious onlooker about the presence of the Harley on the boat. The skipper gave his presentation about their journey, which proved as always to fascinate the listener. As it turned out, the man was on the job. He was responsible for watching the men painting the nearby bridge and if any of them fell into the water, he was to zip out in his boat to retrieve them. Given how bored he looked, the *Acrosswater* team suspected that he planned to sneak out after hours and apply a little axle grease to the girders, just so he might have something to do the next day.

The following morning, captain and crew reversed their typical routine and drove ahead 120 miles rather than boating first. It turned out to work in their favor when a thunderstorm rolled in that afternoon; they sidestepped the torrent because they had already spent time on the water and were busy exploring the towns of Maysville and Portsmouth. Maysville in particular beguiled the visitors with its murals of local history covering the levees. They learned that much of the area was founded just after the Revolutionary War when soldiers received hundreds of thousands of acreage as pay for their service. (It was unclear if the Lytles were the benefactors.)

During their inspection of the murals, a passerby noticed their obvious interest in the town and pointed them to a collection of homes called the Week houses (a series of identical structures painted differently and named after days of the week) and also suggested a restaurant that was a favorite of the townspeople. Still suckers for food that spoke to the tastes of towns they visited, the foursome jogged over to the family-owned diner and went inside. There they found the matriarch of the family running the whole operation by herself that day and doling out orders to other diners about where to fill their drinks and in which bin to put the dirty dishes. When she came to their table, the skipper asked for a chili burger.

"Vat iz…how you say…chilly booger?" She had a thick, thick accent and clearly had never been asked for a chili burger.

"It's just a hamburger with chili ladled on top." Karl mimed opening a bun and pouring something on the sandwich.

"No bun? No chiz?" She still looked puzzled.

"That's alright. I'll find something from the menu." He looked down at the tapestry-sized document in his hands.

"No, no. We make anything you like," she insisted.

Seeing that customer satisfaction was a core value of the shop, the captain again went through the recipe, but this time in more detail, describing step-by-step the construction of the burger. Given the dubious expression on the woman's face at the end of the training, he had serious doubts about what might arrive from the kitchen.

As it turned out, those suspicions were well-founded when she returned with the chef in tow. While the others enjoyed scrumptious, time-tested dishes that had been refined over decades if not centuries, the poor skipper had to choke down what was clearly the restaurant's first attempt at a chili burger while the cook stood table-side, anxiously ringing an apron. It was like being stuck at the dinner table as a child trying to finish a heaping pile of liver and onions while the rest of the family, all of whom had already polished off their meals, sat on the porch downing the last plates of strawberry shortcake.

The next day was a Sunday and since there were river races in the area that weekend, they drove further upstream than normal looking for a boat launch. They found a site in West Virginia and motored back downstream, taking a left off the Ohio to explore the Big Sandy River. It was the dirtiest, the most visually unappealing stretch of water they had encountered - or would encounter - during all their months of travel. The waterway was lined with industry for miles and certainly not gleaming, futuristic factories. They passed by refineries, asphalt manufacturers, petroleum storage, chemical works, gravel mills and coal barges.

Roxa mentioned it was what they had expected the Ohio to look like and Karl noted in his journal a comprehensive list of solid waste he saw float past: old tires (with and without wheels), plastic bottles, hunks of Styrofoam, trash bags, dry rotted basketballs, discarded Big Mac containers and aluminum cans. They half expected to pull around a bend and find a cruise ship evacuating its bowels. Surprisingly, they saw a few fish jump out of the water, but none of them could imagine ever dropping a line into that river. At lunchtime, they tied off on a bank and had a picnic on board *Acrosswater*. Given the nauseating surroundings, it was a good thing the team had packed mild snacks like cucumber sandwiches and canned peaches.

The crew awoke the next morning to the sound of a chainsaw coming from the front of the little RV campground they had pulled into the night before. The adventurers were finding that, just like the contrasting dimensions between the eastern and western states, many of the parks in the east were better suited to smaller, pop-up campers and travel trailers than they were to convoys like *Acrosswater*.

After their trip up the Big Sandy, the team had pulled out of the water and ventured over to Carthage Gap, their accommodations for the night and a rest stop whose name sounded imposing, but which, upon closer inspection, had slips designed to hold a two-man tent at the most. Karl and Larry had gingerly crept onto the grounds with their rigs, but still managed to clear out most of the foliage. The buzz of the saw signaled the efforts of the one-armed caretaker trying to trim off any limbs the Bus and Sportscoach had left on the trees lining the drive. They tipped their caps to him on the way out of camp, thanking him for the effort and hoping the parks further up the road would be more expansive.

The entourage's next planned stop was at the sister communities of Marietta, OH and Williamstown, WV. Because they were already traveling on the Ohio side of the river, they located a truck stop to buy fuel and then decided to park the rigs there while they took the SUV out to explore the towns. Rosemary, Roxa and Larry petitioned for a stop at the Fenton Art Glass factory so the skipper dropped them there while he completed a variety of errands.

At the time, Fenton Art was the largest producer of handmade, colored glass in the United States and one of the largest in the world. More a home to artists than a manufacturer of scale, the company had been producing renowned glass pieces since 1905 and the peek at the process fascinated the *Acrosswater* visitors. (Production ceased at the site just nine years after their visit and the company sold its remaining assets in 2017.)

During his sojourn while the others were at the factory, Karl had gathered some intelligence from the proprietress of an office supply store. Being an old paper clip man himself, he had ducked into the shop to see if it stocked the Acco or OIC brands and struck up a conversation with Sally, one of the owners. She worked part-time as a spokesperson for a trolley tour company and knew all the highlights of the area. Sally informed Karl that, though most of the tourist stops were closed (it was a Monday) there were many things to see. She even gave him a handful of pamphlets, recommended a route to take and noted some meaningful details that a lot of visitors missed.

Better equipped for a day on the town, the captain retrieved the crew at Fenton Art and made for their next stop of the day, lunch at the Lafayette Hotel. Built on the site of the original Bellevue Hotel (which was destroyed in a 1916 fire) and named after the Marquis who had visited the region in 1825, the hotel embraced both its river and Revolutionary lineage.

Sally had told Karl to be on the lookout for bronze plaques marking the height of historic floods and, just as when he had considered high water marks in towns like Cairo, he and his mates stopped and stared in wonder at the medallions affixed fifteen-feet above the sidewalk, and tried to imagine the river running through the town at such depths. After lunch, the team drove the tour route and marveled at the wonderful, old buildings. They learned of the founding of the communities just after the Revolutionary War and discovered that at least nine men from the town of Marietta reached the rank of general during the Civil War. The place was just steeped in history.

After the sightseeing and on the way to its planned camp for the night, the team made an abrupt decision to push on to West

Virginia. They had intended to stay in Woodsfield, OH which was just seventeen miles off the Ohio River Scenic Byway (Ohio State Route 7), but when they reached the turn off to Route 800 which would take them to Woodsfield, they found themselves confronted with what amounted to a U-turn to the left across traffic. Just a week earlier, the convoy had voluntarily made just such a turn when members of the crew thought it would be nice to take a more scenic drive on the way to Rising Sun. That shortcut turned out to be harrowing, with hairpin turns, no shoulder to speak of and three inches or less of clearance on either side.

When the Bus drove with *Acrosswater* in tow, the combination spanned nearly sixty-five feet, essentially the length of a tractor trailer. One huge difference in the comparison, however, is the location of the pivot point between the cab and the object being towed. For a semi trailer forty-eight feet long, the tractor adds an additional nine feet bringing the combined length to fifty-seven feet with the pivot point roughly six feet from the center of the front axle. The Bus-*Acrosswater* combination had its pivot point two thirds of the way down its length which severely limited its capacity for tight turns. Imagine the trailer of the semi towing the tractor instead of the reverse and you get the idea.

The Rising Sun shortcut had caused traffic back-ups for miles, innumerable scraped guardrails and the *Acrosswater* caravan had even forced a Cruise America RV rental into the ditch on one of the turns. (That motorist probably deserved it, though; those rentals were a menace on the roads.) The skipper vowed to avoid similar, future scenarios whenever possible so when he saw the access to the road leading to Woodsfield, he tromped the gas pedal and kept driving. They would have to take their chances at finding space a day early at their appointed campground in Wheeling.

Members of the crew tried calling several times on the way without success to warn the campsite they would be arriving a day ahead of schedule. The campground had earned high marks across the board in Trailer Life, and the front desk certainly did not disappoint, booking the convoy in early and quickly summoning attendants to lead the *Acrosswater* guests to their assigned berths. That's when everyone's optimism and good cheer evaporated.

Driving onto the grounds, Karl and Larry soon suspected that this park must have borrowed the plans to Carthage Gap, then shrank its dimensions and added more trees with lower, longer branches. The attendants directed the Sportscoach to a space just off the main road, but signaled Karl to keep driving into the gloom. When he finally arrived at his assigned space, the captain informed his guides that he would prefer to just park there in the roadway rather than try to maneuver into a slot that was clearly not large enough for the boat trailer alone. Whether it was his white knuckles gripping the steering wheel or his crazed expression that convinced the guides, either way they agreed that parking on the road was best.

The skipper spent twenty minutes trying to connect the power, but after he tripped the breaker for the tenth time, he resigned himself that they would have to dry camp. He also made a mental note to send a letter to Trailer Life and request it update its campground descriptions or at the very least add a warning for larger rigs. He and the crew spent the remainder of the afternoon performing reconnaissance for the next day's launch. They were all determined to not let some camping drawbacks spoil the rest of their time in Appalachia.

In the planning stages of the second leg of their journey across America, the members of the *Acrosswater* party noticed some common themes when they researched the Ohio River Valley. In particular, West Virginia was regularly mentioned near the bottom of state rankings in important indicators like unemployment, education and per capita income. Any preconceptions the travelers had for what they might find when they arrived on the scene near Wheeling were baked into the plan; the region had been underestimated for ages.

Nearby Moundsville was the home of the largest, man-made earthen mound on the continent and for years, people assumed it had been constructed just a few centuries ago when indigenous ancestors would have been advanced enough to pull off such a feat of engineering. Archaeologists were surprised to discover that construction predated the birth of Christ and that its builders made trips - over two million of them - with woven baskets to transport dirt to the mound location.

More recently, the drumbeat of economic woe had echoed through the region and outsiders most often pointed to the decline in coal mining. Realistically, the region had been in transition from having a mining and manufacturing identity to something else for many years. An article by William Stevens that preceded the *Acrosswater* adventure by over a decade noted that coal mining accounted for just six percent of all employment in the state and that the decline was largely driven by automation. Mining companies no longer sent armies of men with picks and jackhammers down into the shafts; they used machines instead. Captain and crew were not sure what they would find but they suspected any manner of abandoned storefronts, ghost towns, toothless old-timers lamenting about the good old days and a parade of communities that modern progress had left behind.

Their first order of business was surveying a path to get the Bus up out of the woods. Even parking on the access road near his assigned slot left Karl with no maneuverability so they had to layout to the foot how far to reverse, when to cut the wheel, which outlets to avoid. It felt like they were trying to adjust the course of Apollo 13 in mid-flight using only the rocket on the LEM. Still, they took their time and, with other team members serving as spotters, the captain managed to safely wind his way back to the main road.

Rather than take a chance snaking their way into their next campsite before launching onto the river, they opted to park in a vacant lot they discovered nearby. Spacious, abandoned and with plenty of room to maneuver, the site provided a perfect location for their regional HQ and the team wondered why nobody else was on the property. They hooked up the SUV to the boat trailer and headed for the river.

Their day in Wheeling turned out to be spectacular. The crew thought that the best launch was back downriver in Moundsville, but that was fine with them because it allowed for a water entrance into Wheeling. The travelers were greeted by the sight of the Wheeling Suspension Bridge which connects Wheeling proper and Wheeling Island. At the time of its construction in the mid-1800's, the bridge was the longest of its kind in the world and was part of the early National Road. It was designated as a National Historic Landmark in 1975 and the *Acrosswater* visitors found it enchanting.

They docked at the waterfront park and were pleased to discover the facilities the finest they had encountered on the trip. In fact, outside of the landing in Nashville on the Cumberland River, the captain could not think of any others even in the same class.

They inspected the park's amphitheater, where they were informed by a local that free concerts were held there every Wednesday night during the summer, and then strolled up into town.

In its heyday, Wheeling was an industrial colossus. The city and its immediate surroundings were home to four coal mines, two steel mills, two commercial porcelain kilns, two clothing manufacturers and the requisite supporting businesses. Peaking in the mid-fifties, Wheeling's population at one time topped 65,000; at the time of *Acrosswater*, it had fallen to roughly half that.

Karl and Larry corroborated the figures they had heard when they ducked into a gun store just off the main drag. The store had first opened in 1908 and carved out a decent business, before eventually being taken over in 1932 by its founder's son, a now ancient fellow with hands terribly crippled by arthritis. He showed his two visitors around the store and patiently answered their questions, grimacing every so often. When asked how he managed to run the store with his hands as painful as they were, he shrugged and asked, "What the hell am I going to do about it?"

Karl and Larry marveled at his collection of museum quality, flintlock rifles and spent over an hour perusing the different displays while alternately quizzing their new friend about the area. He confirmed Wheeling's decline in commercial importance and noted that only two large employers remained in town, the La Belle cut nail factory and the Mail Pouch tobacco plant. (Mail Pouch still operates to this day under the Swisher umbrella, but La Belle shuttered its doors in 2010.) Both had been mainstays in the community since the 1800's and represented Wheeling's last, tenuous hold on industrial importance.

Interestingly, the gun store owner did not seem discouraged, embarrassed or depressed by the evolution of the town's business make up. On the contrary, he spoke with genuine pride about the role the community and its inhabitants had played in the success of the country, from West Virginia's entry into the Union in 1863 (when the state broke from its Confederate sister to the east), to its production of coal and steel as the nation exploded onto the manufacturing stage, to its current status as a city in flux. He seemed to accept it with incredible gumption, which at least partially explained his attitude about his arthritis.

The *Acrosswater* duo bid farewell to their historian, reconnected with Rose and Roxa and spent the rest of the day ambling about town. They visited the museum that resided in the former Independence Hall and strolled the Civil War-era displays until lunch. While they were eating, a ferocious thunderstorm hit and though they took their time and consumed as many iced tea refills as the waitress would bring them, by four o'clock they realized they would have to take action to get the boat off the river.

The skipper caught a taxi back to Moundsville to retrieve the SUV and trailer (skirting a flash flood in Glen Dale along the way) and then crept back to Wheeling to pick up the crew. After he put on his rain gear, Karl hustled onto the boat, dodged a nearby lightning strike and pulled away from the dock while the other three drove the SUV to the ramp located on the other side of Wheeling Island. God knows how many traffic laws Rose broke zipping across the bridge and the island, but in any case, when the captain pulled around the point and saw the boat apron, he was pleased to find the trailer already waiting in the water. Larry and Roxa helped tie everything down and then they were all on their way back to Moundsville.

By the time they arrived at their vacant lot, the storm had finally let up. The rain had rinsed much of the grime and dust off the pavement and, more importantly, allowed the team to see just why nobody else was camping there. The ground was liberally sprinkled with nails and screws of all sizes. They may as well have been parked on La Belle's factory floor. Envisioning every tire turning into a rolling pin cushion, the captain and crew spent the last bit of daylight trying to clear a path for their departure in the morning. Eventually satisfied that they had limited their chances to only having to replace two tires, seeing that the foul weather was gone for good and realizing that they had not spent enough time that day looking at businesses on the decline, they decided to go to a drive-in movie. What a day.

The capstone to their journey through the Ohio River Valley was a series of water entrances into Pittsburgh. Uniquely positioned at the confluence of three rivers (the Allegheny, the Ohio and the Monongahela), the city offered multiple choices of approach. Captain and crew elected to float into the city on the Allegheny and in order to do so, set sail from Sharpsburg, a borough six miles north of Pittsburgh.

They had safely evacuated the Nail and Screw Resort without a serious puncture and had found a campground near Austin Lake with more room, better power, cleaner sewer connections, clearer driveways and fewer sharp objects than the three previous sites. It was halfway between Wheeling and Pittsburgh, however, and a launch out of nearby Toronto into the Ohio would have resulted in minimally a twelve-hour round trip. Still smarting from all the scrapes driving the Bus into Carthage Gap, the skipper also was loath to drag the whole convoy into Pittsburgh, a place with no less than a zillion bridges crisscrossing its rivers. Instead, they found a launch called the Crow's Nest in

Sharpsburg on their maps, locked up the Bus and Sportscoach tight, paid the campground caretaker for another day and headed out with just the SUV and trailer.

The first mate tried to reach the Crow's Nest several times along the way to confirm access, fees, rights-of-way and the like, but she never connected. They pushed on anyway, thanking their lucky stars they had left the Bus behind given all the road construction, and at last found their destination nestled in the lee of Sixmile Island. After the captain convinced the manager on duty that they were willing to pay to launch (apparently locals had a habit of sneaking boats onto the river when nobody was watching), the foursome floated *Acrosswater* free of her trailer, parked the SUV and jetted downriver.

Mile zero of the Ohio starts at Pittsburgh, so captain and crew decided to first hang a right out of the Allegheny and cruise down the Ohio one more time. They locked through at Emsworth and then continued all the way to Montgomery Lock & Dam before making a U-turn and going back upstream. It was a perfect July day and their entrance into the city from the west took their breath away.

They kept cruising east and motored up the Monongahela for about ten miles. Its shorelines were a mix of defunct steel mills and modest restoration. On the way back, the captain noted the Steelers' training facility on the south side of the river. They docked near old Fort Pitt and then walked up near the Point State Park Fountain and the western terminus of the Great Allegheny Passage. They took couples photos with newly-opened Heinz Field (home of the Steelers) and PNC Park (home of the Pirates) in the background.

The view from the point was just sensational and they stood in silence and savored the moment for several minutes. Afterwards, Karl and Rose toured the Fort Pitt Museum while Larry and Roxa stayed with the boat.

They returned to the Crow's Nest and pulled *Acrosswater* out of the river without issue. The same could not be said for another boater whose battery had died after launch and who was then drifting listlessly among the slips. To make matters worse, the man's son had invited friends along. Poor dad was left wasting a precious day off work, wrestling with a faulty boat motor and listening to the teenagers bitch about how terribly unfair their life was. Members of the *Acrosswater* party gave him sympathetic nods in a show of solidarity.

While at the Crow's Nest earlier in the day, the skipper had inquired about the state of the rivers north of the city. The manager strongly advised against going any further up the Allegheny due to water conditions and commercial traffic. Having learned their lesson back in 2000 that acting contrary to local intelligence was a fool's errand, they opted to portage to New York instead of cobbling together an alternate river route.

To that end, they pulled out of the Austin Lake campground the next morning and endured a hair-raising commute to a camp in Rocky Springs, PA. The route they chose had more switchbacks than the Rising Sun shortcut and the skipper had to lay on the horn no less than five times along the way to warn oncoming drivers of his approach.

The park they found in Rocky Springs turned out to be a delight; it was one of those tight-knit, RV communities where residents reunited every summer. The *Acrosswater* convoy arrived during the park's annual, Christmas-in-July celebration and every RV and trailer was covered in lights. What's more, the festival organizers - after hearing about the *Acrosswater* story from the park manager - showed up at the door of the Bus with a plate of sweets and asked the traveling foursome to pick the winner of the light display contest. Sadly, Karl had to decline because the greeters arrived past 9:30 p.m. and (uncharacteristically) the rest of the crew were already in their pajamas. The *Acrosswater* four drifted to sleep that night to the sound of the other campers caroling throughout the park.

The group stopped one more time on the way north at Lake Chautauqua (describing the shape of the lake, Chautauqua was a Seneca word meaning bag-tied-in-the-middle), mostly to play golf, but also to drop the boat into the water for a spin. The course they found had been designed by Donald Ross (a titan among course architects, some of his most famous efforts included Seminole, Oak Hill and Pinehurst No. 2), so its pedigree was too good to pass up. The foursome submitted average rounds for them, but they loved the history and layout of the place.

Even more intriguingly, they were pleased to discover the Chautauqua Institute after trying to spend time out on the water. Stymied by water weeds so thick they fooled *Acrosswater*'s depth finder, captain and crew quickly gave up boating and instead toured through the former, Methodist, training center. There, they learned of the Institute's seasonal impact on the area.

Attracting students of art, music and religion, Chautauqua had been the summer home for educators and intellectuals since the 1870's and swelled the population of the town itself to more than 150,000 when classes were in session. For nine weeks between June and August, the Chautauqua Institute and its enormous, famed amphitheater hosted a dizzying array of performances across a wide spectrum of disciplines: philosophy, opera, piano, theater, jazz, poetry. Rose lobbied to spend a summer there, which the skipper agreed to but only if he could simultaneously attend a training session with Dan Beamer on the Snake River.

The four mates finished the day at a roadside, farmers stand where they collected vegetables and heard an impromptu dissertation by the market's owner about the hours of toil that went into a single gallon of maple syrup. (Forty gallons of sap from a maple tree yielded one gallon of grade A syrup.) Hearing that he was several years younger than them - but looked ten years older - captain and crew again recounted over dinner their good fortune. They shut out the lights that night thinking about the next morning when they would drive straight to Tonawanda and the headwaters of the Erie Canal. A fifty-year-old dream was about to come true.

Chapter 16
The Erie Canal

(AL - BEE - UN)

Karl's journal - August 3, 2002

The skipper helpfully wrote people and places phonetically for future reference. Other examples were Pierre, SD (pronounced "pier"), Loess (LUSS) Hills and Officer Guntle (GUN T LEE).

Lockport, NY

ON a summer day in the early 1800's, two men met in the woods of western New York. One of the men, James Geddes, then in his fifties, had already spent time trekking around in that part of the state when he had surveyed a sizable tract of land in 1808. The other man, Benjamin Wright, had only recently ventured into the area in a professional, surveying capacity. Neither man had formal training in engineering and both men only knew how to survey because they had practiced it out of necessity when they settled property disputes during the course of their normal jobs as judges.

Starting at opposite ends of a miles long section of a route they were assigned to survey, the two men worked their way towards each other and came together somewhere in the approximate middle, their respective measurements missing the mark by all of two inches. It was a remarkable start to an unlikely commission for the two amateurs. They were in the infant stages of the most significant engineering project of the nineteenth century, the Erie Canal.

It is impossible to overstate how important the construction of that canal was for the fledgling nation. Nowadays, if anyone even talks about the venerable waterway, it is either in the context of some fable involving Rip Van Winkle or in a classroom of kindergarten kids during music class. And yet, persuasive evidence points to the completion of the Erie Canal as the launchpad to the economic dominance of the State of New York and the worldwide, financial superiority of the United States. Costing just over $7 million to build – a colossal sum at the time – the Erie Canal generated so much revenue that the fees and tolls collected for use of the waterway allowed the debts associated with its construction to be paid off in just ten years. Moreover, it eliminated the barrier of the Allegheny mountain range, opening a gateway to the west for economic expansion.

What is even more impossible to overstate is how unlikely it was that a group of amateur engineers were able to successfully carve a three-hundred-mile channel - through countryside one European visitor once said filled "...the soul with a sort of religious terror..." - using nothing but hand tools and beasts of burden. Joining Geddes and Wright as a recipient of an assigned leg of the project was Charles Broadhead but he, like the others, was not a formally trained engineer.

The men worked both independently and collectively, spending months at a time on their assigned sections. A fourth, major contributor to the project was Canvass White, without whose intuition and ingenuity the canal surely would have failed. White provided numerous mechanical plans for the various structures scattered along the length of the waterway and, most importantly, developed the watertight cement used to line the canal.

For all those involved, the tension and anxiety was enormous. Governor De Witt Clinton, the tireless proponent and godfather of the project, endured nonstop ridicule from the time he suggested building the Erie Canal to the day he symbolically poured water from Lake Erie into New York City Harbor following the ceremonial first journey. The federal government had refused to fund the project and so the State of New York assumed all the risk.

The builders had to navigate over 1,000 feet of elevation changes, install dozens of locks, build aqueducts, account for water scarcity, remove thousands of trees, hire and train craftsmen and find the best path through the wilds of the New World (no stagecoach service yet existed west of Rome, a town barely a third of the way from the Hudson River to Lake Erie). They were on edge for ten years as they tried to meld their vision of what they hoped the canal would become to what the reality of nature would allow.

Much like his visionary predecessors, Karl felt anxiety as he and the crew rolled into the Buffalo area on July 30. He had recorded in his journal that morning a wide range of emotions: curiosity about how the modern canal would mesh with his childhood memory, fear that his companions would not find it as enchanting as he had described for so many years, worry that problems in the day-to-day execution would sully the experience and apprehension that a lifelong dream fulfilled might lead to crushing depression at its conclusion. Nonetheless, he buried his fears in his journal – his shipmates sensed nothing but child-like excitement – and insisted to the team that they begin this last, primary leg of their adventure in North Tonawanda at Gateway Park and the Erie Canal's western terminus so everyone could receive a proper introduction to the place that had made such an lasting impression on him.

The two couples strolled the paths along the canal, chattering excitedly about what they expected this part of their trip to be like. They happened upon an annual gathering of boating enthusiasts and marveled at the collection of large, cabin cruisers moored along both sides of the waterway. The captain, and indeed the whole crew, realized that the whole length of the canal would not look as pristine or rehabilitated or inviting as Gateway Park, but their brief initiation was more than enough to fill all the visitors with enthusiasm for the journey ahead.

In keeping with the tradition of regional, historical investigation they had practiced over two years, the couples made time to explore other local diversions after they finished walking near the canal. Most notably, they stopped in at the Herschell Carrousel Factory Museum where Larry regaled the other three with insights about the complicated techniques the craftsmen must have used carving and finishing the wooden horses, dogs, pigs and giraffes on display. The foursome also learned about Herschell's marketing plan, first implemented in the 1880's, which simplified the start-up process and therefore made proliferation of carousels as an attraction more likely. They finished the day with a large bucket of chicken wings from the Anchor Tavern, founded in 1935 and the originator of Buffalo-style wings.

They launched for the first time into the Erie Canal on August first and the day could not have gone better. They had already reconnoitered their preferred entry point which enabled them to drive straight from their camp to the water without fretting about parking, road construction or traffic. *Acrosswater* eased effortlessly out of her cradle on the trailer and within minutes she and her crew were gently purring upstream.

They passed under the bridges on Adams and Exchange Streets and cleanly navigated locks 34 and 35 (interlocking). The team members handled their assignments flawlessly, Larry and Roxa holding the vertical lines on the wall of the lock with boat hooks, Rosemary monitoring the wall for clearance and her shipmates for signs of distress and the captain piloting the craft. They soon had dipped the nose of the boat into the Niagara River and added the Buffalo skyline to their collection.

They totaled over four hours on the canal and wished it could have been eight. All four of them took the helm at some point during the day and none of them could stop grinning from ear to ear. The waterway had many places that invited them to stop and at one, Rose and Roxa darted into an ice cream parlor near the water for some cones. They were pleased to find that, not only was it owned by a German family and that it was the grandmother Omi's turn at the fountain, the shop also sold homemade pastries. They already had fresh salmon and salad planned for their celebratory dinner and since it happened to be Larry's birthday, the girls bought some *apfelstrudel*. Karl's journal summary for August 1 said it all. "Perfect day!"

On a journey filled with acts of kindness and miraculous good fortune, the two or three days that captain and crew spent near the towns of Albion, Spencerport and Lyons were notably lucky.

Every day, as if they traveled in the company of guardian angels, that part of their trip could have gone spectacularly wrong had they not heeded the advice of a local, been the recipients of a moment of generosity or simply benefited from a happy coincidence.

It all started when they prepared to depart for Albion. An answered knock on the door of the Bus revealed a policeman asking Karl to come out and check the engine compartment. Soon-to-retire Lieutenant Neuman had noticed the rear door ajar during his patrol and, upon inspection, thought the main drive belt looked damaged. He wanted the owner (Karl) to inspect it himself. It was damaged and would have been catastrophic. The skipper thanked Officer Neuman profusely, wished him luck in retirement and, with Larry's assistance, replaced the belt before they pulled out.

Convinced that they had prevented engine parts from being scattered all over western New York, the team made its way to Albion. The main street of town was littered with sharp, overhanging limbs and turning lanes clearly too small to handle their convoy. The captain in particular was running out of emery cloths and touch up paint for the roof of the Bus so he suggested that they try to find a supermarket parking lot to drop the rigs while they scoped out the city's boat ramp. Given the size of the streets themselves, the launch might have been too small as well.

Finding no lots to speak of, they were starting to run out of road when Karl noticed a small, par-three golf course named Pap Pap's with what appeared to be a large, unoccupied square of lawn near its clubhouse. They opted to duck in and check if it would be willing to host a couple of RV's and, though Pap had died two years earlier, his widow (Bessie) was more than happy to let them camp on the property.

She had a camper herself and understood the difficulty at times finding a safe place to park. She only cautioned that the mowers fired up at 5:30 a.m.

With the din of Toros crawling across the fairways as a soundtrack, the adventurers got an early start on Saturday, August 3, bidding farewell to Bessie and driving first to the water. They planned for Karl and Larry to move the rigs forward and then motor back to join the girls for a day on the canal. They had checked in at Officer Neuman's HQ and were informed that, though the boat ramp was serviceable, it was too remote for the women to wait by themselves. Especially since they were unsure how long it would take for the boys to make the move, Rose and Roxa instead tied off at the wall of the town marina and scrubbed *Acrosswater* while they waited.

Karl and Larry's destination was Allen's Canal Side just east of Spencerport. It turned out to be rather difficult to find, tucked into a nondescript neighborhood, which added at least an hour to their commute. Karl asked John, the owner of the marina, why his property was so discrete. "When people find us, we can't get rid of them," John said, simply.

What added even more time to the rig transfer, however, was the clean up associated with Karl standing on the brakes of the Bus to avoid a collision. Usually before any of them moved their campers, they ran through a checklist of tasks to make sure they were ready to travel: utilities disconnected, storage bays locked, wheel chocks stowed, tow hitch secured. Well, either Karl was distracted by the greens being waxed at Pap's or he thought Rose had done it, but either way, one of them forgot to throw the latch on the refrigerator door. When the skipper hit the brakes, the fridge disgorged its contents and a jar of stuffed olives smashed on the floor as it rolled up the aisle. The upshot was that Karl spent at least an hour picking feta cheese and grape leaves out of the stairwell; six weeks later, visitors were still showing up with pita bread and searching for the bowls of hummus.

Reunited back in Albion, the foursome spent five, relaxing hours on the water that afternoon. They passed under seven of the canal's fifteen lift-bridges along the way and every member of the crew took a turn at the helm. In fact, the captain stayed away from the tiller until entering Allen's marina, which had a narrow ramp. Surprisingly, especially considering John's remarks earlier in the day, the place was swarming with tourists. After pulling *Acrosswater* out of the lagoon, they found John at the front of the camp, wearing a money changer and selling tickets to see the Bus. He had spent his day spreading the word that Dwight Yoakam was parked on the property.

Rumor mongering aside, he turned out to be a delightful host and a great source of Erie Canal lore. He recounted one tragedy from the 1970's when the canal had breached upstream and drained the marina, leaving the boats and docks resting in the mud for the winter. Engineers made their repairs and in the spring, refilled the canal. Nobody noticed that the boats and docks were effectively glued to the bottom and they were soon overrun by the rising water. All were lost.

Their final day in the area, the boaters attempted to add the Rochester skyline to their journals. Since the fall of 1823, when the first packet boat floated down the Erie Canal into town with cargo never seen that far west (fresh oysters), the former outpost for trappers and frontiersmen had exploded into a boomtown. Swiftly outpacing Buffalo to the west, Rochester became a home for innovation, spawning the likes of Xerox, Eastman Kodak and Bausch & Lomb.

In its infancy, the town also saw the construction of one of the most notable engineering achievements on the Erie Canal, the Genesee aqueduct. The aqueduct spanned a particularly treacherous section of the river just below the falls; the water flummoxed the first builders by washing away their construction efforts. The engineers persevered and when completed, the aqueduct, constructed of red sandstone from nearby Medina and limestone from Cayuga, supported the tons of water that filled the canal and carried the boats with their cargo for more than 450 feet across the rushing river below. The sight of the barges floating high above filled spectators with wonder.

Once the initial delight gave way to the mundane, daily order of business, canal overseers soon realized they had a problem. The original structure leaked so badly that just ten years after opening, a new aqueduct had to be built. In due time, the city constructed a dam at the site of the old falls, forcing engineers to move the canal south of the dam and erasing the need for an aqueduct at all. The old Erie Canal thruway was itself transformed into a bridge for automobiles, making the sight of barges maneuvering around the city another relic of days gone by. Approaching from the south and because of the dam, boaters could only hope for a glimpse of the aqueduct remnants more than two bridges away.

That was the strategy the *Acrosswater* foursome followed. They had already moved their camp forward from Allen's and so they had to drive forty miles back to find a suitable ramp. From there it was a twelve mile run downstream on the canal - passing through locks 32 and 33 along the way - and then another four miles north after a hard right onto the Genesee River.

They motored as far north as the marina before the dam warning markers stopped their progress. They snapped some photos of the city and peered into the distance, hoping for a glimpse of the old aqueduct and wishing they were not 170 years too late. The area around the marina was still being revitalized and they all concluded it would be some years before it would become a real draw for visitors. They reversed course and headed for home, stopping only for a bite to eat and to compliment the tender at lock 33 for having such an extraordinary display of flowers.

The next four days were a dream for the happy couples. They ranged between locks 28b and 24 and soaked up as much of the experience as they could. On August 6, they had moved all of their equipment forward which necessitated more backtracking in order to boat along the canal itself. They dropped into the water near Clyde and then alternated between jetting and idling, allowing the attractions along the bank to guide their movements to some degree. They found the lock master (Jerry) at lock 25 to be another fountain of local, historical knowledge.

He invited them up into the lock house for a tour and drew them a small map of spots where they could launch. After leaving Jerry, they also noticed on their charts a small tributary labeled Clinton Ditch; it was a tiny segment of the original, Erie Canal system. They tried to poke the bow of *Acrosswater* into the stream but with a depth of only two and a half feet, they had to settle for essentially a symbolic encounter.

More backtracking on August 7 led them to a trove of antiques, in various forms. It started immediately from the launch near Miller's Marina when Karl spotted what appeared to be converted tug moored at one of the docks. Soon enough, they were all invited on board the *Charity*, a restored Lord Nelson Victory Tug and the pride and joy of Dave and Barb Conroy. Retired and hailing from Florida, the Conroys were spending their third summer in New York. Their cabin cruiser was gorgeous.

A delay at lock 28b caused them to disembark and investigate its cause. A gate had lodged open and the lock master (Gary) was waiting for a diver to arrive on the scene. While they waited, Gary gave them a detailed tour of his station, a building filled with drawings, charts and photos. He also pointed out the semi-restored remains across the frontage road of a double-lock that dated back to the 1850's and the second Erie Canal expansion.

Clearly an enthusiast, Gary had arranged to move a control shed of similar vintage from another location to his post and was in the process of restoring it as well; he had recently replaced the cedar, shake roof. He outlined plans to add new gates to the old double-lock (based on original schematics) and to include original hinges which he had in storage. The *Acrosswater* adventurers wished there were more people like Gary, someone with an appreciation for the forgotten corners of small town America and the passion to preserve it.

After a time, the foursome realized that the diver would not be able to repair the gate soon enough for them to continue forward so they bid farewell to their new friend and departed. As they approached their landing ramp, one of them espied an antique mall; three out of the four threatened mutiny if they were not allowed to at least peruse the wares.

Resigned to the fact he was outnumbered, the captain acquiesced and spent the next hour quietly picking through boxes of old shoelaces and back issues of *Good Housekeeping*. The three amigos struck it rich and walked out of the shop with vintage skis and snowshoes (because, you know, what would be easier to pack across country), a drying rack to pair with a similar discovery from the 2000 expedition and a large hunk of rust that was alleged to have an ax hidden beneath the corrosion.

They stayed off the water on August 8, their last day in the area. After a round of golf at the Geneva Country Club - it was private, but they were granted a reciprocal tee time after Karl contacted the pro at his home course - they filled the remainder of the day driving a loop around the finger lakes of Seneca and Cayuga. At the southern tip of Seneca, they noted signs for the Watkins Glen International Raceway, a mainstay of the NASCAR circuit, but also noted that those signs did not direct them to the track itself. They assumed fans were genetically drawn to the location and thus did not need directions.

Driving east to the southern tip of Cayuga Lake, they passed through Ithaca and the Cornell University campus and did not stop, but the journalists recorded the college as having eclectic building designs, thoughtfully spread out over the hills of the town. They turned north and had almost made it safely home when one of them saw a sign for MacKenzie-Childs. Locals claim that if the wind is blowing in the right direction, the shrieks of delight can still be heard echoing around the lake.

Not even a decade old when the *Acrosswater* party arrived on the property, the whimsical creations of MacKenzie-Childs had already earned a reputation for artistry and quality. Though it made a large number of pieces annually, it was not accurate to describe its process as mass production. Hand crafted and individually painted, works of the same design had a different identity - almost like fingerprints - because the artisans, as skilled as they were, could not replicate each item with the same precision as a machine.

The foursome arrived too late to take a tour but they were in time to visit the gift shop, a building absolutely stuffed with colorful, eclectic wares. It looked like a snow globe had exploded inside. Overcome by the aroma of scented candles, Karl and Larry opted to tour the grounds and gardens instead.

Looking back, August 9 began a time of revelation for captain and crew, not only the beginning of the remaining few weeks of their precious journey on the water, but also the realization that family and friends had been with them all along the way. The travelers had welcomed visitors on occasion since they had started in Astoria, but those all seemed like momentary interludes - almost interruptions - when in fact they were signs of the enormous support from afar, like tips of an emotional iceberg.

The morning of the ninth, Rose stopped at the post office and picked up a care package from Marilee which contained a curated collection of various artists performing *Low Bridge, Everybody down.* (Most people know the song from its familiar line, "fifteen miles on the Erie Canal.") The *Acrosswater* party had already been singing the tune (with some improvisations) at many of the locks along the canal, but Marilee's gift added the likes of Pete Seeger, the Dady Brothers and Suzanne Vega to the ensemble. The whole team was touched by the thoughtfulness and artistic flair that Marilee had poured into the collection. And in the evening of the ninth, Karl received a call from Bill and Laurie Miller, friends who were flying in from Chicago and who would be joining them the following day on the water in their own rented cruiser. Clearly people across the country were dying to be part of the adventure.

To prepare for the Miller's arrival, the team first moved camps from Sylvan Beach to Verona. Sylvan Beach sits on the eastern edge of Oneida Lake and, apparently, was exceedingly popular because every place was worn out (not unkempt, but certainly well used), and a favorite of blue-collar overnighters. In fact, when the *Acrosswater* party pulled into the park for the night - gingerly it must be said for it had those narrow trails with overhanging branches that were so popular with people driving Prevosts - the skipper's foot had just touched the gravel outside his front door when a crowd of campers gathered around him, wanting to have a peek at the Bus.

He spent the next two hours opening every bay, pulling out each slide, answering questions about displacement and torque, pointing out the gage of wire used in the harnesses, passing around old fittings for the dump connections and handing out souvenirs. Although he could not convince anyone to take home any antique snow shoes, the tour was still a roaring success and the guests were so appreciative, that the campsite owner insisted that Karl park *Acrosswater* on the lawn near the office where it would be under the watchful eye of no less than four trusted guardians.

The owner even returned the following day before the adventurers departed to reiterate how grateful he and the other campers were for the time Karl had taken to show them the Bus. Apparently guests in the past with eye-catching equipment would not even look at them, much less let them venture up close unless they were there to shine the chrome or empty a chamber pot. Karl reassured him that, aside from a few breaks in life that had allowed Rose and him to fulfill many of their dreams, he was in essence one of the pipe fitters or welders who had been so enamored with the Bus the day before.

So they shoved off from Sylvan Beach and made it to Verona. The skipper had spent hours putting together a comprehensive itinerary that would seamlessly incorporate the Miller's rental (the *Canadice*) into the *Acrosswater*'s travels. They planned to pick up Bill and Laurie, drive west to retrieve the charter, spend a day west of Oneida Lake to familiarize the Miller's with canal operations and their rental and then leisurely cruise east. There would be time allowed ashore where guests could choose from a variety of excursions that included Revolutionary War sites, golf, the ever-present antique bazaars, quaint, upstate New York towns and, of course, Erie Canal landmarks.

Karl included the ramps they would use to launch, the directional markers to follow on the open water of Oneida, the exits to take when shuttling between campsites and alternative schedules should bad weather or traffic intercede. He felt a little dissatisfied with the scale of his hand drawn map - he had to use 1:1000 instead of the ratio he and the USACE preferred - but he was confident his companions would understand his directions. He even planned a celebratory dinner in St. Johnsville to punctuate their time together. It was just perfect.

Chapter 17
A family affair

*"From mid-lakes to Jct. Oswego River Canal
and Oneida River Canal (prox 6.5 mi)
NOTE: Channel marks reverse upon entering
Oswego River Canal (Red marks Eastside -
Green marks - Westside)"*

Karl's journal - August 11, 2002

A snippet of a canceled itinerary. The skipper
could have filled a three-ring binder with
rewritten agendas and maps alone.

Lock 17

"I beg your pardon?" It was August 11 and Karl was at the rental counter with Bill picking up the Miller's rental. "Did you say that the *Canadice* can only go as far east as Brewerton?" Brewerton was on the western side of Lake Oneida and scant miles into their planned itinerary. Prohibiting travel to the east wiped out most of the agenda that Karl had drawn up.

"Yessir," the attendant said cheerfully, "our charters are not rated to go out onto the lake." He continued reviewing the exhaustive list of prohibitions and restrictions that accompanied the rental. Manhattan real estate transactions have been consummated with less paperwork.

While the rental agent moved on to the amenities list with Bill, Karl took off his embroidered, *Acrosswater II* hat and scratched his head, trying to ignore the ringing in his ears so he could think. After a minute, he whacked Bill on the shoulder with his cap. "Not a prob, Bill. We'll investigate the Oswego Canal today and then regroup." He put his hat back on with a satisfied smile.

"That might work," the attendant chimed in, "but you'll have to hurry. You have to lock up at Baldwinsville before taking full possession so, let's see…" He looked at his watch and did some rough calculations. "It's twenty-seven river miles from Baldwinsville to Oswego and it's three o'clock now. How fast does the *Canadice* go?" He ran his finger over the spec sheet. "Six knots…ok…let's assume you drop into the water at four, there and back is nine hours…" The ringing in the Karl's head drowned out the fellow's voice. He could see they would not be boating on Oswego any time that day.

Limitations aside, the three couples enjoyed themselves immensely. The familiarity with the area may have even helped their cause because the folks from *Acrosswater* shared some of the gems they had discovered that the Millers might have otherwise missed. They showed off most of their favorite canal landmarks and even made another run at MacKenzie-Childs; they still arrived too late the day they visited. The limited cruising speed of the *Canadice* made the pace of each day a little slower and perhaps a touch more relaxed.

In fact, the only source of heart palpitation during the week was the personality of the marina owner who presided over the launch site where the two parties had elected to rendezvous each day; the marina was centralized between the water and the *Acrosswater* camp. The owner had a serious political ax to grind, favored a post near the ramp in his lawn chair for ease of access to his rotating audience and generously lubricated his thoughts with cases of Pabst Blue Ribbon. The travelers thought it may have been an ingenious way to motivate sailors to move boats in and out of their slips more swiftly - they all seemed to pick up the pace whenever he approached - but that seemed unlikely.

The three couples also ran across the old friends of *Acrosswater* (the Conroys) and their rehabbed tug, the *Charity*. Dave and Barb seemed to like the Millers better than the others because it wasn't long into the introductions before Bill sidled up next to the *Acrosswater* skipper and whispered, "Say, would you mind picking us up over at lock 28b? Dave and Barb want to take us for a ride." Before Karl could answer, the Millers were gently chugging away on the *Charity*. Since they had to alter their schedule the next day, it was the last time the skipper saw the Millers on a boat of any kind during their time together.

Their agenda for Wednesday, August 14 had called for a cruise along a section of the canal that was spanned by particularly eye-catching bridges, but from the start those plans were cursed. Though not a Friday nor the 13th, it was close enough and the *Acrosswater* four began the luckless day with an uncharacteristic miscommunication about their rendezvous location. By the time they realized the mistake, Karl had led the troops on a nine-mile trek out into the woods (to the wrong campground) and Larry's RV was again malfunctioning, the gages on the Sportscoach fluttering and crackling like a Geiger counter.

Still undiagnosed, the power failures of the Sportscoach had plagued the travelers randomly across the Mohawk River Valley and seemed to originate in the alternator. Shortly after the Millers had arrived, Bill (an electrical engineer) had disassembled the entire alternator and theorized that the springs on the top of the component had lost their springiness and therefore no longer made consistent contact with the corresponding circuits, thus interrupting the flow of electricity. He had even machined replacement springs out of a #1 paper clip. The temporary fix lasted less than a week, giving out as the convoy shuttled between campgrounds on August 14. Larry and Roxa had no choice but to wait for all the systems to cool down while the other two backtracked to the right campground.

The skipper and first mate arrived at the correct RV park (Elmtree) only to learn that the 50 amp connection at the site had a bad circuit. The region was suffering through a record heat wave (over ninety-nine degrees with high humidity) and without 50 amp power available, the Bus could not run its air conditioner. Even with all the windows open, if the park manager could not repair the circuit, Karl and Rose were looking at a restless night in oven-like conditions. The twosome left the Bus with the hope the power would be fixed and began the long commute (118 miles in one direction) to meet up with Bill and Laurie.

Similarly vexed, the pair on the *Canadice* had inched along at the max speed of the charter to circulate a breeze (the rental did not have air conditioning) and ultimately had passed up their original berth in Newark in favor of one that had none of the romance associated with an evening spent bobbing on the canal, but decidedly more comfort: a Quality Inn. Karl and Rose found them sitting under a large shade tree in front of the motel and since their plans were already shot, the four of them elected to round out the day eating frozen custard. After a more understated ending to their time together than any of them had anticipated, the skipper and first mate said their good-byes to Bill and Laurie and then returned to Camp Hibachi. (The park manager claimed to have fixed the switch, but the Bus still kept tripping the breaker.)

The only good news from the day came from Larry and Roxa who had found a dealer who could repair their RV. The technician they had chatted with on the phone suggested they replace the alternator, belts, water pump and any other ancillary components. Surprisingly, the shop had all the parts in stock and could have the Sportscoach in the garage by 7:30 a.m. The group turned in with fingers crossed that their luck was heading back in the right direction.

In the morning, while the Sportscoach had its alternator, binder clips and toner replaced, the captain and crew took the day to play golf, update the travel website and finalize preparations for a second wave of guests who were joining the expedition. Karl's sister (Karol), brother-in-law (Doug), Karol's daughters (Kelley and Michelle) and Michelle's boyfriend (RJ) were arriving later that afternoon for a weekend of boating and camping.

The *Acrosswater* team's move to the Elmtree HQ (between Utica and Herkimer) was intended to give the much larger party better accommodations, as well as better access to the settings of the events on their tour calendar. (They had a more durable itinerary without the boating limitations of the charter.) Mercifully, the circuit at Elmtree was finally repaired so the group did not have to decide between finding a camp with working, 50 amp power or suffering sleepless nights.

Karl and Larry played at the Crestwood Golf Club while Rose and Roxa spruced up camp. The weather remained unseasonably hot and muggy, but neither it nor the thunderstorms that delayed their round on two occasions dissuaded the guys from having a fun outing. The course had a prison just out of bounds running the length of one of the holes, a clear violation of the Eighth Amendment for any inmate within sight of the fairway. The golfers acquitted themselves, as it were, during their rounds and were waiting at the bag drop when the girls arrived to pick them up.

The foursome then stocked up on supplies, including a tent to expand the sleeping quarters of the campsite. They planned to park

Michelle and RJ in the tent and put Karol and Doug on the spare bed in the Sportscoach. (It had a surprisingly comfortable pull out and was better suited for Doug's creaky back.) Kelley was relegated to the front of the Bus where she would have to sleep through the skipper rising at 3:30 a.m. to brew coffee and write in his journal. After setting up the tent and putting away the groceries, they went into Utica to try to upload some of the text and photos for their travel Web page.

Though the technology had advanced slightly since their first journey, Roxa routinely struggled to find adequate connections during the entire trip in 2002. Utica was no exception. They had called the library and found it had Internet access, but upon arrival were told it was not available for personal laptops. Subsequent calls to the college and multiple PC shops also hit dead ends.

In desperation, Karl suggested they try the Radisson and to their delight, the manager, Eric, turned out to be more than happy to let Roxa camp out in his office while she uploaded every page and picture. Because the connection was on dial up, each upload took so long that two hours into the project, Eric left for home, leaving Roxa with a volley of instructions on how to dispense clean towels to guests, where to find the emergency shut off for the hot tub and how to dim his office lights when she left. Two hours later, she finished the last data transfer and clocked out just as the second shift arrived for work.

After a stroll through the troughs of the Radisson's buffet, the team arrived back at camp at the same instant their guests pulled in, both in the middle of a torrent. They sat in the campers and visited, hoping the storm would pass but it just kept raining. Abandoning hope for a pause in the deluge, Michelle and RJ mustered the nerve to dash out to their tent, cuing the others to turn in themselves. Karl turned out the last light at 1:00 a.m.

If anyone ever needed a reminder of how remote and uncivilized the area was when the Erie Canal passed through in its infancy, they needed to investigate no further than Fort Stanwix. A bulwark against British aggression, the old fortification on the banks of the Mohawk River was all that stood between the Red Coats and a leisurely march all the way to Albany in the summer of 1777. Under normal circumstances, the Brits would have simply rolled in their siege guns and pounded the fort into submission but, because Stanwix was literally in the wilderness, the English chose not to struggle through the woods with heavy armaments and instead, resorted to waiting out the defiant Americans.

And defiant they were. Not only did the militia in the area constantly harangue the invaders, but it was at Stanwix, on August 6 of that year that the Stars and Stripes, cobbled together out of old bloomers and a worn jacket, was raised for the first time in history, a colonial middle finger in the face of the surrounding army. The siege was summarily broken when American forces under the command of General Benedict Arnold marched to the rescue; the British Army lost its nerve when the Seneca and Mohawk fighters supporting the cause of the Empire melted into the trees.

225 years later, reveille at camp *Acrosswater* sounded at 0600; the campers had a full day planned so there was no time to waste. After the presentation of *Acrosswater* regalia to the newest enlistees, the crew

unloaded the Harley off the boat and added some extra folding chairs to give the plebes somewhere more comfortable than the engine housing to sit. They were launching from Rome but before hitting the water, they had planned to visit Fort Stanwix and the Erie Canal Village.

At the fort, Karl and Doug volunteered for the artillery brigade and served with distinction, Doug as a powder and shot handler and Karl as the Commander; the three pound cannon under their charge hit its target with ease. At the Erie Canal Village, the party toured the museum, watched a demonstration of a mule team hauling a packet boat and had lunch. Then it was time to hit the water themselves.

On the way to the launch, they passed a warning sign that indicated a height clearance of just over nine feet. Mysteriously, Kelley had a tape measure in her purse and thus confirmed that the motorcycle hoist topped out at eleven feet. They dismantled the rigging, cleared the bridge and, after confirming the plan to haul out further down the canal thus eliminating a return trip through the low tunnel, reinstalled the hoist. Since they were divided into two SUV's, Larry volunteered to drive one and Michelle and RJ the other to the rendezvous point at lock 20, while the captain and remaining crew jetted over in *Acrosswater*.

They reunited as planned and cruised on the canal for a time, going all the way to the newly built Utica Marine Wall. They tied off and treated themselves to ice cream from a shop nearby and then sat to enjoy the pleasant weather and each other's company. A group of teenagers provided some additional entertainment by jumping off the eight foot canal wall in front of them, one even launching himself on his BMX bike.

After hauling out the boat and showering back at camp, they took another drive into Rome and ate dinner at an Italian restaurant. They reminisced about the day, the newest crewmen expressing wonder at what was a typical day for the core team. Although Michelle and RJ had to return to real life the next day, the other three were so enamored that they reenlisted for an additional tour. They wanted more than a cursory introduction to the *Acrosswater* life.

After Michelle and RJ left for New York City, the expanded party fell into a comfortable, happy rhythm for the next three days. They started later in the day than usual since the newcomers were not accustomed to the strict, regimented schedule of life on the road. The morning routine, the camp moves (Elmtree to St. Johnsville to Scotia), launching into the canal and even meal prep moved at a slower pace, partly because they were all visiting with each other while completing a chore, and partly because the cadets were still learning their assignments. Still, nobody seemed to mind since the original foursome were glad to share the adventure and the other three were delighted to be included.

Karol, Doug and Kelley remained dumbfounded at the amount of work that was expected during the course of a day. Even though it was at once thrilling and relaxing to be on the adventure, the most commonplace task was never completed the same way twice. Take their journey through lock 17 which, at over forty feet in depth, was primed to be a memorable ride for all of them. Everything proceeded like normal with all the crew members fulfilling their duties as ordered but then, right as they exited, a sizable clump of weeds was sucked into the impeller.

Normally, the captain could dislodge a plug by jetting forward and backward but not this time. Try as he might, the debris would not come loose, leaving the boat with little to no power. After a mile of drifting, they puttered over to a homemade dock and everyone disembarked while Karl and Larry took turns trying to scrape off the weeds. Seeing that they had floated to the center of the canal, the captain stripped to his skivvies and swam under the boat so he had a better purchase on the weeds. After two or three dives, full power was restored and the trip down the waterway continued.

Their last day all together, they did not spend any time on the water. The three visitors had to leave for the city by 5:00 p.m. so they did not dare risk getting stuck at a lock or on a bank somewhere. Instead, they did some chores around camp and performed a little maintenance on the equipment. The Harley needed a new battery and an oil change so Karl and Kelley drove into town to find a parts store while the others explored the area. It was a quaint region with gentle hills and charming buildings. Even the weather cooperated with mild temperatures and no humidity. They had a picnic lunch at camp and remained low key all day, sensing that their time together was nearing the end.

When the three departed for the city, the *Acrosswater* four stood in the clearing and watched them go. It was a little sad for all of them and a slight pall stayed over the campsite for the rest of the night, even when Karl and Larry set about finishing their chores and Rose and Roxa went for a ride in a canoe. Alone again, perhaps they all sensed that their great enterprise, the thing that had consumed their thoughts and lives and emotions for the past three years was really almost over.

As with the other landmark segments of their journey, the foursome made a point to connect with as many historical sites all along the Erie Canal as possible. As the day approached when they would leave the canal for good and move onto the Hudson, they found just such a historic juncture outside Scotia, a spot where they could see not only a piece of the ancient, original Clinton Ditch, but also parts of two different expansions, one from 1862 and the modern, still-in-use, barge canal of 1918.

They saw an original lock and viewed the beautiful remains of what was once an eighty-five foot aqueduct spanning Schoharie Creek. (It had been blasted apart years earlier to break up an ice jam.) Rose and Roxa's favorite moment of that stop was walking a trail built on the remains of a bygone tow path along the old canal for two and a half miles. It was simply wonderful.

Their transition into the Hudson began with a trip through the Waterford Flight (the series of five consecutive locks that descended over 170 feet to the Hudson River below). Karl vividly recalled the Flight from his boyhood trip and was eager to share the experience with his mates. Before entering lock 6 (the first of the series since the Erie Canal does not have a lock 1), they passed another boat and asked the skipper if he was planning to go through the Flight too. He looked at them like they had rocks in their heads. "Why the heck would I do that? It takes way too long," he said as he motored away, clearly disgusted. The *Acrosswater* team happily carried along, equally as interested in the journey as the destination.

The descent took just over two and a half hours and all hands performed flawlessly. The only hiccup occurred when they mistook guard gate 2 for lock 5 and they might be waiting there still had Roxa not hiked over and figured out the problem. (She ran into the lock master who was herself walking towards them to investigate the hold up.) Then it was into the Hudson where they took a quick run upriver.

They were all a little quiet as they went, the only sound the hum of the engine and the rush of the water. Three of the four were obviously saddened by the end of the Erie Canal chapter, time barreling forward and them with no chance to slow it. The one exception was a bit of a surprise: the captain himself.

When they had finished their first trip in 2000, it had taken him months to feel normal again. All he could think about then was going back out on the water. This time, as they made the turn at the first lock on the Hudson (C1 for Champlain) and motored back downstream, he felt a satisfying mix of accomplishment and gratitude. The seed his father and uncle had planted in him so long ago had taken time to develop, but he had done it.

They had done it.

Utica Marine Wall

Chapter 18

Liberty

New York City Harbor

WHEN the *Acrosswater* expedition set off from Astoria in the summer of 2000, the members of the team carried with them an emotional stew of elation, anxiety, curiosity, doubt, gratitude and apprehension. Questions abounded. How would their equipment hold up? Would months in confined quarters drive them mad? Would they find the hidden parts of their beloved country a disappointment? And most importantly, would the reality of the experience exceed or fall short of their dreams?

It bears repeating that planning a journey with as much complexity as theirs in 2000 was rife with challenges and had few guarantees. Not once did they see another traveler motoring around with a motorcycle on board and as easy as they made it seem, every hoist of the Harley was a calamity waiting to happen. At the conclusion of the trip, sound connection to the Internet was still woefully scarce, cell phone service was spotty at best, civilian GPS was so rare it may as well have been nonexistent and high-end, digital cameras were still only taking photos in a truly fuzzy 2 MP. Throw in concerns more akin to commercial transportation, like overhead clearance or bridge, weight capacity (the Bus alone weighed close to thirty tons), and it was understandable that the adventurers felt nervous about what they might face every day.

So as they concluded their time on the Erie Canal and began the final, downriver run into the city, they reflected on the answers to all those questions and so many more. They had indisputably rounded into a flexible, capable unit able to adjust to changing conditions immediately. It did not matter if they needed to flip a travel sequence for the day or rotate who would move the equipment, they proceeded with regimental precision, amazing and exhausting any of their familial hitchhikers along the way. Their competence at all the tasks associated with their ambitious travel strategy freed them to absorb the deeper, more enduring impact of the trip.

Their last days on the water were magical and in that final week, they seemed to experience all of the tiny, meaningful nuances that had followed them across the country and that had made the trip so unique. Even potential tragedy was infused with coincidence. When Rose sliced the tip of her finger preparing dinner and they had to make a detour to an emergency room, the doctor who sewed up the wound was a Lewis and Clark enthusiast and listened to the story of their odyssey with great interest.

Passing by West Point, they were treated to a corps of paratroopers rappelling out of a helicopter as it circled the rooftops of the academy, something Karl certainly had not seen when he had traveled through in 1951. They made a stop at Hyde Park and learned about the history and resilience of FDR and then, since it was after 5:00 p.m., hopped over the hedges to peek at a Vanderbilt estate. It was a staggering display of wealth with acres of granite and gardens, but was eerily cold and uninviting. None of the visitors considered it a warm, welcoming place; on the contrary, they all felt it was more comparable to the New York Public Library than a private residence.

On their second to last day on the water, they launched from Newburgh into the Hudson amidst a throng of other boaters (it was a Sunday). It hearkened back to the Lake of the Ozarks with all its pandemonium and excess. There were jet skis zipping over the wakes of the larger boats (few of whom seemed to care about any speed restrictions), and monstrous cruisers out for the day before their owners returned to Wall Street the next morning. The favorite of the *Acrosswater* crew was an eighty-footer flying a Bahamian flag. The foursome completed a forty-mile round trip downriver and back, found that evening's campsite after two or three unintended detours and turned in close to midnight after Roxa finished her latest upload (the camp site happened to have an Internet connection).

Their convoy rumbled into action early on the morning of August 26. The skipper insisted on a prompt start because they were going to a launch site in Jersey City and he had serious concerns about them making the commute without incident, well founded as it turned out. Roxa rode with him in the Bus to help navigate, then Rose followed in the SUV towing the boat and Larry brought up the rear in the Sportscoach. Almost immediately, they missed a turn and were soon on a cross country tour that brought their destination tantalizingly in view, but impossible to reach. They regrouped in a high school parking lot and, after clearing a path through a mob of students crowding around the Bus to see who the celebrity was, returned to the road with what they hoped was a concrete set of directions.

It was, in fact, a wild-goose chase across the old, Tappan Zee Bridge (and its hundred dollar tolls) to a dead end at a park-n-ride. There, like so many times before on their trip, they threw themselves on the good graces of a complete stranger (the parking lot attendant) who gave them step-by-step directions to their actual destination, Liberty State Park. After a quick check-in at the park (during which they heard the manager shouting driving instructions into the phone to another, lost traveler), they hustled over to the launch apron and their destiny. It was 4:40 p.m.

The world had changed since the first leg. Their journal entries from two years earlier on September 11 of 2000 were normal, almost benign, referencing the weather and small details about the events of the day; the most excitement happened when it took them two tries to haul the boat out of the Missouri River. In 2002, as they launched out of Jersey City into the harbor and jetted out to Liberty Island, they realized that the freedom they had enjoyed the whole length of their adventure was not only unique in the world, but precious and fragile.

They took an emotional lap around the island and snapped the final picture for their skyline collection, the adventurers quietly aware that two, towering symbols of their beloved country no longer graced the frame (they visited Ground Zero the next day). It was quite a sight. Four people in a twenty-three-foot, flat-bottomed boat bouncing in the waves, dwarfed by the tugs and the ferries around them. Little did the passengers in those other watercraft know, but the lunatics bobbing about next to them, the two couples trying to steer the boat with a knee, all while they stayed in position for the ideal photo-op, were not just some friends out celebrating an early retirement. And if those other passengers looked a little closer and watched a little longer, they might have noticed the hugs and the high-fives and the tears and wondered what exactly it was that had happened.

Karl, Rose, Larry and Roxa had just completed the most extraordinary adventure of their lives. They had seen parts of the country they had never intended to visit and met people they had previously misunderstood. They had been rescued by poor folks out on the plains of the American West and been hosted by private, rich country clubs in the South. Their eyes had been opened to the unique, complicated history of the country they loved and the people who lived in it. They had met and made friends with an exhaustive list of their countrymen from every walk of life: Sam Duvall, the Longs, the Conroys, Vince and his dubious, romantic conquests, Gary the lock master at 28b, the waitress in Astoria, the family that guided them to Captain Clark's grave, Bessie at Pap Pap's, Jimmy in Paducah and on and on.

They had stood in awe at the power of the Mississippi when they saw the high-water marks in Cairo and wandered in quiet reflection through the Trail of Tears Museum. They had walked in the shadow of landmarks that nearly every American knows (the St. Louis Arch) and rested their hands on historical cairns that almost no one visits (the marker at Reunion Bay). They had been humbled by institutions of education and reflection (Cornell, Lake Chautauqua, Trinity Heights) and reflected on humbling educations (stay off the rocks around locks!). They had looked in sorrow at the many graves that littered Shiloh and felt a shiver gazing at the headstone of an ancestor who perished during a frigid, Montana winter. They had felt their hearts swell with familial pride as they walked amidst the crumbling walls of an ancestral homestead and patriotic pride as the National Anthem rolled across the face of Mount Rushmore.

Nobody could duplicate their journey. The personal qualities that each adventurer brought to the team, the ambition and wherewithal they possessed collectively and their unique ability to ingratiate themselves to those in such varied segments of society would be impossible to replicate today. Moreover, many of the places they visited (Fenton Art, the floating McDonald's, the National Wood Carving Museum) are gone and forgotten.

Beyond all the inspiring encounters, the gorgeous scenery and the singular memories, they had also discovered much of themselves. Larry and Roxa found that they could throw a bowline and tie a clove hitch with the best of them, that driving a boat full throttle at a trailer would not end in catastrophe and that they could enjoy a happy retirement.

Karl and Rose drew closer than ever to each other as the dream that Karl had pursued and that Rose believed in was realized. At the conclusion of his journal, the skipper attributed the unity of the crew and the success of the journey to his beloved first mate.

However they had envisioned the adventure when they first started to craft it in the winter of 1999, it was doubtful they could have predicted all the escapades or charted everywhere they would go, nor could they have predicted the life changing impact of the expedition. They were different people by the time they jetted around Liberty Island, more capable, unified, informed and patriotic than when they started. So as they put *Acrosswater* back in her trailer, their thoughts turned north, to New England and Cape Breton and beyond, because that's what explorers do and who they are at their core; they're awestruck and grateful for where they've been, but they're always excited to keep investigating the road ahead.

And besides, they never knew what they might find around that next bend in the river.

Acrosswater

acknowledgments

My deepest and sincerest gratitude goes first to Karl Klep. Beyond entrusting me with this story, he has been a source of inspriration, wisdom, compassion and friendship for most of my adult life. From the start of the project, he made me caretaker of every source document in existence, a responsibility I did not take lightly. More than that, he provided unvarnished critiques of my telling of his story and gently corrected any stray thoughts.

Rosemary Klep filled in countless gaps and personal details that I either misinterpreted or missed entirely when conducting my research. She was also a bottomless source of encouragement after reading some of the early copies of the project.

Larry and Roxa Bierman gave me their personal journals to use as sources and responded to many inquiries from afar about how they perceived the experience. Even twenty years later, they talked as excitedly about the adventure as if it was yesterday.

Marilee Kimball lent much needed technical and artistic

expertise to the project. Any part that is visually or aesthetically pleasing is attributed to her; anything that is not is attributed to my blundering attempts at creativity.

Christy Klep generously provided a priceless photo of the family homestead.

My mother and sisters not only planted the seeds of a lifelong love of literature, but they read some early chapters of the book and gave thoughtful, apt feedback that proved enormously helpful.

I need to acknowledge two people who have no idea I even exist. First, Bill Bryson has crafted most of my favorite books. His curiosity about life and his clever descriptions of anything, from the most complex to the mundane, are unmatched and have inspired me since I first read *A Short History of Nearly Everything* many years ago. Chris Hardwick, on his Nerdist and later ID10T podcast series, encouraged listeners to do or make or create a "thing", whatever form it takes. It was that suggestion that prompted me to even consider trying my hand at writing.

Lastly, but most importantly, I thank my dear wife, Jeanette, without whom I would have never believed I could do most things in life, especially write a book.

sources

Adler, Johnathan. "Fables of the Cuyahoga: Reconstructing a
     History of Environmental Protection."
     Fordham Environmental Law Journal. New York: 2002.
Ambrose, Stephen. *Undaunted Courage.* New York:
     Simon & Schuster, 1996.
Barry, John M. *Rising Tide.* New York: Simon & Schuster, 1997.
Bergreen, Laurence. *Over the Edge of the World.* New York:
     Harper Collins, 2003.
Bernstein, Peter L. *Wedding of the Waters.* New York:
     WW Norton & Co., 2005.
Beschloss, Michael. *Presidents of War.* New York:
     Crown Publishing Group, 2018.
Bjornstad, Bruce and E. Kiver. *On the Trail of the Ice Age Floods.*
     Sandpoint, ID: Keokee Books, 2012.
Brodkin, Jon. "Bookie Taking Bets on Applie iPad Sales;
     Bookmaker Expects iPad Sales of at Least 2 Million."
     Network World. New York: January 27, 2010.

Bryson, Bill. *The Life and Times of the Thunderbolt Kid.*
New York: Broadway Books, 2006.

Bryson, Bill. *One Summer.* New York: Doubleday, 2013.

Collins, Michael. "Ship of Stools." *Los Angeles CityBEAT,*
26 November 2003.

Davidson, John. *Thinking about Our Polluted Rivers.*
Sierra Club. n.d., n. pag.

Davis, Tony. "Intel, Coors Say They're Saving Water with
Technology, Innovation." *The Arizona Daily Star,*
3 April 2016.

Dell'Acqua, Alexa A. and John Mazzaferro.
"Wireless Communications." *Telecommunications.*
Norwood, MA: March 1996.

Durham, M. (1995 April). "Mound Country."
Gale in Context: U.S. History.

Egan, Dan. *The Death and Life of the Great Lakes.*
New York: WW Norton & Co., 2017.

Ehle, John. *Trail of Tears.* New York: Doubleday, 1988.

EPA Superfund Record of Decision. *Anaconda
Company Smelter, Anaconda, MT.* Omaha, NE:
EPA, 1996.

Fenster, Julie M. *Jefferson's America.* New York:
Crown Publishing Group, 2016.

Flanagan, Patrick. "The 10 Hottest Technologies
in Telecom." *Telecommunications.* Norwood, MA:
May 1997.

Fletcher, Stephanie. "If You Go to Hells Canyon."
The Denver Post, 18 June 2000.

Grant-Marsh, Susan. "Editor's Choice: The Best Products
    Featured in 'Macworld'." *Macworld*.
    New York: December 1993.

Gray, Donna. *Nothing to Tell*. Guilford, CT:
    TwoDot Book, 2012.

Groom, Winston. *Shiloh 1862*. Washington, D.C.:
    National Geographic Society, 2012.

Groom, Winston. *Vicksburg 1863*. New York:
    Vintage Books, 2009.

Haglund, Michael E. *World's Most Dangerous*.
    Astoria, OR: Columbia River Maritime Museum, 2011.

Halberstam, David. *The Fifties*. New York:
    Fawcett Books, 1993.

Hannon, Andie. "Group Effort Nabs Suspect Swimming
    around Lake for More Than an Hour."
    Sun Journal. Lewiston, ME: 22 August 2011.

Hesselbart, Al. *The Dumb Things Sold...Just Like That*.
    Indiana: Legacy Ink Publishing, 2007.

Howard, Joseph Kinsey. *Montana High, Wide, and Handsome*.
    New Haven, CT: Yale University Press, 1959.

Jensen, Jamie. *Road Trip USA*. Chico, CA:
    Moon Publications, 1996.

Johansen, Bruce E. *The Native Peoples of North America*.
    New Brunswick, NJ: Rutgers University Press, 2005.

Jourdan, Katherine M. (2010, December 27). "Bloch Brothers
    Tobacco Company." *e-WV: The West Virginia
    Encyclopedia*. n.p.

Kingsbury, Paul. *The Grand Ole Opry*. New York:
    Villard Books, 1995.

Kingsley, Abby. "Duke Professor Says Hurricane Florence
      Kills Hogs, Destroys Hog-Waste Lagoons."
      The Duke Chronicle. Durham, NC: 2 October 2018.

Least Heat-Moon, William. *River Horse*. New York:
      Houghton Mifflin Co., 1999.

Lonnquist, Lois. *Fifty Cents an Hour*. Helena, MT:
      MtSky Press, 2006.

Martin, James A. "Streetwise: Let Me Guess.
      You Hate to Ask for Directions. Our Road Tests Found
      the Best Street Atlases and Trip Planners." *PC World*.
      New York, May 1998.

Mcdaniel, Chris. "Bonita Mesa RV Park Residents Donate
      $12,931 for Care of Terminally Ill." *The Sun*. Yuma, AZ:
      26 March 2009.

McDaniel, Karina. *Nashville Then and Now*. San Diego:
      Thunder Bay Press, 2005.

McMurtry, Larry. *Oh What a Slaughter*. New York:
      Simon & Schuster, 2005.

O'Daniel, Patrick. *When the Levee Breaks: Memphis and the
      Mississippi Valley Flood of 1927*. Charleston, SC:
      History Press, 2013.

Oldano, Rick. "C-2000 Zoom." *Macworld*.
      New York: October 1999.

Ontko, Gale. *Thunder over the Ochoco:
      Lightening Strikes! Volume III*. n.d., n.p.

Peterson, Susan E. "Will the Payphone Become a
      'New Economy' Casualty?" *Star Tribune*.
      Minneapolis: May 8, 2000.

Philbrick, Nathaniel. *Valiant Ambition*. New York:
      Penguin Books, 2017.

Plaven, George. "Washoe Theater Goes Digital."
Montana Standard, 25 January 2013.

Pollan, Michael. The Omnivore's Dilemma. New York:
Penguin Books, 1996.

Quimby's 2001 Cruising Guide. St. Louis:
The Waterways Journal, Inc., 2001.

Rodriguez, Veronica. "Antique Shops."
http://sbdcnet.utsa.edu, March 2006.

Rolf Klep - A Retrospective. Eugene: University of Oregon Museum of
Art, 1969.

Romine, Linda. Frommer's Nashville & Memphis.
Hoboken, NJ: John Wiley & Sons, Inc., 2012.

Rood, Lee. "Wellspring of Worry about Water Quality."
Des Moines Register, 22 February 2016.

Sandlin, Lee. Wicked River. New York: Pantheon Books, 2010.

Seabrook, Lochlainn. Give This Book to a Yankee.
Springhill, TN: Sea Raven Press, 2014.

Shallat, Todd. Structures in the Stream. Austin:
University of Texas Press, 1994.

Sides, Hampton. Americana. New York: Anchor Books, 2004.

Smith, Rex Alan. The Carving of Mount Rushmore.
New York: Abbeville Press Publishers, 1985.

Stansberry, Rhonda. "Everyone Can Enjoy Powwows."
Omaha-World Herald, 11 August 1995.

Stark, Peter. Astoria. New York: Harper Collins, 2015.

State Farm Road Atlas. Skokie, IL: Rand McNally & Co., 1999.

Stevens, William K. "Economy Reviving in West Virginia."
New York Times, 8 May 1986.

Stewart, Elinore Pruitt. Letters of a Woman Homesteader.
Boston: Houghton Mifflin Co., 1988.

Stringfellow, Kim. (2012). "Safe As Mother's Milk:
The Hanford Project." Thehanfordproject.com

Wilson, James. The Earth Shall Weep. New York:
Grove Press, 1998.

photos and drawings

about the author

Paul Danforth grew up in NH with a family that inspired a love of literature. After moving to Arizona, he began reading non-fiction exclusively and started crafting a bucket-list. Writing a book came in at number five. He can now start working on numbers one through four.

He currently lives in Chandler, AZ with his beloved wife of twenty-two years.

CPSIA information can be obtained
at www.ICGtesting.com
Printed in the USA
BVHW070807230321
603188BV00001B/102